GLOBAL LEADERSHIP FOR SOCIAL JUSTICE: TAKING IT FROM THE FIELD TO PRACTICE

ADVANCES IN EDUCATIONAL ADMINISTRATION

Series Editor: Anthony H. Normore

Recent Volumes:

ADVANCES IN EDUCATIONAL ADMINISTRATION
VOLUME 14

GLOBAL LEADERSHIP FOR SOCIAL JUSTICE: TAKING IT FROM THE FIELD TO PRACTICE

EDITED BY

CHRISTA BOSKE
Kent State University, Kent, OH, USA

SARAH DIEM
University of Missouri, Columbia, MO, USA

Education Resource Center
University of Delaware
Newark, DE 19716-2940

United Kingdom – North America – Japan
India – Malaysia – China

76794

Emerald Group Publishing Limited
Howard House, Wagon Lane, Bingley BD16 1WA, UK

First edition 2012

Copyright © 2012 Emerald Group Publishing Limited

Reprints and permission service
Contact: booksandseries@emeraldinsight.com

No part of this book may be reproduced, stored in a retrieval system, transmitted in any
form or by any means electronic, mechanical, photocopying, recording or otherwise
without either the prior written permission of the publisher or a licence permitting
restricted copying issued in the UK by The Copyright Licensing Agency and in the USA
by The Copyright Clearance Center. No responsibility is accepted for the accuracy of
information contained in the text, illustrations or advertisements. The opinions
expressed in these chapters are not necessarily those of the Editor or the publisher.

British Library Cataloguing in Publication Data
A catalogue record for this book is available from the British Library

ISBN: 978-1-78052-278-4
ISSN: 1479-3660 (Series)

ISOQAR certified
Management Systems,
awarded to Emerald for
adherence to Quality
and Environmental
standards ISO 9001:2008
and 14001:2004,
respectively

Certificate Number 1985
ISO 9001
ISO 14001

INVESTOR IN PEOPLE

CONTENTS

PART 2: PROMOTING SOCIAL
JUSTICE-ORIENTED WORK

PART 3: ENGAGING PRACTITIONERS IN
SOCIAL JUSTICE AND EQUITY-ORIENTED
WORK IN SCHOOLS

LIST OF CONTRIBUTORS

Carl Kalani Beyer	School of Education, Pacific Oaks College, Pasadena, CA, USA
Jill Bickett	Department of Educational Leadership, Loyola Marymount University, Los Angeles, CA, USA
Christa Boske	Educational Administration, Kent State University, Kent, OH, USA
Bradley W. Carpenter	Department of Leadership, Foundations, and Human Resource Education, University of Louisville, Louisville, KY, USA
Heather A. Cole	Department of Special Education, The University of Texas at Austin, Austin, TX, USA
Michelle Collay	Department of Education, College of Arts and Science, University of New England, Biddeford, ME, USA
Sarah Diem	Department of Educational Leadership and Policy Analysis, University of Missouri, Columbia, MO, USA
Thad Dugan	Educational Policy Studies and Practice, University of Arizona, Tucson, AZ, USA
Shernaz B. Garcia	Department of Special Education, The University of Texas at Austin, Austin, TX, USA
Walter S. Gershon	School of Teaching, Learning, and Curriculum Studies, Kent State University, Kent, OH, USA

Mark Halx	Halx Consulting Group, San Antonio, TX, USA
Frank Hernandez	Department of Continuing Studies, Partnerships & Strategic Initiatives, Hamline University School of Education, Saint Paul, MN, USA
Karie Huchting	Department of Educational Leadership, Loyola Marymount University, Los Angeles, CA, USA
Gaëtane Jean-Marie	Department of Educational Leadership and Policy Studies, Jeannine Rainbolt College of Education, The University of Oklahoma, Tulsa, OK, USA
Katherine Cumings Mansfield	Department of Educational Leadership and Policy, School of Education, Virginia Commonwealth University, Richmond, VA, USA
Miriam Bageni Mwita	University of Eastern Africa, Baraton, Kenya
Anthony H. Normore	Graduate School of Education, California Lutheran University, Thousand Oaks, CA, USA
Barbara L. Pazey	Departments of Special Education and Educational Administration, The University of Texas at Austin, Austin, TX, USA
Teresa Wasonga	Department of Leadership, Educational Psychology and Foundations, Northern Illinois University, Dekalb, IL, USA
Anjalé Welton	Department of Educational Policy, Organization and Leadership, University of Illinois at Urbana-Champaign, Champaign, IL, USA
Peg Winkelman	Department of Educational Leadership, California State University East Bay, Hayward, CA, USA

FOREWORD

Within this book *Global Leadership for Social Justice: Taking it from the Field to Practice*, editors Christa Boske and Sarah Diem, along with an array of contributors provide a variety of rich perspectives to the social justice phenomenon from the lens of empirical, and theoretical work in the area of educational leadership. Of equal importance, these scholars reiterate the importance of bridging theory and practice while simultaneously producing significant research and scholarship in the field as their work deepens understandings of what leading for social justice and equity-oriented work looks like within diverse schools. Collectively, the authors seek to give voice to empowering, social justice-focused research – an area that continues to garner much interest in the areas of educational leadership research, teaching, and learning. In conjunction with the theme of this book, the contributors offer research from an international perspective and offer suggestions, and implications for the field of educational leadership on both a national and international level.

The term social justice is an elusive construct, politically loaded, and subject to numerous interpretations (Jean-Marie, Normore, & Brooks, 2009). Its foundation is rooted in theology and social work and it has deep roots in educational disciplines like curriculum and pedagogy. Social justice has also been studied in law, philosophy, economics, political science, sociology, psychology, anthropology, and public policy (Brooks, 2008). However, it is a relatively new term to fields of educational leadership and has become a major concern for educators in many disciplines and is driven by many factors (e.g., cultural transformation and demographic shift of Western society, increased economic gaps of underserved populations, and public accountability pressures and high stakes testing).

The discourse of social justice and leadership are inextricably linked which begs the question of whether there exists any one definition for social justice leadership. Some research (e.g., Bogotch, 2005) insists that social justice has no one specific meaning. Rather, "its multiple a posterori meanings emerge[d] differently from experiences and contexts" (p. 7). Bogotch zeros in on a key component of social justice by stating that "social justice, like education, is a deliberate intervention that requires the moral use of power" (p. 2) and concludes that it is "both much more than what we currently call democratic schooling and community education, and much less than what we hold out as the ideals of progressing toward a just and democratic society and a new humanity worldwide" (p. 8). Other researchers (e.g., Marshall & Oliva, 2006; Normore, 2008) assert that social justice theorists and activists focus inquiry on how institutional norms, theories, and practices in schools and in society lead to social, political, economic, and educational inequities. Further researchers (e.g., Furman & Shields, 2005) argue the "need for social justice to encompass education that is not only just, democratic, emphatic, and optimistic, but also academically excellent" (cited in Firestone & Riehl, 2005, p. 123) while others (e.g., Lee & McKerrow, 2005) argue that social justice is defined "not only by what it is but also by what it is not, namely injustice" (p. 1). Individuals for social justice seek to challenge political, economic and social structures that privilege some and disadvantage others in the name of democracy, equity, care, and compassion. They challenge unequal power relationships based on gender, social class, race, ethnicity, religion, disability, sexual orientation, language, policies, and other systems of oppression.

Crafted from the professional experiences, intellectual engagements, and moral commitments of the editors and contributing authors this impressive piece of scholarly work focuses on the foundation of social justice concerning a multitude of lenses used to view and attempt to understand the intricacies of leadership. A resonating theme throughout the book is the various responses to the fact that while faculty in the field of education have prepared thousands of school leaders over time there exists a limited body of research around the development, training, and preparation of social justice leaders for the daily work in diverse schools in the international context. As readers of this book we embark on a journey that requires us to engage our thinking, and respond to several strands of research about social justice leadership including its history, how leadership preparation is defined internationally, how social justice leadership research is translated into practice, and how various program designs foster and promote inclusive practice, social justice, and equity-oriented work in schools.

Christa Boske and Sarah Diem and the contributing scholars are to be highly commended for undertaking this project and ultimately bringing to light the importance of understanding and honoring the integrity of differences while simultaneously reiterating the significance of leadership preparation that interrupts oppressive practices in schools and the communities in which they serve. The editors and the contributing authors have demonstrated, in Jonathan Sacks words (2007) that, "Difference does not diminish; it enlarges the sphere of human possibilities" (p. 209).

Anthony H. Normore

REFERENCES

Bogotch, I. E. (2005, November 15–18). Social justice as an educational construct: Problems and possibilities. Paper presented at the annual convention of the University Council of Educational Administration, Nashville, TN.

Brooks, J. S. (2008). Freedom and justice: Conceptual and empirical possibilities for the study and practice of educational leadership. In I. Bogotch, F. Beachum, J. Blount, J. S. Brooks & F. W. English (Eds.), *Radicalizing educational leadership: Toward a theory of social justice* (pp. 61–78). Netherlands: Sense Publishers.

Furman, G. C., & Shields, C. M. (2005). How can educational leaders promote and support social justice and democratic community in schools? In W. A. Firestone & C. Riehl (Eds.), *A new agenda for educational leadership* (pp. 119–137). New York, NY: Teachers College Press.

Jean-Marie, G., Normore, A. H., & Brooks, J. (2009). Leadership for social justice: Preparing 21st century school leaders for a new social order. *Journal of Research on Leadership Education, 4*(1). Retrieved from http://www.ucea.org/current-issues/. Accessed on March 6, 2012.

Lee, S. S., & McKerrow, K. (2005). Advancing social justice: Women's work. *Advancing Women in Leadership, 19*(Fall), 1–2.

Marshall, C., & Oliva, O. (2006). *Leadership for social justice: Making revolutions in education.* Boston, MA: Pearson Education.

Normore, A. H. (2008). *Leadership for social justice: Promoting equity and excellence through inquiry and reflective practice.* Chapel Hill, NC: Information Age Publishers.

Sacks, J. (2007). *The dignity of difference.* New York, NY: Continuum.

INTRODUCTION – ADVANCING LEADERSHIP FOR SOCIAL JUSTICE IN A GLOBALIZED WORLD

Today's educational leaders are faced with a myriad of challenges. They must navigate through and meet the demands of a complex and ever-changing educational landscape, amidst the constant scrutiny placed on them by multiple interest groups internal and external to the school context. Further, while the concern for creating more equitable and just schools is given lip service in policy circles, the extent to which social justice and equity are placed in the forefront of existing educational leadership preparation programs remains problematic as those who prepare school leaders continue to grapple with what social justice means, as well as ways to embed such practices throughout their programs of study.

The purpose of this volume is to propose multiple perspectives for conceptualizing the preparation of leaders for social justice and equity-oriented work in schools. Although faculty in the field of education have prepared thousands of school leaders, and the research continues to expand, there is limited research regarding how to prepare leaders for social justice work in schools, especially considering international contexts (Jean-Marie & Normore, 2010; Marshall & Oliva, 2010; Murphy & Vriesenga, 2004; Orr, 2011; Tooms & Boske 2010). There is a need to build on extant empirical and theoretical work in the area of educational leadership preparation, as well as deepen understandings of what leading for social justice and equity-oriented work looks like within diverse contexts. To this end, this volume addresses what it means to prepare leaders for social justice within different contexts as well as practices being implemented within preparation programs to promote entire programs toward preparing school leaders to lead socially just schools. Further, the volume offers common themes in the existent literature and practice regarding preparing leaders for social justice. The chapters also explore how faculty understand to what extent, if any, school leaders are actually engaging in social justice and equity-oriented work in schools that seek to improve the lived experiences of students and their families. This book endeavors to advance the conceptual frameworks presented within the chapters in order to inform future scholarship and pedagogical practices in educational leadership programs.

This book is organized into four parts, or paths of discourse. Part 1, *Turning Research into Practice*, is a summation of how each author's discussion is related to translating theory to social justice education within school administration preparation programs. In conjunction with the foreword by Anthony H. Normore, the first part presents a foundation for understanding international social justice discussions and how this work is embedded within educational administration. In Chapter 1, Teresa Wasonga and Miriam Bageni Mwita address the fragile state of governments in African nations, including policies formulated to deal with social and economic challenges that have been weak on impact, especially for marginalized populations. As reported by various scholars, social, economic, or educational strategies in African nations have not only led to but have also perpetuated gaps that exist between state policy and outcomes, education and employment opportunities, rich and poor, and government and civil societies. Wasonga and Mwita argue the absence of stakeholder participation, bad governance, and perpetuation of colonial rules has compromised the ability of political institutions to deliver services effectively. Together, they present perspectives about leadership actions that reduce the negative effects of educational policies, socioeconomic status, and regional marginalization. In Chapter 2, Katherine Cumings Mansfield, Anjalé Welton, and Mark Halx illustrate the value of student voice in educational leadership research and practice. While much research has explored leading schools for social justice, it has rarely considered the student perspective as an integral component of leadership decision-making. They emphasize how often student voice should be the sine qua non of leadership responsibilities and investigations. Together, they provide examples of this more inclusive approach to researching and leading school in global contexts. In Chapter 3, Bradley W. Carpenter and Sarah Diem investigate the impact of school leaders increasingly being held accountable for the significant increase in the number of public schools labeled as chronically low-performing. They explore the potentiality of using Q-methodology as an evaluative instrument in reformation efforts of educational leadership preparation programs attempting to better equip school leaders for diverse contexts.

In Part 2, *Promoting Social Justice-Oriented Work*, authors examine educational administration programs and strategies utilized to promote social justice work in schools. Carl Kalani Beyer, in Chapter 4, uses Pacific Oaks College as an example of how educational leadership programs can combine democratic community, social justice, and school improvement to reculture the profession of educational administration as a democratic community. Beyer argues positive changes in schools and school districts can occur by preparing the next generation of social justice leaders who can foster democratic communities and bring about the school improvements necessary to ensure that all members of their school communities have a chance to reach their full potential as teachers and learners. In Chapter 5, Karie Huchting and Jill Bickett focus on Loyola Marymount University's school leadership preparation program in Los Angeles, California. They emphasize practices to promote leaders who can advocate for social justice in educational settings, implement theory into practice, and lead to facilitate transformation in the field of education. In the final chapter of this part, Frank Hernandez provides a review of preparation programs that are infusing social justice curricula that more effectively prepare aspiring school leaders to meet the increased diversity of public schools as well as exemplars of field-embedded internship with a social justice framework in preparation programs across the United States.

Part 3, *Engaging Practitioners in Social Justice and Equity-Oriented Work in Schools*, provides a collection of chapters that specifically focus on the role of practitioners in promoting social justice and equity. Chapter 7 presents Thad Dugan's examination of racial identity development theory and how it should be a fundamental element of school principals' preparation and practice. The chapter includes a brief examination of the related research that merges school leadership and racial identity, and a description of three racial identity development theoretical models (Black, White, and Latino/a); after suggesting questions that still exist regarding racial identity development theory, the author highlights specific ways in which racial identity development can be incorporated principal preparation programs. In Chapter 8, Walter S. Gershon presents a pilot study as part of the International Successful Principal Project (ISSPP). ISSPP is a vast project spanning more than eight countries. While the study emphasizes the knowledge, disposition, and skills principals have used in successful schools across national and international contexts, other findings emerged that extend beyond capacity building. In chapter 9, Christa Boske examines how public school educators understand what it means by leading for social justice in US public schools. The empirical study contributes to the extant literature, because it explores the impact of innovative methods being used at a university to prepare aspiring school and district leaders regarding what it means to lead for social justice and equity in US preK-12 public schools. The findings suggest those interested in leading for social justice must engage in a complex process in which candidates deepen their understanding of self to lead in authentic ways to make meaningful actions aligned with the needs of the individual or community. In Chapter 10, Peg Winkelman and Michelle Collay describe the applied research of two scholar-practitioners leading for equity, and explore how site leaders addressed inequities at their sites by collaborating with and empowering those positioned to make a difference for students.

In Part 4, *The Future of Educational Leadership Programs*, authors conclude with imaginative possibilities associated with embedding social justice work throughout school leadership preparation programs. In Chapter 11, Barbara L. Pazey, Heather A. Cole, and Shernaz B. Garcia highlight the limited preparation of many educational leadership faculty related to disability, and the need to develop frameworks for leadership preparation that will produce candidates with the requisite dispositions, knowledge, and skills to serve students with disabilities. They present a preliminary, integrated framework for the design of educational leadership preparation programs to explicitly situate disability in the vision of social justice leadership and equity for all students. In Chapter 12, Christa Boske and Sarah Diem contend there is a need for practitioners, school community members, universities, and national organizations to seek out ways to build upon each others' efforts to overcome resistance as an alliance versus school leaders naively thinking their efforts alone will change both the school and external environment.

We would like to thank the scholars and practitioners who have graciously contributed chapters as well as Anthony H. Normore and Gaëtane Jean-Marie for their words of encouragement and support throughout the process. Many of the chapters presented here are the first tellings of seminal work done to promote international social justice work in preparation programs. We are particularly pleased that authors agreed to share their experiences, strategies, and empirical work to facilitate a formal discussion in the field of educational administration about what it means to prepare school leaders for international social justice work. It is our hope that this book will continue and expand the conversation on what it means to be a leader of social justice and equity in a globalized world; our children certainly deserve it.

Sarah Diem
Christa Boske
Editors

REFERENCES

Jean-Marie, G., & Normore, A. H. (2010). The impact of relational leadership, social justice, and spirituality among female secondary school leaders. *International Journal of Urban Educational Leadership*, 4(1), 22–43.

Marshall, C., & Oliva, M. (Eds.). (2010). *Leadership for social justice* (2nd ed.). Boston, MA: Allyn & Bacon.

Murphy, J., & Vriesenga, M. (2004). *Research on preparation programs in educational administration: An analysis.* Columbia, MO: University Council for Educational Administration.

Orr, M. T. (2011). Pipeline to preparation to advancement: Graduates' experiences in, through, and beyond leadership. *Educational Administration Quarterly*, 47(1), 71–113.

Tooms, A. K., & Boske, C. (2010). *Bridge leadership: Connecting educational leadership and social justice to improve schools.* Charlotte, NC: Information Age Publishing.

PART 1
TURNING RESEARCH INTO PRACTICE

CHAPTER 1

MITIGATING THE IMPACT OF EDUCATIONAL POLICIES IN RURAL KENYA

Teresa Wasonga and Miriam Bageni Mwita

ABSTRACT

In this chapter, we argue that injustices experienced by children in Kenyan schools can be traced back to educational policies and corruption in government. However, few studies have focused on the links between policies, injustices, and the work of principals. Data collected on the work of school principals indicated that individual commitments and developing capacity for leadership in schools through the practice of dispositional values resulted in success.

There are very few studies that have focused on the link between educational policies and social injustices in schools in developing countries like Kenya. In this chapter, we argue that injustices experienced by children in Kenyan schools can be traced back to educational policies and corruption in government. In addition, our research shows that the actions of school principals can make a difference. We start by highlighting issues that plague the Kenyan government, followed by the structure of schooling, and educational policies. The conclusion in this chapter provides data that

Global Leadership for Social Justice: Taking it from the Field to Practice
Advances in Educational Administration, Volume 14, 3–20
Copyright © 2012 by Emerald Group Publishing Limited
All rights of reproduction in any form reserved
ISSN: 1479-3660/doi:10.1108/S1479-3660(2012)0000014005

shows what school leaders are doing to mitigate the effects of government
policies.

Given the fragile state of governments in African nations, policies formulated to deal with socioeconomic challenges have been weak on impact.
Mostly, policy strategies used are reactive, short-term, or expedient
(Buchmann, 1999; Mitullah, 2004; Mwiria, 1990). Over time, these strategies
have forestalled both quality and equity in the public sector. As reported by
various scholars; socioeconomic and educational strategies in African
nations have not only led to, but have also perpetuated the gaps that exist
between state policy and outcomes, education and employment opportunities, the rich and the poor, and government and civil societies (Buchmann,
1999; Cubbins, 1991; Mitullah, 2004; Transparency International [TI],
2010). In Kenya, the Education Sector Integrity Study Report (TI, 2010)
found discrepancies between stated policy, governance, and implementation. With widespread mismanagement and general lack of accountability
in the education sector, most projects that are "implemented are not
well deliberated, leading to the haphazard implementation" and failure of
policy (p. v). The report highlights the absence of policy guidelines on
educational expansion, stakeholder involvement, and quality management.
Consequently, the absence of stakeholder participation, bad governance,
and perpetuation of colonial rules has compromised the ability of political
institutions to deliver services effectively (Mitullah, 2004). Scholars concur
that the main source of inefficiency in government including the education
sector is politics, often exemplified by patronage, non-procedural appoint-
ments, lack of clear criteria for appointees, and self-interests (Buchmann,
1999; Mitullah, 2004; Muhula, 2009).

Historically, the Kenyan government has failed to control the balance
between expansion and quality of education, and employment opportunities. Instead, it has continued to promote education as the key to social
mobility and economic development (Buchmann, 1999; Mwiria, 1990). This
conundrum has led to what has become an extremely competitive education
system with uncontrollable imbalance between education and the labor
market (Buchmann, 1999). The confluence of high demand for education
and weak government has created an environment with high levels of
inequity, inefficiency, and ineffectiveness in the education sector. The "great
faith in education" (Buchmann, 1999, p. 96) that poor Kenyans have had
since independence has declined and quality education has become both
expensive and scarce. Education through schooling that was intended to
be the great equalizer in social mobility and economic development has
slowly and consistently become the instrument of inequality. Lackluster

policy implementation, wealth and gender gaps, and regional politics have consistently worked together against the poor, the politically marginalized, and the regionally sidelined. In this context, social injustices are likely to persist and policies are the invisible instruments used to perpetuate them in the education sector. The data reported in this study were analyzed to discover strategies used by principals to mitigate the effects of policies. This chapter draws from qualitative data that include policy documents, observations in schools, and the perspectives of students, teachers, school leaders, and other members of the school community. Of particular interest were perspectives about leadership actions that reduce the negative effects of educational policies among marginalized communities.

STRUCTURE AND THE SCHOOLING SYSTEM IN KENYA

Inherent in the Kenyan education system are structures that perpetuate injustice. A close look at the education system in Kenya indicates that the type of school attended may or may not give advantage to the students. While on the surface it would seem like merit is the criteria for selecting students to national or provincial schools, in reality this is seldom the case. Wealth determines who gets selected to schools that are considered to be the "top schools" especially after primary school. To comprehend the hidden discrepancies in student outcomes, the schooling system has to be interrogated. The system of education features two major categories of schools – public and private. Public schools are government owned and are highly subsidized by the public. Government assistance is in the form of teacher salaries, text books, equipment, and meals. Local communities and parents provide the funds for physical development, salaries for nonteaching staff, boarding fees, and other operations. On the other hand, private schools are owned by entrepreneurs, companies, churches, or corporations. They are funded through school fees and sponsorships and are diversely resourced depending on who owns them (Onsomu, Mungai, Oulai, Sankale, & Mujidi, 2004). In recent times, Kenya has witnessed a re-emergence of "community schools." These are quasi-public schools that are built and financed by local communities and nongovernmental agencies mainly for populations that are grossly underserved by the government (*ibid.*) – poor urban slums or marginalized rural areas like the Arid and Semi-Arid Lands (ASALs). Typically, these schools are subsidized by charitable organizations and government agencies.

Schools, mostly at secondary level, are further categorized by gender and residence. There are single-sex and mixed (coeducation) schools, and there are residential (boarding) and nonresidential schools. The majority of Kenyan secondary schools are single-sex residential schools. It is widely assumed that single-sex residential schools offer more stable learning environments especially for girls and the poor (Bosire, Mondoh, & Barmao, 2008; Sax, 2009). Girls are generally disadvantaged because of traditional expectations and gender roles at home (FAWE, 2000; Grown, Gupta, & Kes, 2005; Kanyike & Piwang-Jalobo, 2003). The demands placed on children, especially those from poor families, range from working to feed the family to house chores, leaving no time for study. However, the number of day schools and students attending them has increased, mostly because of the high cost of boarding in residential schools.

Secondary schools are further classified by hierarchy, placing national schools at the top, followed by provincial and district schools. National schools are the most prestigious public schools. They are well-resourced in terms of facilities, personnel, honor, and finance. They admit students with the highest scores on the Kenya Certificate of Primary Education (KCPE) – a national examination at the end of 8 years of primary education. Because of their status, these schools are coveted, competitive, expensive, and out of reach for majority of Kenyans. In 2012, of the 700,000 students who sat the exams in 2011, only 10,000 were admitted to national schools. The fierce competition means that some poor deserving students do not get into these schools. Provincial and district schools, although predominantly under-resourced, educate the majority of Kenyan students. Government subsidies to these schools are inconsistent and most of the students served come from the lower middle to low socioeconomic strata. Facilities and equipment are limited in relation to the number of students served. These schools are often overcrowded and have high teacher/pupil ratios. And yet they serve the children with the highest needs due to deficiencies occasioned by poor preparation in primary schools. Researchers have found that student outcomes at the end of primary education depend, predominantly, on the quality of primary schools attended (Sawamura & Sifuna, 2008). On average, 40% of the students who complete primary do not transition to secondary schools (RoK, 2007) mostly because they are poor or have attended poorly resourced schools. These students are also less likely to qualify for admission to national and provincial schools, and if they do, they are too poor to afford it. Invariably, the education system including admission policies to national and provincial schools has tended to favor students from well-resourced private or public schools.

EDUCATIONAL POLICY IN KENYA

The definition of policy depends on one's philosophical understanding about the "nature of society, the meaning of power, and the proper role of government" (Fowler, 2009, p. 3). Fowler defines policy as a "dynamic and value laden process through which a political system handles a public problem" including a government's expressed intentions, official enactments, as well as patterns of activity and inactivity (p. 4). In Kenya, policy is broadly understood, and ranges from presidential pronouncements, government intentions, to patterns of political activity and inactivity. Educational policies have mostly been derived from presidential mandates or commissions, committees, and taskforces appointed by the president (MoEST, 2004). At present, presidential mandates and five commissions are noted to have been instrumental in the formulation of the current educational policies. The commissions include The Kenya Education Commission – Ominde Report of 1964; The National Committee on Educational Objectives and Policy – Gachdhi Report of 1976; The Presidential Working Party on the Second University in Kenya – Mackay Report of 1981; The Presidential Working Party on Education and Manpower – Kamunge Report of 1988; and The Commission of Inquiry into the Education System of Kenya – Koech Report of 2000. These commissions were mostly set up in response to crises in the education sector and political self-interest. It is, therefore, not surprising that policies formulated by these commissions have been found to favor the sitting government. Whenever findings of commissions did not favor the government (president), the reports were shelved or rejected (Amutabi, 2003; Sawamura & Sifuna, 2008). Expediency has tended to precede educational reforms to the detriment of the public. According to Ojiambo (2009, p. 141), well thought out commission reports have been rejected because they do "not agree with the political motives of the government."

A historical perspective of policy development would help explain how the interests of a few have survived in Kenya. Before independence, the Kenyan formal education was provided mostly by religious missionaries and managed by the colonial government. In this system, although the Africans paid the bulk of the taxes, the British administration spent 50% less on the education of Africans that was limited to basic literacy and numeracy (Sifuna & Otiende, 2006). Government policy favored the education of Europeans and Asians and the advantages provided by a superior education enabled them to occupy positions of power and wealth in both the private and the public sectors. African leaders saw outright discrimination in this system of education. In response, they, through the Local Native Councils

(LNC), took an active role in providing education for Africans by applying part of their local tax levies to the building of independent schools.

After independence in 1963, Kenya continued with the colonial system of education that had marginalized Africans. They were pressed with the immediate need for skilled labor. Working from the assumption that the knowledge needed to run the government was the knowledge that the British provided for themselves, the government increased access to it. The immediate policy initiative was to expand access to British education for Africans. The curriculum that was reserved for Europeans and Asians was made available to all, including Africans in independent schools. This was the beginning of the national curriculum. Primary school was extended from 4 to 7 years and the high stakes exam (taken after fourth grade) that kept 80% of African children from proceeding to upper primary was abolished. These actions led to the introduction of the 7-4-2-3 (7 years of primary, 4 years of secondary, 2 years of advanced secondary [A-levels], and 3 years of university) in 1964. In addition, the government initiated a bursary scheme to enable some African pupils attend "high cost" European and Asian schools (racial integration), and English was established as the medium of instruction in all schools (Sifuna & Otiende, 2006). What the education policy of access and integration did was "open access to the emerging African political elites who could afford to pay the fees charged in what had been well-equipped, formerly European-only schools" (Oketch & Rolleston, 2007, p. 133). While these few Africans proceeded to acquire secondary education needed to take up jobs in the government, majority of Kenyans only attained primary education. Government policy that was aimed at expanding higher (secondary) education mainly for manpower realized expansion at the primary level for the common people (Bogonko, 1992) and secondary level for the elite. These policies set the stage for what has now become a hierarchical system of schooling where public schools, especially national schools that are funded by tax payers, mostly serve the wealthiest.

Besides the administrative and power vacuum created by the exit of the British at independence, there was also uncertainty about national unity and identity among Kenyans. The British had divided Kenyans by race and ethnicity. Seeking to unite Kenyans, African leaders decided that "education had the task of uniting the different racial and ethnic groups making up the nation" (Sifuna & Otiende, 2006, p. 240). Beginning with the Ominde Commission of 1963, other education commissions (Koech Report of 2000 and Gachathi Report of 1976) have not only considered education to be the facilitator of national unity, but also implied that national unity is and should be an objective of education (MoEST, 2004). Residential national and provincial schools were used as proxies for national unity, admitting students from all over the country based on merit. This policy ensured that secondary school students from different parts of the country, ethnicity, and socioeconomic backgrounds converged at boarding schools where they learned together and about each other. It did not last.

Following recommendations of the Mackay Report of 1981 (a Presidential Working Party on the establishment of a second university in Kenya), the 8-4-4 structure of education replaced the 7-4-2-3 (MoEST, 2004). Through a presidential mandate, the education system was restructured to ensure that students exiting primary and secondary schools acquired "scientific and practical knowledge that can be utilized for self-employment, salaried employment or further training" at the end of any of the different levels of school (Sifuna & Otiende, 2006, p. 256). Previously, the Gachathi Report (RoK, 1976, pp. 33–34) had raised questions about the gaps between the education structure and employment. The report said, "One of the largest problems confronting the country is that of unemployment" following the enormous expansion of the education system in the first years of independence. The report noted that unemployment had extended to both high school and university graduates. International Labor Organization (ILO) World Employment Program had also published a report on unemployment in Kenya in 1972 (Sifuna & Otiende, 2006). The report recommended a restructuring of education to focus on basic education for more people, integration of curriculum into community activities including rural development, and devoting a proportion of the curriculum to prevocational subjects. However, the burden of providing this new curriculum fell on local communities in what was known as "cost sharing" irrespective of their ability to raise capital to deliver the curriculum (Amutabi, 2003; Eshiwani, 1993). Over time, the 8-4-4 system has revealed regional disparities because resources were unevenly distributed depending on ethnicity and political patronage. Of significance is the fact the 8-4-4 system of education localized school funding, reduced the number of students traveling across provinces, and paved way for segregation by ethnicity and socioeconomic status. Poor regions and rural areas that lack infrastructure and capital have had to contend with poor educational facilities and poor educational outcomes. The converse is true for more affluent communities especially in the urban area and regions that are home to the political elites. We note that Kenya's educational policies have led to a skewed system of education characterized by significant gaps in student enrollment, educational outcomes, and socioeconomic status by region and ethnicity. Consequently, while the intention of national schools and boarding facilities was to enhance national unity, they have become a purview of the rich who can afford well-resourced primary schools (mostly private). Provincial and district schools have become ethnic and socio-economic enclaves, because educational policies have significantly reduced inter-ethnic and inter-socioeconomic class interactions.

In the current dispensation, Kenya has a national curriculum at both the primary and secondary levels of education, and all schools must be registered by the Ministry of Education, Science and Technology (MoEST). These two may be the only common factors among schools across socio-economic strata and regional boundaries. Historically and regionally, the majority of Kenyan Africans who were marginalized by the colonial government are still marginalized by the independent Kenyan government. The rural poor and those in the ASALs are still excluded from new educational opportunities. They experience very high school dropout rates and there is still a lack of responsiveness to nontraditional students in these areas. These challenges persist despite the introduction of "free primary education" in 2003 for the third time, and the increased number of students going to school (primary). Government policy has not mitigated persistent problems of access, equity, and quality, especially among the poor and regionally marginalized (De Souza & Wainaina, 2009; MoEST, 2004). Uwezo's (2011) findings show significant disparities in education by region and socioeconomic status. Central province leads in most aspects of education, including attendance, reading, books, funding, teacher/pupil ratio, and students attending private schools. Of the three Kenyan presidents since independence, two have come from central province, giving the region unparalleled political advantage. But all is not lost. Despite these disparities, there are school leaders who are working and succeeding in poor rural schools against policy odds.

EDUCATIONAL LEADERS DEFYING POLICY IMPACTS

Reported here are findings from research on International Successful School Principals Project in Kenya. This research focused on identifying actions of successful school principals. Successful principals as identified by research-ers (e.g., Day, Parsons, Welsh, & Harris, 2002; Leithwood, Jantzi, & Steinbach, 1999; McBeath, 1998; Southworth, 2002) are those who attend to the broad moral, social, and ethical issues in educating students. They were found to succeed by setting directions, developing people, and redesigning the organization. This chapter presents the work of four school principals in marginalized schools (poor rural) in Kenya. Based on school visits and interviews with students, teachers, community leaders and school heads in successful rural schools, themes that demonstrate actions mitigating negative impacts of educational policies include elbow leadership, focus on common purpose, and dispositional values. Successful school principalship was defined by significant improvement in physical facilities, student outcomes, student and teacher retention, and/or school turnaround.

Elbow Leadership

Why elbow leadership? Kenya is a hierarchical society where leaders including principals have unprecedented authority. With this authority, they are expected to implement educational policies that include the Children Act of 2001, safety standards, and quality assurance. These policies provide guidelines for the safety of children and the management of schools. However, principals complain that limited resources often impair the implementation of policies. For example, most parents especially of students in provincial and district level schools do not pay school fees on time, nor does the government. Operating schools without enough funding has forced leaders to think differently – give up their ego. To be successful, these leaders have to practice leadership that is quintessentially human, leadership that engages the community in ways that can sustain the schools as they wait for funds. These engagements often include seeking overdrafts, facilities, supplies, and favors. Success necessitates developing personal "elbow to elbow" relations with various constituents including traders, doctors, bankers, police, and other stakeholders.

Traditionally, principals have rarely related on a one on one basis with subordinates (teachers) or ordinary members of their communities. Social architecture, "the sum of the systems, processes, beliefs, and values that determine an individual's behaviors, perspectives, and skills in an organization" (Prahalad & Krishnan, 2008, p. 148), has been absent, and still is absent in many schools. Principals have ruled alone. However, in all of the four schools, in addition to leading from the front and the back, "elbow leadership", where principals worked alongside teachers, parents, and students, was the norm. In doing so, they built respect, commitment, and trust, factors that were instrumental in transforming the people. As explained by a teacher, "in working together, we recognize each other's humanity, strengths and weaknesses, and we appreciate each other." This partnership has led to higher levels of engagement, stimulated thought, action, and inspired many people to take up responsibilities. Such responsibilities include teachers working long hours after school and weekends without extra pay in order to cover the syllabus as required by state policy. In these schools, there were very few books (1:6, i.e., one book used by six children), crowded classrooms (1:50/60, i.e., a classrrom for 50–60 children), and many students missed lunch (too poor to pay for it). Success demanded "more hands," a change in leadership style. Leading from the side (elbow) enhanced bonding among stakeholders as they joined in and created committees. Different schools had different committees including School Committees, which focused on the overall management of schools under the jurisdiction of local authorities (TI, 2010); parent/teacher associations, focusing on student and teacher welfare; curriculum teams, focusing on developing affordable local teaching aids; professional teams, focusing on ways and means to help teachers grow in the profession; and school community teams, focusing on school- and community-related social issues. In these schools, the teams functioned because of the leadership style that included leadership from the side (elbow leadership).

Unlike these schools, in the other schools that were visited, leadership was highly embedded in the formal leader and was rarely experienced in the school community. In most cases, principals were perceived as functionaries of politicians and the government, and were therefore feared rather than respected. On the other hand, in the successful schools, leadership was felt throughout the schools as principals joined with others "elbow to elbow" in teaching, communicating with villagers and political leaders, advising students, and working with funding agencies. Principals worked from the premise that there was untapped capacity for leadership among teachers and community members. They harnessed this capacity by meeting people at their level (elbow), sharing experiences and therefore building trust. In doing so, they helped others identify and use their talents to help the children succeed socially, emotionally, and academically.

In one school, a community member described the principal as focused on creating a "true democracy," which he defined as "getting people to talk for themselves and their children." He also stated that teachers were engaged in meaningful activities, including "taking turns to supervise sporting activities in the evenings, leading workshops on civic education, meeting with parents, visiting the community, and preparing students for exams." The students in these schools were engaged and empowered through debates on policies that impact them directly. A teacher claimed that "while debating students became critical about civic knowledge and internalized values." Groups of students were observed debating the roles of student leadership and current events including corruption in public service. They were encouraged to read and critique daily newspaper reports in what was called "parliament" in one school. In three schools, shared governance was achieved through rotations in which teachers substituted the deputy headmaster and headmaster. Through this process, teachers have mastered the operations of the school; they have evolved and they are leaders in their own rights.

Focus on Common Purpose

Participants in this study (students, teachers, and community) repeatedly cited "self-interest" among principals as the reason behind woes in schools. Numerous examples demonstrated this: principals doing personal business on school time; purchasing a bus at the expense of a laboratory because the principal can hire the bus out for money; tenders go to the highest bidder because the principal gets a kick back; hiring of less qualified staff due to nepotism; using reward and punishment against teachers unfairly; abusing students; and covering up abuse by teachers, staff, and adults in the community. None of these comments focus on the purpose of school. According to Begley (2008), educational leaders should keep the fundamental purposes of education in mind as they make decisions, manage people or resources, and generally provide leadership within their organizations. It is very difficult to focus on the purpose of school in a policy environment where personal interests trump public interest and resource allocation is based on political interests. And while wealthy established schools have the luxury of focusing on purpose, the impoverished schools focus on basic needs.

In this study, we noted that successful principals focused on public interest and the purpose of school. They pushed their communities to recognize the role of school in society and their moral obligation to do right for their children. For one principal, the common purpose for community was to "improve learning and the learning environment for children by creating order." He stated that "children cannot learn when and where there is no order." He explained that a safe orderly school was a welcoming place where children could go to despite their circumstances. He revealed that when he arrived at the school, it was in chaos with parents and school staff at loggerheads. The chair of the school committee confirmed this and added, "The Headmaster is focusing on order because when there is order, then we can talk about purpose." The headmaster uses stories, analogies, and experiences in everyday life to help the local people connect what is going on in public discourse and their own lives to the purpose of school. For example, at a meeting with parents, the principal explained how a new statute [all members of parliament would need to have a college education and all ministers must have a bachelor's degree] would impact the community. He said, "A frog's large eyes will not stop a cow from drinking water," a common saying used by locals to emphasize understanding of the bigger picture. He continued, "If we proceed in this way [not supporting children], if our children cannot go to high school, we will not have a member of this community in parliament." The use of familiar cultural experiences in sharing ideas seemed to appeal to all including those who did not go to school. What we observed were principals impacting people's consciousness by helping them develop shared understanding about the organization and its goals that can frame a sense of purpose (Leithwood & Riehl, 2005). Data indicated that knowing the common purpose enabled people to work toward a common goal.

Dispositions/Values

Based on our observations, the hierarchical nature of Kenyan society means that the gap between government policy and what happens in schools is wide. "Our government policies are good on paper and that is how far they go," one teacher said. He explained that requirements of the curriculum were not achievable with the limited resources in rural schools. "It takes a lot of heart to succeed with children whose parents have so little," a community leader said. "The good work in poor rural schools is driven by moral values and principals going beyond the call of duty," said an education officer. Research has indicated that leadership values determine in large measure what transpires in a school (Reyes & Wagstaff, 2005). In this study, values were cited by interviewees as being core to the work of principals in successful rural schools. Two of these principals were described as being spiritual. One used a lot of proverbial analogies and biblical stories during the interviews and conversations. To him, dispositions were the radar for leadership and, he emphasized, the ethical purpose in life and ones profession. He explained that value orientations were the intuitive tendencies that motivated his actions and the resulting consequences. In our view, failures in the implementation of policies that regulate the behaviors of principals elevate the value of dispositions. Interviews revealed that the ministry of education's idea of quality assurance (overseeing school management) has been marred by corruption among its officers and principals. Quality Assurance and Standards in Education (QASE) is a sector within the ministry that monitors and reports on the performance of school personnel (Ministry of Education, 2012). Data in this study shows that patronage and nepotism thrive in this sector. Merit is rarely considered in recommendations in the appointment of principals and their deputies; schools underperform for years under their watch; and bad principals including those who abuse children continue to serve. In this kind of environment, moral values seem to be the only recourse for justice among the despondent.

Tendencies that favor egalitarian leadership (elbow to elbow) were central in co-creating engaging leadership in these schools. Literature indicates that such tendencies include humility, patience, collaboration, resilience, active listening, cultural anthropology, trust, and subtlety (Bruffee, 1993; Collins, 2001; Follett, 1927; Freire, 1990). In responding to the question "Why would you work for this principal?" most participants responded by describing the principals as responsive, patient, humble, willing, persistent, and/or trustworthy. These characteristics were perceived as factors that enable the leader to reach out to people in the community and motivate them to want to work with him/her. One teacher noted, "He [principal] has qualities that enable him to have continuous conversations that sometimes challenge our assumptions, and we respond positively because he is trustworthy." This, the teacher added, "has helped to build trust among us and therefore instead of focusing on him, we focus on purpose of school." The principal at this school explained that dispositions, "the attitudes that I bring to work," can either make it easier or more difficult to work as a team. He continued, "The education policies we have in this country do not favor poor children and when they do, we do not have the right attitudes to make them work for all children." For example, he asked, "Why provide free primary education to the rich and ask the poor to build their schools when they cannot even afford school uniform? Why ban corporal punishment when the government cannot protect children from it?" We observed teachers under the watch of principals ignore the ban and swat students regularly even for issues beyond their control [coming to class late because of too few toilets and missing school due to lack of sanitary towels for girls]. In discussing how education policies have influenced their actions, these principals agreed that educational policies per se were not the problem. They felt that patronage, political interest, and, mostly, the inability of the government to provide funding to execute policies made it difficult for them to operate schools in a fair and just manner. Even though the government has recognized that access to education is every child's right, it has failed in making this a reality for over 60% of students who do not finish high school.

REFLECTIONS

The framework for the International Successful School Principals' Project (ISSPP) and the meta-analyses of what is known about educational leadership (Leithwood & Riehl, 2005) reveals that we already "know" what successful school leadership looks like in the West (America, Canada, and Europe). What we do not know are how other cultures, nations, or policy contexts in other countries function to suppress or enhance success for school children. Kenya's case, in many respects, is congruent with what has been found to be core policy failure in African states (Chabal & Daloz, 1999; Ward, Bourne, Penny, & Poston, 2003) and successful school leadership (setting direction, developing people, and restructuring organization) in the West (Leithwood & Riehl, 2005). However, cultural differences present new challenges in understanding policy intentions, success, and school leadership from a global perspective. What we have observed in Kenya is a culture where policies serve a few, and the absence of written policy promotes self-interest. We noted and agreed with a parent whose praise for the principal indicated that the selfless leadership and bonds that had emerged between the principal and teachers, students, and community had liberating effects from both marginalization and injustice. Schools in this study were stable in leadership, orderly, had enhanced student achievement, and, in one case, turned around from a failing to thriving school.

Unlike the West, in Kenya, the government's input in education is dismal, especially when it comes to physical development (Bold, Kimenyi, Mwabu, & Sandefur, 2009), accountability, and the greater good. Despite government promises and policies, the poor, mainly rural folks, have not benefitted proportionately from the country's resources compared with the wealthy and politically connected. The disenfranchised continue to rely on the goodwill of nongovernmental organizations, donor agencies, and skills of individuals for proper management, funding, and physical development. Disproportionate resource allocations follow in the footsteps of the colonial government. While the colonial government spent less on the education of Africans, independent Kenyan government is spending even less on the education of poor students. This situation is made worse by the unabated corruption in government, rampant patronage in public institutions, and lack of accountability among leaders. Government policies make these possible. For example, the hiring of teachers and principals is centralized and managed by a government agency, Teachers Service Commission (TSC). The extremely hierarchical bureaucracy embedded in the management makes it very difficult for the agency to be accountable to the local people and children. One principal elaborated that he is paid whether or not he does anything. There is no transparent systematized objective evaluation or accountability system for head teachers. The communities they serve are far removed from TSC and they have very little in terms of legal or other recourse in case of mismanagement by headmasters. The total quality assurance sector of the Ministry of Education charged with ensuring proper management of schools has failed to develop sustainable procedures for the same. Without procedures, their self-interest comes first (corruption), and their effect minimal. Basically, in this context, moral qualities and dispositions are the major reasons principals will do the right thing. Indeed, this research demonstrates that the personal qualities of principals were the factors that differentiate success from failure in schools. This is because dispositional values were useful in instigating personal accountability, engaging the strengths of others, and thereby co-creating egalitarian communities that were instrumental in directing the focus of communities on children's education, raising money for development, equipment and supplies, and surmounting the odds that educational policies have failed to remedy.

In sum, these findings indicate that (1) commitment of individuals (the heart, the soul, the body, the time, the intellect, the energy, the passion, the person) can turnaround a school where government policy is not supportive and (2) to sustain progress, the leaders must develop collective capacity including capacity of the affected (poor students and their families). Initiating success may depend on individual competencies, but sustaining success depends on the collective capacity that is co-created as is articulated in the African adage, "It takes a village to educate a child." These four schools are examples of how a leader can weave in and out of multiple identities and cultures to position self and others to influence society and change the course of government policy.

ACKNOWLEDGMENTS

This research was done in Kenya and funded through the Fulbright Scholarship award.

REFERENCES

Amutabi, M. N. (2003). Political interference in the running of education in post-independence Kenya: A critical retrospection. *International Journal of Educational Development, 23*, 127–141.

Begley, P. T. (2008). The nature and specialized purposes of educational leadership. In J. Lumby, G. Crow & P. Pashiardis (Eds.), *International handbook on the preparation and development of school leaders* (pp. 21–42). NewYork, NY: Routledge.

Bogonko, S. N. (1992). *Reflections on education in East Africa.* Nairobi, Kenya: Oxford University Press.

Bold, T., Kimenyi, M., Mwabu, G., & Sandefur, J. (March, 2009). Free primary education in Kenya: Enrollment, achievement and local accountability. Paper presented at Annual Conferences at the Center for the Study of African Economies, Oxford University, UK.

Bosire, J., Mondoh, H., & Barmao, A. (2008). Effect of streaming by gender on student achievement in mathematics in secondary schools in Kenya. *South African Journal of Education, 28*, 595–607.

Bruffee, K. A. (1993). *Collaborative learning: Higher education, interdependence, and the authority of knowledge* (2nd ed.). Baltimore, MD: The Johns Hopkins University Press.

Buchmann, C. (1999). The state of schooling in Kenya: Historical developments and current challenges. *Africa Today, 46*(1), 95–117.

Chabal, P., & Daloz, J. P. (1999). *Africa works: Disorder as political instrument.* Oxford, UK: James Curry.

Collins, J. (2001). *Good to great: Why some companies make the leap... and others don't.* New York, NY: HarperCollins.

Cubbins, L. A. (1991). Women, men, and the division of power: A study of gender stratification in Kenya. *Social Forces, 69*(4), 1063–1083.

Day, C. W., Parsons, C., Welsh, P., & Harris, A. (2002). Improving leadership: Room for improvement? *Improving Schools, 5*(1), 36–51.

De Souza, A., & Wainaina, G. (2009). Kenya's three initiatives in universal primary education. In L. Brown (Ed.), *Maintaining universal primary education: Lessons from Commonwealth Africa.* London, UK: Commonwealth Secretariat. Differences in their characteristics and the transition to college. http://heri.ucla.edu/PDFs/Sax_FINAL%20REPORT_Sing_1F02B4.pdf

Eshiwani, G. (1993). *Education in Kenya since independence.* Nairobi, Kenya: East African Educational Publishers.

FAWE. (2000). Impact of HIV/AIDS on girls' education in sub-Saharan Africa. *FAWE Newsletter, 8*(2).

Follett, M. P. (1927). Leader and expert. In H. C. Metcalf & L. Urwick (Eds.), *Dynamic administration: The collected papers of Mary Parker Follett* (pp. 247–269). New York, NY: Harper & Brothers.

Fowler, F. C. (2009). *Policy studies for educational leaders: An introduction* (3rd ed.). Boston, MA: Pearson.

Freire, P. (1990). *Pedagogy of the oppressed.* New York, NY: Continuum.

Grown, C., Gupta, G. R., & Kes, A. (2005). *Taking action: Achieving gender equality and empowering women.* UN Millennium Project: Task Force on Education and Gender Equality 2005. London, UK: Earthscan.

Kanyike, F., & Piwang-Jalobo, G. (2003). *Bridging the rural villages urban gender gap in education in Uganda.* Kampala, Uganda: Forum for African Women Educationalists.

Leithwood, K. A., Jantzi, D., & Steinbach, R. (1999). *Changing leadership for changing times.* Buckingham, UK: Open University Press.

Leithwood, K. A., & Riehl, C. (2005). What do we already know about leadership? In W. A. Firestone & C. Riehl (Eds.), *A new agenda for research in educational leadership* (pp. 81–100). New York, NY: Teachers College.

McBeath, J. (1998). *Effective school leadership: Responding to change.* London, UK: Paul Chapman Publishing.

Ministry of Education. (2012). *Quality assurance and standards.* Retrieved from http://www.education.go.ke/ShowPage.aspx?department=5&id=260

Mitullah, W. V. (2004). Making institutions work for the poor in Kenya: A search for institutional strategies. In J. M. Buhemuka & J. L. Brockington (Eds.), *East Africa in Transition: Images, institutions and identities* (pp. 124–139). Nairobi, Kenya: University of Nairobi Press.

MoEST. (2004). *A policy framework for education, training and research: Meeting the challenges of education, training and research in Kenya in the 21st century.* Sessional Paper No. 1. MoEST, Nairobi, Kenya.

Muhula, R. (2009). Horizontal inequalities and ethno-regional politics in Kenya. *Kenya Studies Review, 1*(1), 85–106.

Mwiria, K. (1990). Kenya's Harambee Secondary School Movement: The contradictions of public policy. *Comparative Education Review, 34*(3), 350–368.

Ojiambo, P. C. O. (2009). Quality of education and its role in national development: A case study of Kenya's educational reforms. *Kenya Studies Review, 1*(1), 133–149.

Oketch, M., & Rolleston, C. (2007). Policies on free primary and secondary education in East Africa: Retrospect and prospect. *Review of Research in Education, 3,* 131–158.

Onsomu, E. N., Mungai, J. N, Oulai, D., Sankale, J., & Mujidi, J. (2004). *Community schools in Kenya: Case study on community participation in funding and managing schools.* Paris, France: International Institute for Education Planning.

Prahalad, C. K., & Krishnan, M. S. (2008). *The new age of innovation: Driving co-created value through global networks.* New York, NY: McGraw-Hill.

Republic of Kenya. (1976). *The National Committee on Educational Objectives and Policies (Gathachi Report).* Nairobi, Kenya: Government Printer.

Republic of Kenya. (2007). *Kenya vision 2030: A globally competitive and prosperous Kenya.* Nairobi, Kenya: Government Printer.

Reyes, P., & Wagstaff, L. (2005). How does leadership promote successful teaching and learning for diverse students? In W. A. Firestone & C. Riehl (Eds.), *A new agenda for research in educational leadership* (pp. 101–118). New York, NY: Teachers College.

Sawamura, N., & Sifuna, D. N. (2008). Universalizing primary education in Kenya: Is it beneficial and sustainable? *Journal of International Cooperation in Education, 11*(3), 103–118.

Sax, L. (2009). *Women graduates of single sex and coeducational high schools: Differences in their characteristics and the transition to college.* Retrieved from http://heri.ucla.edu/PDFs/Sax_FINAL%20REPORT_Sing_1F02B4.pdf

Sifuna, D. N., & Otiende, J. E. (2006). *An introductory history of education* (Rev. ed.). Nairobi, Kenya: University of Nairobi Press.

Southworth, G. (2002). Learning-centered leadership in schools. In L. Moos (Ed.), *Educational leadership: Understanding and developing practice* (pp. 33–52). Copenhagen, Denmark: The Danish University of Education.

Transparency International. (2010). *The Kenya education sector integrity study report 2010.* Retrieved from http://www.afrimap.org/english/images/documents/Education + Integrity + Report.pdf

Uwezo. (2011). *National annual learning assessment report (Kenya).* Retrived from http://www.uwezo.net/index.php?c=67

Ward, M., Bourne, J., Penny, A., & Poston, M. (2003). Why do education policies in East Africa fail? What's changing? *Journal of Education, 30,* 127–148.

CHAPTER 2

LISTENING TO STUDENT VOICE: TOWARD A MORE INCLUSIVE THEORY FOR RESEARCH AND PRACTICE

Katherine Cumings Mansfield, Anjalé Welton and Mark Halx

ABSTRACT

The purpose of this chapter is to illustrate the value of student voice in educational leadership research and practice. While much research has explored leading schools for social justice, it has rarely considered the student perspective as an integral component of leadership decision-making. In fact, listening to the student voice should be the sine qua non of leadership responsibilities and investigations. This chapter provides examples of this more inclusive approach to researching and leading schools. It operationalizes student-focused and social justice practices that hold promise to sensitize our research efforts, destabilize oppressive school leadership structures, and create positive and innovative environments for students in all global contexts.

Global Leadership for Social Justice: Taking it from the Field to Practice
Advances in Educational Administration, Volume 14, 21–41
Copyright © 2012 by Emerald Group Publishing Limited
All rights of reproduction in any form reserved
ISSN: 1479-3660/doi:10.1108/S1479-3660(2012)0000014006

Research on educational leadership and social justice rightly contends that it is imperative for school leaders to recognize the ways in which their leadership practices may reproduce marginalizing conditions (Dantley & Tillman, 2009). Indeed, it is essential that school leaders critically examine the social, cultural, and economic dynamics of their school communities and reflect on how personal attitudes and beliefs are influenced by their own position of privilege and oppression (Rodriguez & Fabionar, 2009). Moreover, research demonstrates if school principals make their students' identities an integral part of their leadership practice, the result will inevitably be a more caring pedagogy where children who find their realities represented in school curriculum, class dialogue, and school policies are encouraged to engage and connect to school and learning, and in turn, experience greater school success (Shields, 2004).

While much research suggests that listening to student voice facilitates a more insightful approach to educational research and practice (Fielding, 2001, 2004; Mitra, 2004), the student perspective is not prioritized in most educational leadership research and practice. Including and honoring the students' perspective not only yields richer and more authentic results, it also increases student engagement. Yet, as Sands, Guzman, Stephens, and Boggs, (2007) have noted, "Despite intense endeavors to promote educational change to affect student achievement, one voice, perhaps the most critical voice that could inform the debate of how to increase student achievement, is sorely lacking: that of students themselves" (p. 324).

The purpose of this chapter is to illustrate the value of student voice in educational leadership research and practice. While much research has explored leading schools for social justice, it has rarely considered the student perspective as an integral component of leadership decision-making. We argue that listening to the student voice should be the sine qua non of socially just leadership, and we provide examples of this more inclusive approach to researching and leading schools. Listening to and considering the voice of the student inherently operationalizes student-focused and social justice practices that sensitize our research efforts, destabilize oppressive school leadership structures, and create positive and innovative environments for students in all global contexts.

STUDENT VOICE LITERATURE

Much current U.S. education policy at the federal and state levels encourages educational research activity that is intended to advocate for students by utilizing quantitative testing data to shed light on achievement gaps. The 2001 No Child Left Behind (NCLB) Act, and its successor, the 2009 ED Recovery Plan (which included Race to the Top Fund), are two unfortunate macro examples of this quantitatively based policy focus. Likewise, research inquiries that reach further than quantitative test score analyses tend to prioritize researcher interpretation over the perspective of the research participants themselves (Fielding, 2001). As such educational policies and research that represent students as statistics and numerical ratings disregard the contextual realities of students, trivialize the student experience, and fall short (on many levels) of achieving their purposes (Fielding, 2001). Surveying students and counting their responses does not yield an authentic picture of the educational reality of the individual students; it provides only a portrait of an amalgamated "average" nonexistent being. Similarly, surveying students, and then interpreting their words, is comparably inauthentic. Researcher advocacy efforts to emancipate students are certainly at least partially negated when the researchers speak for students rather than letting the students speak for themselves (Fielding, 2001). Prioritizing the authentic student voice in educational research is the only genuine means of evaluating current school reform efforts and facilitating more socially just educational environments and outcomes.

For the last several decades, student voice has played a significant role in igniting social and educational change in the United States and throughout the world. In 1960, the Student Non-violent Coordinated Committee (SNCC) organized the first series of sit-ins at lunch counters where Black students were denied service. In 1968, the Brown Berets' students and supporters organized the first high school walkout to challenge the treatment of Chicano students – for example punishment for speaking Spanish in school – in the California educational system. Similarly, in 1995 high school students in Salt Lake City, Utah, in order to counter state and local board of education resistance to the establishment of gay–straight student alliances, staged walkouts and facilitated community and teacher education workshops on the challenges LGBT student face (Mayberry, 2006). In 2011, youth protest in Greece and Egypt roused consciousness concerning undemocratic sociopolitical, structural, and economic issues. Even today, Chicano youth continue to use walkouts as demonstrations of resistance to aversive policies such as SB 1070 (the Arizona anti-immigration law). These events illustrate the ways in which students across the globe have demonstrated that they are capable of impacting leadership and affecting change.

Defining Student Voice

There is some disagreement among student voice scholars as to what "counts" as research and practice that speaks with (rather than for) students (i.e., research that is grounded more in a democratic belief system than a more neoliberal/capitalism-based business model desire to control students and meet accountability standards). For example, Michael Fielding (2001) argues teachers and other adults "speak too readily and too presumptuously on behalf of young people" (p. 123). And, Mitra (2008) laments, "most schools are not structured in ways that encourage student voice" (p. 24). Mitra (2008) argues that age and ability segregation, coupled with unmanageable school and class sizes, increases student alienation.

Scholars have recognized that the potential of student voice in research and practice can be represented on a continuum (see Fig. 1) that moves from using students as simple data sources to empowering students to lead the research team that defines and directs school reform efforts (Fielding, 2001, 2004; Mitra, 2008; Mitra & Gross 2009; Sands et al., 2007; Schultz, 2011). Mitra (2008) identified three levels of student voice. At the most basic level, students share their opinions concerning school problems. At the next level of intensity, the students collaborate with adult practitioners to identify and

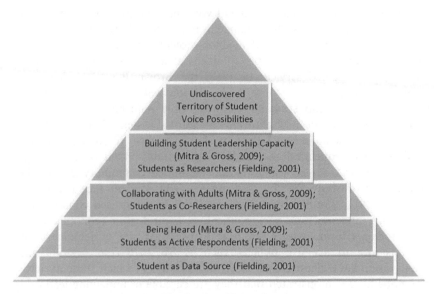

Fig. 1. The Student Voice Continuum.

address school reform. The most intensive student voice initiatives train students to assume leadership roles in researching problems and in identifying and implementing solutions. Mitra and Gross (2009) also outlined three levels of student engagement with school improvement processes: (1) being heard; (2) collaborating with adults; and (3) building capacity for leadership (p. 523).

Mitra (2004), and Mitra and Gross (2009), suggested that conducting surveys and focus groups with students is clearly a viable means to improve practice. While asking what students think is important, Mitra (2004) went on to suggest "young people [collaborate] with adults to address the problems in their schools" (p. 651). Shifting the focus to research *with* youth rather than *on* youth (Torre & Fine, 2006) and speaking *with* students rather than *for* students (Fielding, 2001, 2004) is not only appropriate developmentally (Sands et al., 2007) but is a more comprehensive and ethical way to approach educational research and school improvement efforts (Fielding, 2001, 2004; Sands et al., 2007). Torre and Fine (2006) made the case succinctly: student voice initiatives "counter neoliberalistic perceptions of marginalized youth as disengaged, passive, and blind consumers who lack connection" (p. 269). Indeed, instead of being positioned as "the problem," students identify issues and offer solutions (Irizarry, 2009, 2011b). Thus, student voice and engagement become a strong force of resistance against hegemonic structures that reproduce societal inequities (Ginwright, Noguera, Cammarota, 2006; Giroux, 1986; Schultz, 2011).

Advantages of Including Student Voice

There are several important reasons to change the way we engage in educational research and practice. For example, there is empirical evidence that allowing the students to have a voice, even at the most basic level, results in the development of civic habits essential to democracy. Moreover, engaging students at a higher level results in curricular improvements and strengthens teacher–student relations (Fielding, 2001, 2004; Mitra, 2008; Mitra & Gross, 2009; Sands et al., 2007).

According to Lenoir (2011), personal and academic resilience is strengthened when students are their own advocates. Indeed, as Welton (2011a) argued, "As educational leaders, we must listen to, collaborate with, and assist youth in taking power over navigating their educational trajectories" (p. 4). Numerous researchers agree that ignoring student voice results in feelings of alienation, anonymity and powerlessness, and disengagement on the part of the students (Fielding, 2001, 2004; Mitra, 2008; Mitra & Gross, 2009; Sands et al., 2007). Moreover, disengaged students exhibit lower self-esteem, lower academic achievement, and higher dropout rates (Mitra & Gross, 2009; Valenzuela, 1999).

Seeking student voice is also supported by motivation theory, self-determination theory, and constructivist learning theory. All support active student engagement and feedback to the educational process (Sands et al., 2007). In addition to strengthening their civic skills, positioning students as transformative intellectuals helps build written and oratory skills and contributes to college aspiration (Duncan-Andrade & Morrell, 2008). Students who are given voice also learn how to be agents of change in their communities (Duncan-Andrade & Morrell, 2008), which positions them to work within a framework of social justice in youth policy. Student voice allows marginalized youth to gain critical awareness of oppressive structures and reclaim a sense of power through collective action (Ginwright, Cammarota, Noguera, 2005). "Enabling youth to interrogate and denaturalize the conditions of their everyday oppression inspires a process of community and knowledge building" that benefits all (Torre & Fine, 2006, p. 269). The greater the interaction and leadership of students in school reform efforts, the greater the return will be (Fielding, 2001, 2004; Mitra, 2008; Mitra & Gross, 2009; Sands et al., 2007).

STUDENT VOICE THEORETICAL FRAMEWORK

In the model shown in Fig. 1, we illustrate our interpretation of the student voice framework based on our readings of the literature. The pyramid represents a continuum of the level and role of student involvement in educational leadership research and practice. Level one, *students as data sources*, is seen as the lowest level and level four, *students as researchers/ building capacity for leadership*, is seen as offering the highest level of student involvement. We purposely left the apex as an unknown entity because we believe that future work in this area will certainly add to our understanding.

Limitations of the Model

While the model in Fig. 1 outlining the student voice literature is helpful, we believe there are some limitations that should be acknowledged and explored. For example, we do not believe that the current student voice literature adequately explores issues of identity, power, and context. Nor does the current model do an adequate job of explaining why, in certain circumstances, higher levels of student participation are achieved. Thus, we revisit the literature to discover and explain the missing elements that might serve as a better model for future educational leadership research and practice.

Issues of Context and Power

Although Fig. 1 indicates the added value of elevating all students' voices, it does not address the fact that in particular settings certain students' voices have less power than others. Marginalized students' voices are often muted by the dominant forces in institutional contexts (see Irizarry, 2011a; Valenzuela, 1999). While the framework above does allude to more democratic fostering of the students' own research involvement and leadership capacity, Scheurich (1998) suggested that social justice-minded researchers and practitioners use caution when endorsing democratic rhetoric in schools because democracy does not always guarantee equity. In fact, when democratic ideals are practiced in educational contexts where both students from dominant groups and students from historically marginalized groups are in attendance, resistance is inevitable, and those interested in listening to the student voice must contend with the struggle among groups over whose cultural capital will "count" as meaningful or whose cultural capital "will prevail in legitimating particular ways of life" (Giroux, 1986, p. 50).

Educational settings often tacitly facilitate the silencing of students from marginalized groups (Delgado Bernal, 2002). Institutional and structural classism, racism, homophobia, and xenophobia silences students who are not members of the dominant group, and in many cases students are rendered virtually invisible in a given context. The silencing of students from nondominant groups comes in many forms. For example, micro-aggressions (Nadal et al., 2011; Solórzano, Ceja, & Yosso, 2000) – or subtle, daily discriminatory acts toward any student from an oppressed group – and blatant racial stereotyping clearly have a negative impact on the academic performance of students of color (Steele & Aronson, 1998) and incline them toward silence. Students who identify as LGBTQ often experience overt forms of school-sponsored silencing via tolerated bullying and harassment, and when schools fail to address this abuse, LGBTQ identified youth experience lower levels of belongingness, higher levels of truancy, and contemplate suicide more than straight-identified students (Robinson & Espelage, 2011). Moreover, a number of researchers have documented the ways in which inequities such as course tracking, teacher attitudes, the policing of students' native language, and egregious disciplinary sanctions deplete the positive capital of students of color (Irizarry, 2011a, 2011b; Rubin et al., 2006; Valencia, 2010; Valenzuela, 1999).

While struggle might be inevitable, we believe school leadership practices can act as mediating factors that bridge student voice efforts in challenging contexts. A socially just educational leader must challenge the power structures that silence the voices of students, especially those who are marginalized in a particular educational context. In the following sections we highlight elements of educational leadership literature that specifically addresses issues of identity, power, and context when underscoring students' voices.

Leadership Practices as Mediating Factors
Neoliberal policies such as *No Child Left Behind* and the ideology of global competitiveness place school leaders at odds with holding to established democratic principles (Hursh, 2007; Lipman, 2004). As a result, schools have detoured from what Giroux (1986) called the "Deweyian vision of public schools as democratic spheres" where students can express, interact, negotiate, and "engage the politics of voice and representation" in "order to make sense of their lives in schools" (p. 48). The school leader is pivotal in fostering student voice and the restoration of such democratic ideals. In this section we highlight specific concepts within educational leadership literature – democratic practices, transformative leadership, leadership for social justice, and critical pedagogy – that serve as critical mediating factors for addressing issues of identity and power in schools with an eye toward increasing student voice.

Just as the student voice literature points out that students are more engaged and stay in school when power is shared with them, the school leadership literature points out that when principals practiced democratic or shared leadership, they found teachers felt a higher level of commitment and greater sense of effectiveness (Miller & Rowan, 2006). In fact, several researchers (Bogler, 2001; Brooks & Miles, 2008; Bryk & Schneider, 2002; Dantley & Tillman, 2009; Deal & Peterson, 2009; Marks & Printy, 2003; Miller & Rowan, 2006; Shields, 2004; Tschannen-Moran, 2004) advocate a leadership stance that emphasizes democratic or shared leadership since that stance usually produces the most positive, balanced school climate.

According to Bogler (2001) and Copland (2003), leaders who managed by democratic or distributed leadership principles fostered collaboration, trust, professional learning, and reciprocal accountability that grew over time. Furthermore, group-made democratic decisions establish an atmosphere of trust and inspire individuals to become personally responsible for the specific elements of the collective goals (Ouchi, 1981). We argue that these democratic leadership principles hold true for students as well as teachers and administrators in educational settings. According to Brooks, Jean-Marie, Normore, and Hodgins (2007):

> social justice leaders strive for critique rather than conformity, compassion rather than competition, democracy rather than bureaucracy, polyphony rather than silencing, inclusion rather than exclusion, liberation rather than domination, and action for change rather than inaction to preserve inequity. (p. 400)

Furthermore the essence of a democratic environment revels in the multiple voices, identities, and perspectives of the school community (Dantley & Tillman, 2009). Thus, leaders practice democratic leadership by laboring to "see democratic practice and equitable treatment of all members of the learning community, regardless of race, gender, class, ability, age, or sexual orientation" (Dantley & Tillman, 2009, p. 26). The development of democratic coalitions within schools and other community organizations provides strength to disrupt and undo oppression. Lott and Webster (2006) purported that:

> The practicing of democracy can take place within young people's groups, classrooms, businesses, and local community groups. This involves supporting access, inclusion, and participation in processes and decisions. Having one's capacities respected, and having access to multiple roles and responsibilities can be a powerful stimulus to engage in social action for justice. (p. 132)

As such, democratic schools and societies consider the design and implementation of socially just policies as the only assured method to globally sustain and build capacity for tolerance, peace, and harmony (Zajda, Majhanovich, & Rust, 2006).

The leadership for social justice literature is clear that school leaders who are transformative recognize contextual issues and practice self-reflective behavior in order to lead schools more justly (Dantley & Tillman, 2009; Shields, 2004). As school leaders, we must critique how our "educator voice" may silence the "student voice" and explore the ways that our "educator voice" can help empower the "student voice" (Giroux, 1986). A transformative leader recognizes the notion of power and privilege in schools and provides space for change-agent dialogue that challenges and dismantles oppressive structures (Shields, 2004, 2010). Furthermore, transformative leaders use critical pedagogy and dialogue as a means to enhance, not subtract, students' lived experiences and cultural assets (Shields, 2004). Rightly, a socially just educational leader must challenge the power structures that silence the voices of students who are most marginalized in any given context.

Alternate pedagogies, like critical pedagogy (Duncan-Andrade & Morrell, 2008; Freire, 1970; Kincheloe, 2008; McLaren, 2003), provide additional insight into the value of student voice. Critical pedagogy builds from a student's cultural knowledge base and "fundamentally repositions students as actors and contributors to the struggle for social change" (Duncan-Andrade & Morrell, 2008, p. 13). And, as Irizarry noted, "education should be about helping students learn more about how the system works and working with them to develop a voice to speak up against issues they find troubling or in favor of ideas they support" (p. 119). However, when educators help students develop a voice, *they* must also listen to it. A more critical pedagogy sets the stage for more authentic teacher and administrator engagement with the students. Critical pedagogy *requires* a level student/ teacher dialogue that creates an authentic and engaging educational environment. Students live and speak authentically, and that authenticity is worth hearing. Where traditional lecture-style pedagogy fails to take advantage of the perspective and lived experience of the student, a more critical pedagogical approach requires and honors student voice. Pedagogical reform that privileges student voice must be advocated by educational researchers and practitioners who see students as the subject, not the object, of their research activity and leadership decision-making practice.

A MORE INCLUSIVE THEORY FOR RESEARCH AND PRACTICE

The notions of democratic research and practice are well represented in both educational leadership and the student voice literature; hence, we propose a unification of the two in order to develop a more comprehensive theory. Research on leadership and social justice affirms that leaders who nurture democratic spaces enjoy the greatest gains in school personnel effectiveness and student achievement. However, we believe it is clear that educational leaders need a greater arsenal – the voices of students – to contend with a history of educational policies that have only deepened the "education debt" (Ladson-Billings, 2006) they owe to students. In Fig. 2, we graphically illustrate this theoretical unification of leadership for social justice and student voice as a stronger approach for destabilizing oppressive school structures in order to ultimately create positive and innovative learning environments for all students. Instead of the student voice continuum standing alone, it is placed within the sociocultural context of schools with leadership practices acting as a possible buffer and bridge between these two conceptual elements.

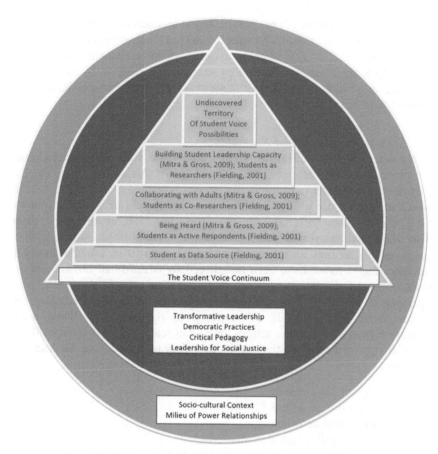

Fig. 2. Integrating the Missing Pieces Toward a Holistic Visioning of Research and Practice.

From the Field: Empirical Examples as Illustrations

As demonstrated in the previous sections, we assert democratic practices, critical pedagogy, transformative leadership, and leadership for social justice are critical components of educational leadership that foster students' voices and leadership capacity. In addition to engaging conceptually with the research literature, we also reflected on empirical findings from our own research experiences (see Halx, 2011; Halx & Ortiz, 2011; Mansfield, 2011a,

2011b, in press; Welton, 2011a, 2011b). In the sections that follow, we share how our research exemplifies the conceptual theoretical framework presented in Fig. 2 as well as critique our work in terms of its limitations. We conclude the discussion section by suggesting further study as we work toward a more inclusive model of student voice for educational leadership research and practice.

One Student Voice Raps and Resonates
The voice presented in Halx's (2011) study is the pure, unenhanced, and uninterrupted voice of one student participant: Alejandro, a selectively chosen non-completer (sometimes disparagingly termed, "dropout") student who had much more to say than the researcher sought or was prepared to hear. How ironic, fortunate for the researcher, and at the same time disturbing, that this young man had written and memorized a rap song that conveyed his feelings about education and his status in life. Alejandro's thoughts might never have been heard/read by educational researchers or practitioners if the students' voice had not been sought. Alejandro was interviewed for a larger study on the viability of critical pedagogy in urban south Texas schools. In response to the question, "How does education here at your high school make you feel?" Alejandro asked if he could answer in a rap lyric that he wrote. Below is a portion of Alejandro's response.

Wanna wait but I'm dreamin'
weeks pass my thoughts, but I'm schemin'
of completing great achievements
and with all my unforeseen demons
trying to deal with what I'm given, so now just look at me singin'
look, I don't care
I ain't worried
but in reality I'm hurtin'
living's becoming a burden ...
I'm stressed out, I'm agitated
the life I lead's complicated
what's up ahead there's no tellin'
can you direct where I'm headin'?

The import of this example, and the story conveyed by this one student, serves both as a detailed presentation of a life being lived, but it also inspires the notion that there may be many other students who feel as he does, yet who do not show it outwardly. Alejandro was an 18-year-old high school "dropout" who made the decision to return to school. Like the other participants in the study, Alejandro took a while to warm up and engage more fully with the interviewer, and he initially answered the questions as would be expected. However, when the researcher engaged Alejandro and asked him to reflect on his emotional reaction to his school experience, Alejandro responded authentically through his rap music. The authentic student perspective is too often missing from quantitative educational research and traditional school leadership decision-making practice.

A Collective Voice for Change

Welton (2011b) conducted a yearlong case study of the educational opportunity networks of students and school personnel at Green High School, a high poverty–high minority (HPHM) semirural high school. Green High School was in its third consecutive year of poor academic performance under NCLB federal and state accountability guidelines. This "academically unacceptable" designation placed the school under review by the state education agency, which required immediate improvement in student academic achievement.

The first academically unacceptable designation lowered the morale of school personnel and students and mandated principal and teacher turnover. The stigma of low performance that plagues many HPHM schools (see Reddick, Welton, Alsandor, Denyszyn, & Platt, 2011) affected Green High School cultural climate as both teachers and students were embarrassed of the "ghetto" school stereotype. Then, a new principal, and a few dynamic teachers, took charge and began to serve as transformative leaders. They decided that empowering student voices would be the best way to improve school's cultural climate while at the same time serving to "internally motivate" students.

A coalition of teachers and students initiated the *Students for Change* project by facilitating a series of student-led dialogue sessions where students problem solved and crafted action plans to improve school climate. Students designed motivational posters that were placed all around the school to advertise the *Students for Change* agenda. Students also designed a number of incentives for creating positive peer relationships as well as incentives for increasing student academic engagement. Finally, the students crafted a teacher advocate program in order to enhance student belongingness and academic support. Each student selected a teacher advocate, and the student and teacher advocate signed a contract that included agreed upon student short-term and long-term goals. Though social justice observers might question accountability ratings as a mechanism to determine the fate of a school, Green High School was elevated to academically acceptable the following school year and remained open largely as a result of the *Students for Change* initiatives.

Democratic Leadership and Student Engagement

In a study emphasizing the utility of student voice, Mansfield (2011a) conducted a two-year ethnography at a public school for young women. Mansfield's study emphasized the importance of democratic engagement in the development of school culture. In this study, school leadership sought input from adult stakeholders and was committed to engaging students in the decision-making processes at the school from the start. For example, at the end of each year the principal administered a school-wide student survey entitled, "How are we doing so far?" seeking feedback to gauge student opinions on a wide variety of important issues.

In addition to seeking feedback from students on school climate, the principal also included students in the selection process for faculty hires each spring. School leaders conducted training sessions where students helped select interview questions and practiced the art of interviewing. Students asked interviewees tough but important questions. The prospective faculty members also presented lessons during the interviews, and the student interviewers offered critical feedback. Students were given a figurative and literal voice in the selection of new faculty members.

All voices in this study, including those of students, described a school culture devoted to learning and flourishing; a place where people respected each other, grew, and learned together. Interestingly, it was not until Mansfield (2011a, 2011b) interviewed students directly that one of the most important themes emerged. The students shared that neighborhood peers disapproved of their academic attitudes and behaviors, which resulted in name-calling and rock throwing. Prior to these conversations with students, school administration was not aware that this harassment was occurring, and thus, was not in a position to intervene. As a result of shared findings from this study, the school administrators are developing coaching programs to address the students' needs. The willingness of school leadership to extend student voice efforts from paper–pencil surveys to interviews with a researcher facilitated social justice efforts that directly addressed student needs that might have otherwise gone unnoticed.

DISCUSSION: A CRITICAL REFLECTION
ON OUR SCHOLARSHIP

While each of these research vignettes offers an example of how our proposed theory in Fig. 2 can be put into practice, we also acknowledge limitations in our own work as we critically reflect on ways in which students' voices could be included even further. In our first example (Halx, 2011), the pursuit of student voice enabled Alejandro to express his schooling experiences in a way that would not have occurred through conventional quantitative surveys or structured qualitative methods. Alejandro's authentic voice, like that of several other students in the study, exposed his internalized oppression. These students blamed themselves for their academic stressors, and they did not consciously recognize how school structures and curricula contributed to their stress. A more critical pedagogy would offer students an opportunity to critique their schooling experiences, and allow their voice to be shared with school leaders and personnel. This more comprehensive engagement would facilitate a critical examination of how leadership practices contribute to students' disconnectedness from school while at the same time *connecting* leaders more holistically to the school.

In our second example (Welton, 2011b), the principal and teacher leaders were transformative in the sense that they empowered students to change the school climate and challenge negative school stereotypes. However, there was insufficient interrogation of contextual constraints, and students were still framed as part of the problem. It was the students who in large part recognized the changes that were necessary to improve school climate, but school administration did little to use this opportunity as a means to reflect further on how *their practices* also contributed to the stigma of failure. Several school staff members still viewed the student's community and home lives as the source of the school's academic struggles. The school administrators failed to exhibit authentic transformative leadership by failing to engage in critical self-reflection and recognize how student-level inequities can often largely be attributed to greater institutional and school-level forces (see Shields, 2010).

Study three (Mansfield, 2011a) offered a robust example of how integrating concepts from the literature (democratic practices, transformative leadership, leadership for social justice, critical pedagogy, and student voice) can give students a safe space to excel academically. However, the somewhat serendipitous discoveries that illuminated student struggles are disconcerting. The latent nature of the student voice findings serve as a poignant reminder of the importance of strategically and purposely giving students an opportunity to candidly converse with teachers, principals, and other adult stakeholders. Moreover, while the school in this study can offer a "safe academic space" (Mansfield, in press) for those lucky enough to win such an opportunity via the magnet school lottery, a troubling question lingers: *What about the others?* Students who do not have the luck-driven privilege of gaining access to this school must continue to contend with disempowering school experiences. Too often, school leadership, at the highest levels, is not practicing democratic leadership; and thus, most students in this district, and other districts like it, are left to contend with the unsatisfactory status quo.

These research examples, taken in aggregate, illustrate that listening to the voice of the student is not only vital toward the advancement of socially just policies, but it also provides valuable insights toward immediate improvement in student performance, retention, and progress. One student voice illuminated internalized oppression that could potentially be addressed by pedagogical reforms. Multiple student voices helped to dramatically reform a failing school that might have otherwise closed. An inclusive school administration created an environment that enabled the discovery of discrimination that might have otherwise hindered student safety and success.

The reoccurring theme that links all of these research studies was that listening to student voice not only facilitated solutions to the problems of individual students and student groups, but it also positively impacted the overall school environment, the decision-making processes of the school leaders, and by extension, the well-being of the surrounding community. A more socially just community begins with listening to the students who will soon become the leaders within it.

IMPLICATIONS AND RECOMMENDATIONS

Much of the literature demonstrating how to engage student voice and practice comes from the field of teacher education (Duncan-Andrade & Morrell, 2008; Irizarry, 2011b). Though we shared snapshots of how we incorporate student voice in our scholarship, the field of educational leadership still has a way to go in offering more examples of educational leaders who integrate student voice with their personal theories of action. Hence, we proposed a means to do so via an enhanced model for student voice by adding principles of democratic practices, leadership for social justice, transformative leadership, and critical pedagogy from educational leadership literature.

We recognize that forefronting student voice and contesting the status quo is challenging and difficult. As Marshall and Anderson (2008) noted, school leaders are often discouraged from engaging in matters of social justice activism for fear that being identified as an open activist might negatively impact their careers. In fact, many school districts and educational leadership preparation programs urge current and future school leaders to take a neutral stance or refrain from political engagement altogether. Yet conversely, the Interstate School Leaders Licensure Consortium (ISLLC) standards, adopted by the Council of Chief State School Officers (ISLLC, 2008), *encourages* learner-centered leadership *and* political advocacy.

Regrettably, educational leaders often receive little or conflicting instruction on how to engage in matters of social justice because leadership preparation programs tend to avoid dialogue on social justice leadership practices (Marshall & Anderson, 2008). However, as demonstrated by our review of the student voice literature in this chapter, encouraging student voice is one method in which school leaders can at least make micro political ripples that align with their personal social justice values (see Marshall & Anderson, 2008; Santamaria & Santamaria, 2012). Thus, it is evident that school leaders should consider the student perspective if they hope to make enduring changes to equity in schools.

Educational leadership programs should commit to providing school leaders with the skill sets necessary to integrate student voices – especially those from marginalized groups – and mediate the political backlash that may arise from the dominant population. Educational leadership programs should move beyond the restrictive pedagogy of current school "reform" and accountability and move toward innovative and creative instruction that recognizes how student voice is instrumental to school improvement and policies. As Pasi Sahlberg, author of the book *Finnish Lessons* has noted, "Accountability is something that is left when responsibility has been subtracted" (Partanen, 2011, p. 2). School leaders have the responsibility to include students in the process of school leadership. As the studies above suggested, schools that embed student voice in school improvement efforts will inevitably flourish because student voice not only helps develop leadership capacities and critical consciousness of students, but it also builds positive relationships between those students and school personnel (Delgado & Staples, 2008).

The future success of social justice pursuits depends on researchers and practitioners who are willing to step outside the conventional box and try something that might seem counterintuitive. It is indeed ironic that sharing power with others actually strengthens one's power, and that engaging students in school leadership actually enhances the outcome of that leadership, but these ironies are nonetheless true. Professors in school leadership programs and current school leaders should all step back from the expected and allow the perhaps unexpected student "wisdom" to help them do their job.

The pursuit of excellence is important, but should not supersede the pursuit of equity. This notion may also seem counterintuitive, but empirical studies in Finland and elsewhere provide evidence that excellence follows equity (Partanen, 2011; Sahlberg, 2011). However, we believe that both equity and excellence are concurrently achievable in our schools. The model we have proposed is just one means to facilitate that process. Clearly, we believe that listening to student voice is equity and excellence in action. Social justice-minded educational researchers and school leaders do not need to reinvent the proverbial wheel. They just need to start listening to the students.

REFERENCES

Bogler, R. (2001). The influence of leadership style on teacher job satisfaction. *Educational Administration Quarterly, 37*(5), 662–683.

Brooks, J. S., Jean-Marie, G., Normore, A. H., & Hodgins, D. W. (2007). Distributed leadership for social justice: Exploring how influence and equity are stretched over an urban high school. *Journal of School Leadership, 17*(4), 378–408.

Brooks, J. S., & Miles, M. T. (2008). From scientific management to social justice … and back again? Pedagogical shifts in the study and practice of educational leadership. In A. H. Normore (Ed.), *Leadership for social justice: Promoting equity and excellence through inquiry and reflective practice* (pp. 99–114). Charlotte, NC: Information Age Publishing.

Bryk, A. S., & Schneider, B. (2002). *Trust in schools: A core resource for improvement.* New York, NY: Sage Foundation.

Copland, M. (2003). Leadership of inquiry: Building and sustaining capacity for school improvement. *Educational Evaluation and Policy Analysis, 25*(4), 375–395.

Dantley, M. E., & Tillman, L. C. (2009). Social justice and moral transformative leadership. In C. Marshall & M. Oliva (Eds.), *Leadership for social justice: Making revolutions in education* (2nd ed., pp. 19–34). New York, NY: Allyn and Bacon.

Deal, T. E., & Peterson, K. D. (2009). *Shaping school culture: Pitfalls, paradoxes, and promises* (2nd ed.). San Francisco, CA: Wiley.

Delgado, M., & Staples, L. (2008). *Youth-led community organizing: Theory and action.* New York, NY: Oxford University Press.

Delgado Bernal, D. (2002). Critical race theory, Latino critical theory, and critical race-gendered epistemologies: Recognizing students of color as holders and creators of knowledge. *Qualitative Inquiry, 8*(1), 105–126.

Duncan-Andrade, J. M. R., & Morrell, E. (2008). *The art of critical pedagogy: Possibilities for moving from theory to practice urban schools.* New York, NY: Peter Lang Publishing.

Educational Leadership Policy Standards: As Adopted by the National Policy Board for Educational Administration (ISLLC). (2008). Retrieved from http://www.wallace foundation.org/knowledge-center/school-leadership/principal%20evaluation/Documents/ Educational-Leadership-Policy-Standards-ISLLC-2008.pdf

Fielding, M. (2001). Students as radical agents of change. *Journal of Educational Change, 2*(2), 123–141.

Fielding, M. (2004). Transformative approaches to student voice: theoretical underpinnings, recalcitrant realities. *British Educational Research Journal, 30*(2), 295–311.

Freire, P. (1970). *Pedagogy of the oppressed.* New York, NY: Continuum.

Ginwright, S., Cammarota, J., & Noguera, P. (2005). Social justice and communities: Toward a theory of urban change. *Social Justice, 32*(3), 24–40.

Ginwright, S., Noguera, P., & Cammarota, J. (Eds.). (2006). *Beyond resistance: Youth activism and community change: New democratic possibilities for policy and practice for America's youth.* New York, NY: Routledge.

Giroux, H. (1986). Radical pedagogy and the politics of student voice. *Interchange, 17*(1), 48–69.

Halx, M. D. (2011). A more critical pedagogy: Could it reduce "dropout" rates of disadvantaged male Latino students? The student perspective. Paper presented at University Council for Educational Administration, Pittsburgh, PA.

Halx, M. D., & Ortiz, M. (2011). Voices of Latino male high school students on the meaning of education: Perspectives of "drop-outs" and those-on-the-brink. *Latino Studies, 9*(4), 416–438.

Hursh, D. (2007). Assessing No Child Left Behind and the rise of neoliberal policies. *American Educational Research Journal, 44*(3), 493–518.

Irizarry, J. G. (2009). Reinvigorating multicultural education through youth participatory action research. *Multicultural Perspectives, 11*(4), 194–199.

Irizarry, J. G. (2011a). Buscando la libertad: Latino youths in search of freedom in school. *Democracy and Education, 19*(1). Retrieved from http://www.democracyeducation journal.org/home

Irizarry, J. G. (2011b). *The Latinization of U.S. schools: Successful teaching and learning in shifting cultural contexts.* Boulder, CO: Paradigm Publishing.

Kincheloe, J. L. (2008). *Critical pedagogy primer.* New York, NY: Peter Lang.

Ladson-Billings, G. (2006). From the achievement gap to the education debt: Understanding achievement in U.S. schools. *Educational Researcher, 35*(7), 3–12.

Lenoir, G. C. (2011). *Study and analysis of academic skills of newcomer high school students who are foreign born in central Texas.* Doctoral dissertation. The University of Texas at Austin, Austin, TX. Retrieved from http://repositories1.lib.utexas.edu/bitstream/handle/ 2152/ETD-UT-2011-0%202817/LENOIR-DISSERTATION.pdf?sequence=1

Lipman, P. (2004). *High stakes education: Inequality, globalization, and urban school reform.* New York, NY: Routledge.

Lott, B., & Webster, K. (2006). Carry the banner where it can be seen: Small wins for social justice. *Social Justice Research, 19*(1), 123–134.

Mansfield, K. C. (2011a). *Troubling social justice in a single-sex public school: An ethnography of an emerging school culture.* Unpublished dissertation. The University of Texas at Austin, Austin, TX.

Mansfield, K. C. (2011b). "They throw rocks at us and call us 'Oreos' and 'Dykes'": Student voices cry out for school administration intervention. Paper presented at University Council for Educational Administration, Pittsburgh, PA.

Mansfield, K. C. (in press). "I love these girls, I was these girls": Women working for social
    justice in a single-sex public school. *Journal of School Leadership, 23*(4), forthcoming.
Marks, H. M., & Printy, S. M. (2003). Principal leadership and school performance: An
    integration of transformational and instructional leadership. *Educational Administration
    Quarterly, 39*(3), 370–397.
Marshall, C., & Anderson, A. (2008). *Activist educators.* New York, NY: Routledge.
Mayberry, M. (2006). The story of a Salt Lake City gay–straight alliance: Identity work and
    LGBT youth. *Journal of Gay & Lesbian Issues in Education, 4*(1), 13–31.
McLaren, P. (2003). Critical pedagogy: A look at the major concepts. In A. Darder,
    M. Baltodano & R. Torres (Eds.), *The critical pedagogy reader* (pp. 69–96). London:
    Routledge Falmer.
Miller, R., & Rowan, B. (2006). Effects of organic management on student achievement.
    American Educational Research Journal, 43(2), 219–253.
Mitra, D. (2004). The significance of students: Can increasing "student voice" in schools lead to
    gains in youth development? *Teachers College Record, 106*(4), 651–688.
Mitra, D. L. (2008). Amplifying student voice: Students have much to tell us about how best to
    reform our schools. *Educational Leadership, November,* 20–25.
Mitra, D. L., & Gross, S. J. (2009). Increasing student voice in high school reform: Building
    partnerships, improving outcomes. *Educational Management Administration and Leader-
    ship, 37*(4), 522–543.
Nadal, K. L., Issa, M., Leon, J., Meterko, V., Wideman, M., & Wong, Y. (2011). Sexual
    orientation microaggressions: 'Death by a thousand cuts' for lesbian, gay, and bisexual
    youth. *Journal of LGBT Youth, 8*(3), 234–259.
Ouchi, W. G. (1981). The Z organization. In J. M. Shafritz, J. S. Ott, Y., & S. Jang (Eds.),
    Classics of organizational theory (6th ed., pp. 424–435). Belmont, CA: Wadsworth.
Partanen, A. (2011). What Americans keep ignoring about Finland's school success. *The
    Atlantic,* December 29. Retrieved from http://www.theatlantic.com/national/archive/
    2011/12/what-americans-keep-ignoring-about-finlands-school-success/250564/#disqus_
    thread. Accessed on January 4, 2012.
Reddick, R., Welton, A., Alsandor, D., Denyszyn, J., & Platt, S. (2011). Stories of success:
    Pathways to higher education for graduates from high minority, high poverty public
    schools. *Journal of Advanced Academics, 22*(4), 594–618.
Robinson, J. P., & Espelage, D. L. (2011). Inequities in educational and psychological outcomes
    between LGBTQ and straight students in middle and high school. *Educational
    Researcher, 40*(7), 315–330.
Rodriguez, G. M., & Fabionar, J. O. (2009). The impact of poverty on students and schools:
    Exploring the social justice leadership implications. In C. Marshall & M. Oliva (Eds.),
    Leadership for social justice: Making revolutions in education (2nd ed., pp. 55–73).
    New York, NY: Allyn & Bacon.
Rubin, B. C., Yonemura Wing, J., Noguera, P. A., Haydé Fuentes, E., Liou, D. D., Rodriguez,
    A. P., & McCready, L. T. (2006). Structuring inequality in Berkeley High. In
    P. A. Noguera & J. Y. Wing (Eds.), *Unfinished business: Closing the achievement gap
    in our schools* (pp. 29–86). San Francisco, CA: Jossey Bass.
Sahlberg, P. (2011). *Finnish lessons: What can the world learn from educational change in
    Finland?* London: Teachers College Press.
Sands, D. I., Guzman, L., Stephens, L., & Boggs, A. (2007). Including student voices in school
    reform: Students speak out. *Journal of Latinos in Education, 6*(4), 323–345.

Santamaria, L. J., & Santamaria, A. P. (2012). *Applied critical leadership in education.* New York, NY: Routledge.

Scheurich, J. J. (1998). The grave dangers in the discourse on democracy. *International Journal of Leadership in Education, 1*(1), 55–60.

Schultz, B. (Ed.). (2011). *Listening to and learning from students.* Charlotte, NC: Information Age Publishing.

Shields, C. M. (2004). Dialogic leadership for social justice: Overcoming pathologies of silence. *Educational Administration Quarterly, 40*(1), 109–132.

Shields, C. M. (2010). Transformative leadership: Working for equity in diverse contexts. *Educational Administration Quarterly, 46,* 558–589.

Solórzano, D., Ceja, M., & Yosso, T. (2000). Critical race theory, racial microaggressions, and campus racial climate: The experiences of African American college students. *Journal of Negro Education, 69,* 60–73.

Steele, C. M., & Aronson, J. (1998). How stereotypes influence the standardized test performance of talented African American students. In C. Jencks & M. Phillips (Eds.), *The Black White test score gap.* Washington, DC: Brookings Institute.

Torre, M. E., & Fine, M. (2006). Researching and resisting: Democratic policy research by and for youth. In S. Ginwright, J. Cammarota & P. Noguera (Eds.), *Beyond resistance: Youth activism and community change: New democratic possibilities for policy and practice for America's youth* (pp. 269–285). New York, NY: Routledge.

Tschannen-Moran, M. (2004). *Trust matters: Leadership for successful schools.* San Francisco, CA: Jossey-Bass.

Valencia, R. R. (2010). *Dismantling contemporary deficit thinking: Educational thought and practice.* New York, NY: Taylor and Francis.

Valenzuela, A. (1999). *Subtractive schooling: US-Mexican youth and the politics of caring.* Albany, NY: State University of New York Press.

Welton, A. (2011a). The courage to critique policies and practices from within: Youth participatory action research as critical policy analysis. A response to "Buscando la Libertad: Latino Youths in Search of Freedom in School". *Democracy and Education, 19*(1). Article 11.

Welton, A. (2011b). *Navigating networks of opportunity: Understanding how social networks connect students to postsecondary resources in integrated and segregated schools.* Unpublished doctoral dissertation, University of Texas, Austin, TX.

Zajda, J., Majhanovich, S., & Rust, V. (2006). Introduction: Education and social justice. *Review of Education, 52,* 9–22.

CHAPTER 3

RE-THINKING THE PREPARATION OF EDUCATIONAL LEADERS: UTILIZING Q-METHODOLOGY TO FACILITATE THE DEVELOPMENT OF SOCIALLY JUST LEADERS

Bradley W. Carpenter and Sarah Diem

ABSTRACT

The continued move toward high-stakes accountability has significant consequences for public schools located within communities occupied by historically marginalized populations, as the majority of chronically low-performing (CLP) schools are housed within metropolitan areas where students of color are the primary population (Noguera & Wells, 2011). Consequently, over the course of the last decade, college- and university-based educational leadership preparation programs have been placed on the defensive (Cibulka, 2009; Goldring & Schuermann, 2009), as school leaders and those who prepare them are being increasingly held accountable for the significant escalation in the number of CLP schools. With such issues as the contextual backdrop, the purpose of this chapter is to further examine two issues critical to the field of educational leadership preparation: the need for leadership preparation programs to develop and

Global Leadership for Social Justice: Taking it from the Field to Practice
Advances in Educational Administration, Volume 14, 43–57
Copyright © 2012 by Emerald Group Publishing Limited
All rights of reproduction in any form reserved
ISSN: 1479-3660/doi:10.1108/S1479-3660(2012)0000014007

provide curricula and pedagogical offerings that better prepare leaders to serve within diverse communities, and the potentiality of using Q-methodology as an evaluative instrument in the reformation efforts of educational leadership preparation programs attempting to better equip school leaders for diverse contexts.

Over the course of the last decade, college- and university-based educational leadership preparation programs have been placed on the defensive (Cibulka, 2009; Goldring & Schuermann, 2009), as school leaders are increasingly being held accountable for the significant increase in the number of public schools labeled as chronically low-performing (CLP). The escalation of the accountability pressures being placed upon school leaders was recently intensified when President Barack Obama unveiled the latest iteration of the Title I School Improvement Grant (SIG). Embedded within the policies structuring the Obama/Duncan version of the Title I SIG are four "turn-around" strategies – turnaround, restart, school closure, and transformation – from which schools failing to meet the standardized definition of success defined by Adequate Yearly Progress (AYP) must select (U.S. Department of Education, 2009).

Much like the previous version (Bush/Spellings Title I SIG), the current SIG program was crafted to promote dramatic increases in the student achievement of CLP schools. However, unlike its predecessor, each of the strategies listed in the Obama/Duncan iteration calls for the removal of the school leader. Therefore, even without the necessary research to support turnaround policies that promote the removal of school leaders (Ravitch & Mathis, 2010), the values that inform the Obama/Duncan Title I SIG program endorse the continued shift away from policies focused on the importance of educational inputs (e.g., adequate funding) to policies focused on the measurement of educational outputs (e.g., effectiveness of school leaders working with low-performing schools).

The continued move toward high-stakes accountability and the value being placed upon the effectiveness of educational outputs has significant consequences for public schools. Furthermore, schools located within communities occupied by historically marginalized populations are particularly vulnerable, as the majority of CLP schools affected by the Obama/Duncan Title I SIG programs are housed within metropolitan areas where students of color are the primary population (Noguera & Wells, 2011).

With such issues as a contextual backdrop, this chapter has two guiding foci. First, we provide a brief review of how issues pertaining to race and racism are often marginalized within the explicit curricula guiding educational leadership preparation programs. Next, we examine the potentiality of using Q-methodology as an evaluative instrument in reformation efforts of educational leadership preparation programs attempting to better equip school leaders for diverse contexts. The first focus – programs preparing leaders for diverse communities – was chosen on the basis of our belief that during this moment, where CLP schools have become a highly prioritized policy issue, the effectiveness of educational leadership programs seeking to prepare educational leaders for highly diverse communities must be further examined. The second focus – the potential use of Q-methodology in the evaluation of leadership preparation programs – was chosen after our initial exploration of this methodology revealed an approach to research considered to be "inclusive" in nature; its methods require researchers to gather and value a diverse range of voices when evaluating the effectiveness of programs (Militello & Benham, 2010). The inclusivity of Q-methodology aligns well with our broader research agenda, which aims to answer two primary questions: (1) how should preparatory programs investigate the ways in which dialogical relationships between professors and students, administrators and teachers, and teachers and students affect the enactment of anti-racist and racially conscious practices within public schools that house historically marginalized populations? and (2) what types of evaluative tools are available that can be used by preparatory programs seeking to examine the formal and informal variables that influence the dialogical relationships around issues of social justice present in university or college classrooms between professors and students, administrators and teachers, and teachers and students?

The purpose of this chapter is to further examine two issues critical to the field of educational leadership preparation: (1) the need for leadership preparation programs to develop and provide curricula and pedagogical offerings that better prepare leaders to serve within diverse communities and (2) the potentiality of using Q-methodology as an evaluative instrument in the reformation efforts of educational leadership preparation programs attempting to better equip school leaders for diverse contexts.

THE RACIALLY CONTINGENT CONTEXT OF HIGH-STAKES ACCOUNTABILITY: IMPLICATIONS FOR LEADERSHIP PREPARATION

Embedded within the regulatory language of No Child Left Behind (NCLB) is the stipulation that standardized measures of success would increase each year until 2014, when every child would be expected to meet levels of proficiency on all assessed subjects. In 2009, at the time of Arne Duncan's confirmation as the Secretary of Education, it was estimated that 5,000 schools – or 5% of the nation's total – would qualify as CLP (Duncan, 2009). In addition, from the 2004–2005 school year to the 2008–2009 school year, the number of schools categorized as in need of improvement rose about 30% (from 9,690 to 12,597) (Planty, Kena, & Hannes, 2009). These statistics have major implications for a great number of school communities. While such statistics are alarming, they are especially troublesome for communities of color where the majority of CLP schools are housed. As noted by Balfanz and Legters (2004),

> Schools that have Blacks or Hispanics as the largest racial/ethnic group make AYP [Adequate Yearly Progress] about one third of the time, whereas schools with Whites as the majority group make AYP 53% of the time. (p. 568)

The increased pressures of high-stakes accountability and the increasingly publicized failures of public schools have contributed to the growing amount of concern as to the effectiveness of college- and university-based leadership preparation programs (Shakeshaft, 1999). Consequently, when considering the inequalities stressed by Balfanz and Legters (2004), restructuring educational leadership preparation programs through the use of more inclusive evaluative measures such as Q-methodology must be considered in efforts to better equip educational leaders for diverse settings.

LEADERSHIP PREPARATION FOR DIVERSE COMMUNITIES

In the field of educational leadership, the preparation of school leaders oriented toward issues of social justice is of primary importance, given the inequities apparent in the predominance of CLPs populated by historically marginalized populations. Likewise, as public schools continue to grow more segregated along racial and socioeconomic lines (Orfield, 2009), educational leadership preparation programs must develop and implement curricula and pedagogies that equip future leaders to participate in critically oriented dialogues within diverse school communities. Moreover, scholars within the field must hold programs accountable for the ways in which professors are/are not incorporating anti-racist pedagogies into their classrooms. Leadership preparation programs must share best practices, seeking to learn from one another as they work to make social justice an educative component found along all points of the continuum during the leadership development process.

Within the field of educational leadership, a greater emphasis has been placed upon issues of social justice during the course of the last several years (Blackmore, 2009; Jean-Marie, 2010; Jean-Marie, Normore & Brooks, 2009; Marshall & Oliva, 2006; McKenzie et al., 2008; Theoharis, 2007, 2009, 2010). Yet, while efforts to orient programs toward issues of social justice have been celebrated, scholars within the field have expressed concerns with the historical failure of such efforts to adequately address issues of diversity and race (Brown, 2004, 2006; Cambron-McCabe & McCarthy, 2005; Dantley, 2002; López, 2003; Parker & Shapiro, 1992; Shields, 2004; Tillman, 2004; Young & Laible, 2000). Hawley and James' (2010) recent study of University Council for Educational Administration programs validates such concerns. Seeking to determine the ways in which preparatory program courses, resources, and strategies are aligned in a way that would ensure students of diverse school communities could learn at high levels, Hawley and James' findings suggest preparatory programs may not be equipping future leaders with the necessary skills to meet the needs of students housed within diverse public schools.

Specifically, Hawley and James (2010) found leadership preparation programs often (a) marginalized issues of diversity to singular course offerings, (b) focused more on sociological and economic hardships encountered by students of color, thus failing to address race-related issues school leaders are asked to confront during their daily interactions with students, parents, and school communities, and (c) failed to fully integrate readings, film, and other pedagogical tools specifically focused on issues of race and ethnic diversity, choosing instead to orient most activities toward broader issues of social justice.

Our own research efforts (Carpenter & Diem, 2010, forthcoming; Diem & Carpenter, 2012) support the exploratory findings presented by Hawley and James (2010), as we discovered that the purposeful addressing of race, racism, and race relations within the classroom is often prevented by a number of formal and informal barriers. As an example of formal barriers, our study suggested that programs lack the formal structures (e.g., curricular committees) and resources (e.g., release time) necessary to encourage or sustain efforts to purposefully examine how and why educational leadership programs should address issues of race within the classroom. As for informal barriers, we found the persistence of race-related conversations within preparatory programs is often dependent upon the "commitment level" of colleagues within the department. Though issues of commitment may be attributed to lack of formal structures, our conversations with scholars from the field suggest that professors, unless personally "committed," may relegate themselves to individual silos, thus limiting opportunities to engage with peers about issues of race, racism, and race relations and how they should be addressed within the classroom (Carpenter & Diem, forthcoming).

Even when professors overcome issues attributed to the formal and informal barriers discussed above and are able to address socially just themes in the classroom, they often fail to provide the full range of race-specific offerings necessary to prepare leaders for diverse communities (Carpenter & Diem, forthcoming). Consequently, if programs fail to formally structure courses so they directly focus on the variety of complicated issues surrounding race, the probability of students participating in the reflexive consideration of such issues will be determined by whether or not individual professors teaching the course feel personally equipped to facilitate such conversations. Therefore, a variety of personal factors such as the extent of one's past experiences, the understanding of one's positionality, and/or one's overall interest in race-related topics govern the pedagogical and curricular experiences offered to those asked to lead school communities located within highly racialized contexts (Carpenter & Diem, 2010, forthcoming; Diem & Carpenter, 2012).

While both theoretical critiques from scholars within the field (Brown, 2004, 2006; Cambron-McCabe & McCarthy, 2005; Dantley, 2002; Diem & Carpenter, 2012; López, 2003; Parker & Shapiro, 1992; Tillman, 2004; Young & Laible, 2000) and empirically based studies such as Hawley and James (2010) point toward the continued deficiencies of educational leadership programs in addressing the learning needs of leaders serving diverse communities, questions still remain. First, even if structural factors are addressed (e.g., insistence upon a fully integrated curriculum, offering of a diverse range of pedagogical practices), how exactly should preparatory programs investigate the ways in which dialogical relationships between professors and students, administrators and teachers, and teachers and students encourage the enactment of anti-racist and racially conscious practices within public schools that house historically marginalized populations? Second, are there evaluative tools that could be used by preparatory programs seeking to examine the formal and informal variables that influence the dialogical relationships existent in university or college classrooms between professors and students, administrators and teachers, and teachers and students? In the next section we provide insight into these guiding questions by examining the potentialities of Q-methodology as an evaluative instrument for the development and delivery of curricula within educational leadership preparation programs.

Q-METHODOLOGY AND THE CRITICAL ANALYSIS OF MARGINALIZED VOICES

Introduced by William Stephenson in 1935 (Brown, 1980; Stephenson, 1935), Q-methodology is an analytical approach that examines participants' subjectivity when considering highly complex issues (e.g., the ways in which to construct purposefully direct conversations concerning race) (Brown, 1996; Watts & Stenner, 2005). Combining qualitative and quantitative research methods, Q-methodology offers an "inclusive" investigatory lens, placing specific emphasis on the appreciation of a diverse range of voices (Militello & Benham, 2010, p. 620). Consequently, Q-methodology, as a mixed-methods framework for analysis, is a methodological approach that underscores the empowerment of a studied population by allowing participants to examine their own beliefs while engaging in critically reflexive activities (Militello & Benham, 2010). Brown (2006) claims Q-methodology is a "match made in heaven" when studying marginalized populations, highlighting the advantages of a methodology with "built-in features, that, while not providing guarantees, certainly loads the dice in favor of seeing things from the native's or any other point of view, marginalized or otherwise" (p. 365).

Consequently, if the reformatory goal of leadership preparation programs is to better promote the enactment of anti-racist leadership practices in public schools serving historically marginalized populations, perhaps Q-methodology should receive further consideration as an evaluative tool for the design and implementation of curricula being offered. In the next section, we describe the "doing" of Q-methodology by highlighting the efforts of scholars within the educational leadership field.

Q-METHODOLOGY AND THE PREPARATION OF EDUCATIONAL LEADERS

Though scholars within the field of educational leadership have used Q-methodology as an analytical tool to guide their research efforts, there are strikingly few that currently use the methodology to study educational leadership and leadership preparation programs. Using the *Academic Search*

Premier database, we conducted the following *Boolean* searches, scanning peer-reviewed articles published from 2000 to 2010 in order to determine how often Q-methodology is used as a research method to study educational leadership preparation programs: (a) Q-methodology AND education leadership; (b) Q-methodology AND leadership preparation; and (c) Q-methodology AND principal preparation.[1]

As shown in Table 1, there is very little evidence within peer-reviewed journals in the educational leadership field that Q-methodology is being used in the study of issues pertaining to educational leadership preparation. Of the seven articles found within our initial searches, two address issues relating to leadership preparation within European countries (Presthus, 2006; Woods, 2011); two focus on issues concerning counselor leadership within the United States (Curry & DeVoss, 2009; Janson, Stone, & Clark, 2009; West, Bubenzer, Osborn, Paez, & Desmond, 2006); and the seventh article, though published for an international audience, most closely addresses our focus, which is how Q-methodology can be used to better develop educational leaders (Militello & Benham, 2010). The purpose of the Militello and Benham's (2010) study was to "measure the perceived growth in collective leadership with participants in the Kellogg Leadership for Community Change (KLCC) initiative[2]" (p. 620), and to investigate the ways in which leadership development scholars and evaluation development scholars can collaborate to better evaluate the development of collective leadership skills.

Though we highlight the absence of Q-methodology-specific articles within our field's peer-reviewed journals, we certainly acknowledge the existence of researchers who use mixed-methods approaches to address issues

Table 1. The Use of Q-Methodology within the Field of PK-12 Educational Leadership Preparation.

Search Terms	Number of Citations in the *Academic Search Premier* Database	Types of Academic Articles
Q-methodology AND education leadership	6	Leadership Preparation (International) (2), Counselor as Leader (United States) (3), Collective Leadership Development (International) (1)
Q-methodology AND leadership preparation	1	Counselor as Leader (1)
Q-methodology AND principal preparation	0	

pertaining to social justice and leadership preparation. However, we do feel as if this absence is noteworthy, as we acknowledge the purposefully inclusive aims of Q-methodological specific research, viewing its investigatory intent as a valuable tool when attempting to evaluate the ways in which leadership preparation programs plan for and discuss issues pertaining to race.

In the next section, we briefly describe each step involved in the enactment of a Q-methodology study. After highlighting the guiding structure of a Q-methodological study (Watts & Stenner, 2005), we illustrate how researchers form the field of educational leadership (Militello & Benham, 2010) were able to use Q-methodology to evaluate the development of educational leaders through their examination of the KLCC initiative.

Q-METHODOLOGY AND ITS POTENTIALITY WITHIN EDUCATIONAL LEADERSHIP RESEARCH

Step 1

To conduct a study using Q-methodology, researchers must first develop a Q-sample, the set of statements selected participants will choose from when participating in the study (Watts & Stenner, 2005). As described by McKeown and Thomas (1988), Q-samples either can be developed in a structural fashion, meaning the adoption of prefabricated statements (i.e., published standards such as Interstate School Leaders Licensure Consortium (ISLLC) standards), or can be developed in the naturalistic sense, meaning a group of evaluators would develop a set of agreed-upon themes and/or statements based upon a review of literature. After determining how the Q-samples are to be constructed, researchers identify emergent themes and sort Q-samples into related families. In their study, Militello and Benham (2010) chose to develop Q-samples in a naturalistic manner, beginning with a review of documents provided by the KLCC initiative. Initially, the researchers provided participants with 79 statements. They then "discarded duplicate statements or combined items that expressed similar ideas" (Militello & Benham, 2010, p. 624). Next, statements were edited for clarity, retaining the original wording provided by participants. These statements were then "pilot tested" (p. 624) with KLCC members in an effort to ensure content validity, which lead to a consolidation of the initial statements. The final product of these efforts resulted in 33 statements, which Militello and Benham assigned random numbers from 1 to 33.

Step 2

After researchers compile an initial working list of Q-samples, they must establish collaborative relationships with participants so they are able to monitor the participants' evaluation of chosen Q-samples; this is also referred to as Q-sorting (Watts & Stenner, 2005). Militello and Benham (2010) selected six different KLCC sites to evaluate the prioritized Q-samples within their study. KLCC fellows at each site were asked to sort each of the 33 statements into 9 categories. They were then asked to select a value for each response, ranging from a score of $+4$ (most representative of the participants' work with KLCC) to -4 (least representative of the participants' work with KLCC). Next, after completing the value-assigned sort, researchers asked participants a number of questions, seeking to gather the subjective reasoning behind their choices. The researchers stress the importance of this step claiming, "These questions helped us understand better the participants' rationales for sorting the cards in the manner they did" (p. 625). Citing the work of Brown (1980), Militello and Benham (2010) explain that this step within the investigation provides researchers with an opportunity to clarify points that may have otherwise been left unclear.

Step 3

The final step in a Q-methodology study involves the statistical analyses of gathered data, which includes factor extrication, rotation, and estimation (Watts & Stenner, 2005). Militello and Benham (2010) chose to use software (MQ Method 2.06) to help facilitate the quantitative analysis of Q-component data. The component analysis conducted through the use of the MQ software allows researchers to "find associations among the different Q-sorts", provides "z scores for each statement on each factor," and helps to "identify how each individual correlates to each of the model sorts" (pp. 625–626).

Although the Q-methodology previously described allowed Militello and Benham (2010) to provide evaluative data for six sites working with the KLCC initiative, they are quick to caution readers that the conclusions drawn from their evaluation of KLCC's ability to help develop collaborative leadership skills cannot be completely tied to the analysis of Q-data. Offering a summative explanation of their findings the researchers state:

> Our findings have helped us learn that community-based, collective leadership has many dimensions. We have also learned that leadership is about building trusting relationships and alliances, as well as managing tasks to achieve goals. And we have learned that

learning leadership is a lifelong commitment that builds on the epistemological knowledge of place, the organic and participatory nature of learning organizations, and the values of compassion, and inclusivity. (p. 631)

While such findings add value to the field of educational leadership preparation, our desire was to highlight the ways in which Q-methodology could serve as an evaluative tool for programs seeking to prepare educational leaders for highly diverse communities. Thus, the insights Militello and Benham (2010) offer as to the overall effectiveness of Q-methodology are perhaps the greatest insights how such a methodology may address our overall desire.

Through Q-methodology, participants were invited to make decisions as to 'what is meaningful' and hence what does (and what does not) have value and significance from their perspectives. Consequently, this process can afford leadership program developers better insight into participants perceptions of individual leadership abilities, the use of leadership principles, and the effect this work might have on community change and policy agendas. (p. 630)

Therefore, as school leaders, and by extension school leadership preparation programs, are being increasingly held accountable for the significant increase in the number of public schools labeled as CLP, perhaps it is time for our field to further investigate Q-methodology as an evaluative tool that offers a more inclusive focus on the identity and voice of participants in the field. Clearly, if preparation programs are still not adequately implementing curricula throughout all of their courses and programmatic activities that address issues of diversity, equity, and social justice (Hawley & James, 2010), there is no excuse not to explore new methods of understanding why this is occurring.

DISCUSSION: Q-METHODOLOGY AS A FACILITATOR OF PROGRAMMATIC REFORM

The purpose of this chapter is to further examine two issues critical to the field of educational leadership preparation: (1) the need for leadership preparation programs to develop and provide curricula and pedagogical offerings that better prepare leaders to serve within diverse communities and (2) the potentiality of using Q-methodology as an evaluative instrument in the reformation efforts of educational leadership preparation programs attempting to better equip school leaders for diverse contexts. Additionally, our broader agenda focuses on the further development of anti-racist leadership preparation programs, pushing us to continue investigating the ways in which dialogical relationships between professors and students, administrators and teachers, and teachers and students affect the enactment of anti-racist and racially conscious practices within public schools that house historically marginalized populations. This agenda also challenges us to continue searching for evaluative tools that may be used by preparatory programs seeking to examine the formal and informal variables that influence the dialogical relationships present in university or college classrooms between professors and students, administrators and teachers, and teachers and students.

Principals today work within a context defined by the continued emphasis on high-stakes accountability and the inequitable distribution of CLP schools. Therefore, it is extremely important that educational leadership preparation programs include the pursuit of equity and social justice as a central priority. Scholars responsible for preparing PK-12 administrators must better evaluate their programs' ability to offer adequate exposure to purposeful conversations focused specifically on issues of race and racism. We believe Q-methodology addresses this evaluative need by affording leadership preparation programs "better insight into participants' perceptions of individual leadership abilities, the use of leadership principles, and the effect this work might have on community change and policy agendas" (Militello & Benham, 2010, p. 630). The purposeful construction of Q-methodological studies can help faculty and students work together in a critically reflexive manner, systematically probing the issues that inform the ways in which leaders must be prepared to work in diverse communities. Thus, Q-methodology can be used to assist leadership preparation programs in evaluating, developing, and maintaining the curricula and pedagogy necessary to cultivate leaders able to enact an agenda of student success through practices built upon a social justice agenda (Militello & Benham, 2010).

Although the demographic make-up of public schools continues to dramatically shift and the federal government continues to place more of a policy-enforced emphasis on increasing accountability standards, scholars within the field of educational leadership must challenge themselves to seek out new techniques that will better facilitate the development of socially just leaders. We feel Q-methodology addresses this particular challenge by allowing professors within preparation programs to critically reflect at themselves, their curricula, and their practices while also seeking input from a more diverse constituency, those who are asked to realize their role as anti-racist leaders within diverse school communities. We believe Q-methodology, as a purposefully inclusive and critically reflexive approach to research, may benefit the field of educational leadership by providing an investigative approach that allows leadership preparation programs to examine the ways in which teacher and administrator relationships hinder and/or facilitate the actualization of anti-racist and racially conscious practices and conversations within public schools.

NOTES

1. Searches were constructed as inclusive as possible, using *All Text* as the modifying search category.
2. The KLCC initiative was designed by the W.K. Kellogg Foundation to "strengthen community leaders as they address their own local issues" and "focus on cultivating a group of community leaders on specific issues over a two-year period" (http://www.iel.org/programs/klcc.html).

REFERENCES

Balfanz, R., & Legters, N. (2004). *Locating the dropout crisis: Which high schools produce the nation's dropouts? Where are they located? Who attends them?* Report No. 70. Center for Social Organization of Schools, Johns Hopkins University, Baltimore, MD.

Blackmore, J. (2009). Leadership for social justice: A transnational dialogue. *Journal of Research on Leadership Education, 4*(1), 1–10.

Brown, K. M. (2004). Leadership for social justice and equity: Weaving a transformative framework and pedagogy. *Educational Administration Quarterly, 40*(1), 77–108.

Brown, K. M. (2006). Leadership for social justice and equity: Evaluating a transformative framework and andragogy. *Educational Administration Quarterly, 42*(5), 700–745.

Brown, S. R. (1980). *Political subjectivity: Applications of Q methodology in political science.* New Haven, CT: Yale University Press.

Brown, S. R. (1996). Q methodology and qualitative research. *Qualitative Health Research, 4,* 561–567.

Brown, S. R. (2006). A match made in heaven: A marginalized methodology for studying the marginalized. *Quality & Quantity, 40*(3), 361–382.

Cambron-McCabe, N., & McCarthy, M. M. (2005). Educating school leaders for social justice. *Educational Policy, 19*(1), 201–22210.1177/0895904804271609.

Carpenter, B. W., & Diem, S. (2010). Narrative explorations of race and racism: Interrogating the education of tomorrow's leaders. Paper presented at the American Educational Research Association Annual Meeting, Denver, CO.

Carpenter, B. W., & Diem, S. (forthcoming). Talking race: Facilitating critical conversations in educational leadership preparation programs. *Journal of School Leadership.*

Cibulka, J. G. (2009). Declining support for higher-education leadership preparation programs: An analysis. *Peabody Journal of Education, 84*(3), 453–466.

Curry, J. R., & DeVoss, J. A. (2009). Introduction to special issue: The school counselor as leader. *Professional School Counseling, 13*(2), 64–67.

Dantley, M. E. (2002). Uprooting and replacing positivism, the melting pot, multiculturalism, and other important notions in educational leadership through an African American perspective. *Education and Urban Society, 34*(3), 334–352.

Diem, S., & Carpenter, B. W. (2012). Exploring the blockages of race-related conversations in the classroom: Obstacles or opportunity? In J. S. Brooks & N. W. Arnold (Eds.), *Educational leadership and racism: Preparation, pedagogy and practice*. Charlotte, NC: Information Age Publishing.

Duncan, A. (2009). *Turning around the bottom five percent* [Speech]. U.S. Department of Education. Retrieved from http://www2.ed.gov/news/speeches/2009/06/06222009.html

Goldring, E., & Schuermann, P. (2009). The changing context of K-12 education administration: Consequences for Ed.D. program design. *Peabody Journal of Education, 81*(1), 10–43.

Hawley, W., & James, R. (2010). Diversity-responsive school leadership. *UCEA Review, 52*(3), 1–5.

Janson, C., Stone, C., & Clark, M. A. (2009). Stretching leadership: A distributed perspective for school counselor leaders. *Professional School Counseling, 13*(2), 98–106.

Jean-Marie, G. (2010). "Fire in the belly": Igniting a social justice discourse in learning environments of leadership preparation. In A. K. Tooms & C. Boske (Eds.), *Bridge leadership: Connecting educational leadership and social justice to improve schools* (pp. 97–124). Charlotte, NC: Information Age Publishing, Inc.

Jean-Marie, G., Normore, A., & Brooks, J. S. (2009). Leadership for social justice: Preparing 21st century school leaders for a new social order. *Journal of Research on Leadership in Education, 4*(1), 1–31.

López, G. R. (2003). The (racially neutral) politics of education: A critical race theory perspective. *Educational Administration Quarterly, 39*(1), 68–94.

Marshall, C., & Oliva, M. (2006). *Leadership for social justice: Making revolutions in education*. Boston, MA: Pearson.

McKenzie, K., Christman, D., Hernandez, F., Fierro, E., Capper, C., Dantley, M., et al. (2008). Educating leaders for social justice: A design for a comprehensive, social justice leadership preparation program. *Educational Administration Quarterly, 44*(1), 111–138.

McKeown, B. F., & Thomas, D. B. (1988). *Q methodology*. Newbury Park, CA: Sage.

Militello, M., & Benham, M. K. P. (2010). "Sorting Out" collective leadership: How Q-methodology can be used to evaluate leadership development. *The Leadership Quarterly, 21*(4), 620–632.

Noguera, P. A., & Wells, L. (2011). The politics of school reform: A broader and bolder approach to Newark. *Berkeley Review of Education, 2*(1), 5–25.

Orfield, G. (2009). *Reviving the goal of an integrated society: A 21st century challenge*. Los Angeles, CA: University of California, The Civil Rights Project/Proyecto Derechos Civiles.

Parker, L., & Shapiro, J. (1992). Where is the discussion in educational administration programs? Graduate student voices addressing an omission in their preparation. *Journal of School Leadership, 2*(1), 7–33.

Planty, M., Kena, G., & Hannes, G. (2009). *The condition of education 2009 in brief*. Washington, DC: National Center for Education Statistics.

Presthus, A. M. (2006). A successful school and its principal – Enabling leadership within the organization. *International Studies in Educational Administration, 34*(2), 82–99.

Ravitch, D., & Mathis, W. J. (2010). A review of college- and career-ready students. In W. J. Mathis & K. G. Welner (Eds.), *The Obama education blueprint: Researchers examine the evidence* (pp. 9–22). Charlotte, NC: Information Age Publishing, Inc.

Shakeshaft, C. (1999). The struggle to create a more gender-inclusive profession. *Handbook of Research on Educational Administration, 2*, 99–118.

Shields, C. M. (2004). Dialogic leadership for social justice: Overcoming pathologies of silence. *Educational Administration Quarterly, 40*(1), 109.

Stephenson, W. (1935). *The study of behavior: Q-technique and its methodology.* Chicago, IL: University of Chicago Press.

Theoharis, G. (2007). Social justice educational leaders and resistance: Toward a theory of social justice leadership. *Educational Administration Quarterly, 43*(2), 221.

Theoharis, G. (2009). *The school leaders our children deserve: Seven keys to equity, social justice, and school reform.* New York, NY: Teachers College Press.

Theoharis, G. (2010). Sustaining social justice: Strategies urban principals develop to advance justice and equity while facing resistance. *International Journal of Urban Educational Leadership, 4*(1), 92–110.

Tillman, L. C. (2004). (Un)intended consequences? The impact of the Brown v. Board of Education decision on the employment status of black educators. *Education and Urban Society, 36*(3), 280–303.

U.S. Department of Education. (2009). *Guidance on fiscal year 2010 school improvement grants under section 1003(g) of the Elementary and Secondary Education Act of 1965.* Retrieved from http://www2.ed.gov/programs/sif/guidance-20091218.doc

Watts, S., & Stenner, P. (2005). Doing Q methodology: Theory, method and interpretation. *Qualitative Research in Psychology, 2*(1), 67–91.

West, J. D., Bubenzer, D. L., Osborn, C. J., Paez, S. B., & Desmond, K. J. (2006). Leadership and the profession of counseling: Beliefs and practices. *Counselor Education and Supervision, 46*(1), 2–16.

Woods, C. E. (2011). Using Q methodology to explore leadership: The role of the school business manager. *International Journal of Leadership in Education, 14*(3), 317–335.

Young, M. D., & Laible, J. (2000). White racism, antiracism, and school leader preparation. *Journal of School Leadership, 10*, 374–415.

PART 2
PROMOTING SOCIAL
JUSTICE-ORIENTED WORK

CHAPTER 4

A PROGRAM DESIGNED TO RECULTURE EDUCATIONAL LEADERSHIP

Carl Kalani Beyer

ABSTRACT

The purpose of this chapter is to share a higher education leadership program at Pacific Oaks College that aims to prepare the next generation of administrators. The goal of this program is to prepare school administrators who are capable of leading school districts or schools so that they exemplify environments committed to democracy, social justice, and school improvement. The purpose of sharing this information is to get Schools of Education to consider a similar approach so that the next generation of social justice leaders can foster democratic communities and bring about the school improvements necessary to ensure that all members of their school communities have a chance to reach their full potential as teachers and learners.

INTRODUCTION

The purpose of this chapter is to share a higher education leadership program that aims to prepare the next generation of administrators. The goal of this

Global Leadership for Social Justice: Taking it from the Field to Practice
Advances in Educational Administration, Volume 14, 61–78
Copyright © 2012 by Emerald Group Publishing Limited
All rights of reproduction in any form reserved
ISSN: 1479-3660/doi:10.1108/S1479-3660(2012)0000014008

program is to prepare school administrators who are capable of leading school districts or schools so that they exemplify environments committed to democracy, social justice, and school improvement. To meet this purpose, this chapter includes the following: a brief introduction of Pacific Oaks College, the institution sponsoring this program; the connection of this educational leadership program to a call for reforming educational leadership programs made by experts in the field more than a decade ago; the design of the program; the alignment of the program to both the California and National Board leadership standards; the description and resources connected to each course in the program; the five-year plan of assessment; and a conclusion that links this program to what the experts stated educational leadership programs needed in order to transform our schools.

PACIFIC OAKS COLLEGE

Pacific Oaks College is an independent institution of learning influenced by its Quaker heritage and dedicated to principles of social justice, respect for diversity, and value of individual uniqueness. For over 65 years, it has been the goal of a Pacific Oaks College education to encourage learners to find their own voices, to take stands in the face of opposition, and to exercise competence while collaborating with others. In the past, the ability of Pacific Oaks College to impact education was limited to early childhood education; however, due to the creation of a new School of Education, Pacific Oaks College is ready to prepare educators who can have a positive impact on children throughout the pre-K-12 age groups. The newest program in the School of Education is its educational leadership program, a program intended to help low-performing students and/or schools and school districts by credentialing California administrators who are committed to democracy, social justice, and school improvement. This degree results from collaboration between the Education and Human Development Departments at Pacific Oaks College and our alumni. It was during our focus discussion groups with alumni that the faculty and administrators learned that a call for reforming administrative preparation had been around for over 10 years.

THE CALL FOR REFORM

Over 12 years ago, Murphy (1999) challenged educational leadership programs to combine democratic community, social justice, and school improvement to form "three powerful synthetic paradigms" that would "reculture the profession of educational administration" (p. 54). He defined "democratic community" based upon John Dewey's assertion of democracy as being a mode of associated living and the perspective of Furman and Shields (2003) that democratic community includes the following:

> respect for the worth and dignity of individuals and their cultural tradition; reverence for, and proactive facilitation of, free and open inquiry and critique; recognition of interdependence in working with the common good; responsibility of individuals to participate in free and open inquiry; and the importance of collective choices and actions in the interest of the common good. (p. 9)

Social justice principles that relate to schools include the following strategies: foster inclusion in schools; plans that close the achievement gap; ways to address barriers to social justice; and measurable goals and evaluation systems (Beck & Malley, 2011; Cambron-McCabe, 2005; Cambron-McCabe & McCarthy, 2011; Larson, 2001; Self, 2009). Murphy refocused social justice to involve educational leadership programs developing "cultural knowledge; knowledge about [the candidates] own culture and cultural biases, [and] other cultures," and dealing with conflicts, which derive from cultural sources. Finally, he called for the need for educational leadership programs to address school improvement from the perspective of the study of teaching and learning, including "learning theory, school change, curriculum theory, assessment, and data analysis" (p. 57).

DESIGN OF PROGRAM

The Master of Arts (MA) degree program in Educational Leadership is a 44-semester unit, post-baccalaureate program, which intends to provide candidates with the fundamental knowledge base to become leaders in curriculum and promote democratic community, social justice, and school improvement. The design of this program is to produce transformative leaders who can ensure the success of all members of the learning community he or she leads. Moreover, while every course in the program has an assessment feature that prepares teachers to know how to instruct and assess student performance, one course in the program focuses entirely on accountability, an area that is vital to achieving the success of all children. More importantly, this degree prepares educational leaders for urban and suburban schools and school districts populated by low-income and culturally diverse families and students in order to help children and certified and uncertified staff reach their full potential.

The proposed MA in Educational Leadership offers a curriculum that prepares leaders for self-reflection, experiential learning, best practices, and the leadership skills necessary to promote social justice, equity, and student success in meeting the demands of No Child Left Behind (NBCT). This model of education permits candidates to examine knowledge through multiple cultural lenses and be transformed by the educational experience in an environment that treats every member of the school community with dignity and respect.

In preparing leaders who can change school environments through a systemic transformational process, this program relies on the following set of principles: human development theories, which assume learning is a cumulative and lifelong process; the principles of cultural-centered education, which are instructional strategies that derive from the belief that every human being has an innate value, strengths and abilities, and infinite potential; constructionist theory, which purports that humans generate knowledge and meaning from an interaction between their experiences and their ideas; and transformative theories, which provide candidates with the means to transform organizations and society to be places where social justice and equality are realized.

The MA in Educational Leadership program is unique in providing aspiring school leaders with the tools for leadership that empower them to help everyone in schools discover their fundamental worth and human potential. During the program, candidates investigate the social justice principles that relate to schools and identify skills and traits of social justice leaders (Fuller, 1998; Gaetane, 2008). This process is one that needs to be transformational. According to Taylor (2011), "social justice must do more than touch us; it is meant to move us." School leaders learn how to develop strategies that foster inclusion in schools (Anderson, 2001), which involves preparing candidates to understand diversity, promote an anti-bias curriculum, manage conflicts through conflict resolution strategies, and support professional development, collaboration, and community building (Cambron-McCabe, 2005; Cambron-McCabe & Dantley, 2001; Cambron-McCabe & McCarthy, 2011). Moreover, this program helps candidates learn how to construct a plan that closes the achievement gap by establishing measurable goals and evaluation systems and addressing barriers to social justice (Fuller & Johnson, 2001; Haycock, 2001). Through problem-solving experiences, observations of practicing social justice leaders, and role-playing exercises, this program examines how to create the modern learning organization poised for adaptation in a global economy and environment of uncertainty, and will draw upon diverse perspectives and ethical considerations (Cameron & Quinn, 2006; Changing, 2011; Fullan, 2001a, 2001b; Gordon, 2003; Gupta, 2009; Schein, 1993).

ALIGNMENT OF PROGRAM TO STANDARDS

The MA in Educational Leadership program utilizes the standards of both the California Commission on Teacher Credentialing (CTC) and the National Board Certificate for Educational Leaders (NBCEL). Interestingly, the three powerful synthetic paradigms of democratic community, social justice, and school improvement are integral to these two sets of standards. Thus, utilizing the CTC Standards of Candidate Competence and Performance and the NBCEL Standards, and the College's traditional mission regarding fostering social justice and equity and culture-centered education made it easy to develop a program that more than meets Murphy's challenge for an educational leadership program.

The CTC Standards of Candidate Competence and Performance Standards involve candidates demonstrating competence in developing, articulating, and implementing a vision of learning that is supported by the school community; promoting student learning and professional growth; ensuring organizational management for student learning; collaborating with diverse community interests and mobilizing community resources; modeling personal ethics and leadership capacity; and understanding, implementing, and influencing the larger political, social, economic, legal, and cultural context (Standards, 2009). The NBCEL Standards involve preparing accomplished principals who lead with a sense of urgency and achieve the highest results for all students and adults; lead and inspire the learning community to develop, articulate, and commit to a shared and compelling vision of the highest levels of student learning and adult instructional practice; ensure that teaching and learning are the primary focus of the organization; ensure that each student and adult in the learning community is known and valued; inspire and nurture a culture of high expectations, where actions support the common values and beliefs of the organization; skillfully lead the design, development, and implementation of strategic management systems and processes that actualize the vision and mission; consistently demonstrate a high degree of personal and professional ethics exemplified by integrity, justice, and equity; and view their own learning as a foundational part of the work of school leadership (National, 2010).

DESCRIPTION AND RESOURCES OF COURSES

Besides the required field experience and clinical practice and research capstone course, the courses in this program include education and human development courses that together serve to prepare candidates to be social justice leaders and meet the CTC and NBCEL Standards. The "Social Justice, Equity, and School Reform" course investigates the social justice principles that relate to schools, develop strategies that foster inclusion in schools, construct a plan that closes the achievement gap, reflect on ways to address barriers to social justice, identify skills and traits of social justice leaders, and establish measurable goals and evaluation systems for social justice leaders (Beck & Malley, 2011; Cambron-McCabe, 2005; Gaetane & Normore, 2009; Larson, 2001; School climate, 2004; Self, 2009).

The "Legal and Ethical Dimensions of Leadership" course provides a comprehensive coverage of the theories, frameworks, and ethics of leadership practice and the evaluation of leadership theories, concepts, and approaches. It integrates ethical decision-making processes and assesses the potential impact of leadership strategies on organizations, including organizational social responsibility (Beyer, 1997; Boyd & Crowson, 2002; Bull & McCarthy, 1995; Carney, 2000; Equal protection, 2011; Free speech, 2011; Mattocks, 1985; Reamer, 2008; Traditional teaching, 2011).

The "Transformational Leadership" course investigates advanced leadership theory, acquisition of power and influence, and participative and transformational forms of leadership. Through problem-solving experiences and exercises, this course examines how to create the modern learning organization poised for adaptation in a global economy and environment of uncertainty, and will draw upon diverse perspectives and ethical considerations. It focuses on organizational redesign and the essential skills necessary for leaders to initiate organizational transformations. Finally, examining resistance and acceptance of change initiatives, including the impact on organizational culture completes the content of this course (Baron, 2011; Blackmore, 2002; Bolger & Somech, 2004; Collaborative skills, 2011; Frattura & Capper, 2007; Lawrence, 2007; Markewicz, 2005; Prichard, 1996; School mission, 2011).

The "Contemporary School Finance Theory and Policy" course is an introduction to organizational finance policies and practices. Included in this course is an exploration of federal, state, and local revenue sources, and organizational budgeting and financial management procedures. This course examines the financial reports that aid school leaders in making business decisions that promote an environment focused upon social justice and equity. In doing so, this course covers issues such as long- and short-term budgeting, key financial statements, the role of the outside auditor, reporting financial information, and valuation of assets and equities (Critical race theory, 2011; Dearden, Ferri, & Meghir, 2002; Marx, 2002; Partnering, 2011; Torres & Burnett, 2011; Utt, 1999; Why School, 2011; Wilde, 2011).

The "Leadership for System Accountability" course focuses on the role of leaders in the development and implementation of monitoring systems. It prepares candidates to analyze development and methods of aligning standards, instruction, and assessment in order to develop a perspective of instructional theory, development, and design methods, which aligns educational content to articulated goals and applies valid and reliable assessment to the evaluation of the instructional program. The intention of this course is to move candidates beyond consideration of test scores as the sole vehicle for accountability and provide candidates with the knowledge and skills to develop quantitative and qualitative elements of a multi-dimensional monitoring system for their organization (Angelo & Cross, 2011; Assessing, 2011; Critical issues, 2011; DuFour, 2004; Ellis & Hughes, 2002; Finding, 2011; Klassen & Willoughby, 2011; Lusthaus, Anderson, Carden, & Montalván, 2002; No child, 2007; 9 principles, 2011; Principles, 2007; Professional, 2011; What are promising, 1996).

The "Human Resources and School Culture" course provides an analysis of organizational culture and change and offers ideas and strategies on how stories, rituals, traditions, and other cultural practices can be used to create positive, caring, and purposeful schools. In addition, this course enables candidates to analyze how leaders can balance cultural goals and values against accountability demands in order to transform negative and toxic school cultures so that trust, commitment, and sense of unity can prevail (Gordon, 2003; Heathfield, 2010, 2011a, 2011b; Krüger, 2011; Schein, 1993; What is culture, 2011).

The "Supervision for Effective School Community" course investigates the theoretical and practical framework for supervising and evaluating the performance of all members of the school community (administrators, teachers, and staff). While the theoretical perspectives of development supervision theory provide the basis for engaging in the practice of super-vision of instruction, assessment, program quality, and standards-based instruction, candidates in this course construct a supervision plan based upon supervising all school employees toward creating a school community that is successful academically and treats all its members with dignity and respect. In this course, professional development is a strategy to increase the effectiveness of all members of the school community. Finally, it addresses the impact of collective bargaining on human resources and community relationships. For candidates seeking to do the master's degree research project, they must select an area of interest directly linked to educational leadership that transforms schools by the completion of this course (Aseltine, Faryniarz, & Rigazio-Digilio, 2011; Hattie & Timperley, 2007; Tracy, 1995; Transformational, 2011; Twadell, 2008; What is supervision, 2011).

The "Communication for Empowerment" course empowers candidates to make connections with other people. This course addresses the following five areas of communication: active listening for meaning; concise, organized, and reflective writing; analysis and critique of diverse modes of scholarship; creating collaborative structures of group facilitation and leadership; and demonstrating organized verbal communication and presentation of self together with reflective feedback. In addition, students evaluate their ability to think critically, synthesizing the subjective and the objective, in all the areas of communication. They will critique the impact of their values and biases on communication across cultural, racial, class, and gender lines (Acculturation, 2011; Aneas & Sandin, 2009; Barstow, 2008; Common, 2011; Communication models, 2011; Dialogue, 2011; Intercultural, 2011; Jory & Yodanis, 2011; MacFarlane, 2011).

The "Conflict Resolution and Mediation" course provides candidates with the tools to evaluate the nature of human conflict, create effective strategies, and develop programs for the peaceful resolution of conflict. Candidates evaluate and critique techniques and models for conflict resolution and mediation, and engage in creative problem-solving in various conflict areas at the micro and macro levels of society. Communicating across cultures and bias awareness issues will be evaluated within all content areas (Brahm, 2004; Bush & Folger, 2005; Causes, 2011; Conflict resolution education, 2011; Facts for teens, 2011; Inger, 1991; Johnson, Johnson, Dudley, & Burnett, 1992; Johnson, Johnson, Stevahn, & Hodne, 1997; Moore, 2003; Spangler, 2003; Stevahn, 1998; Stevens & Stevens, 2011; Tallinn, 1997; Understanding conflict, 2011; Who should, 2011; Winslade & Monk, 2000).

The "Implementing the Anti-Bias Curriculum" course provides candidates with skills for working with adults within an anti-bias framework. Class format includes discussions, interactive activities utilizing case studies and policies, readings, and written assignments. Candidates engage with each other in critical evaluation of educational practices and societal obstacles to deepen their theoretical knowledge and to define levels and models of advocacy work (Hespe, 2011; Hohensee & Derman-Sparks, 1992; Lamantia, 2008; Normore & Blanco, 2011; Seahorn, 2011; Tetlock & Mitchell, 2011; 101 ways, 2011).

The "Working with Families in a Diverse World" course enables candidates to assess the psychosocial developmental stages/tasks of families, the critical importance of culture/ethnic traditions, values, and beliefs and how these all affect our work as advocates. Within this context, candidates create strategies to be more successful individual, interpersonal, and institutional change agents. Candidates engage in active, experiential learning, synthesize theory and practice, and evaluate the impact of social, ethnic, gender, and class contexts on themselves and their work with diverse families (Akey, 2006; Besaw et al., 2004; Caspe, 2003; Cuevas De Caissie, 2011; Developing, 2011; Fuller, 2002; Newbury, 2005; Spagola & Fiese, 2007).

The "Leadership in Education" course prepares candidates to work effectively with diverse colleagues and families; program development and administration; strategies for facilitating empowerment, responsibility, and advocacy; adult supervision; and professional growth and survival. Candidates critically evaluate their own practice and values, to observe and assess other adults working with children and their families or with other adults, and to synthesize values with practice (Blasé & Blasé, 1999; Clair & Adger, 1999; Cohen, 2007; Graue, 2011; Guide, 2011; Howard, 2007; Lewis, 2003; Meeting, 2011; Mitra, 2011; Sullivan, 2011; Whelan, 2011).

FIVE-YEAR ASSESSMENT PLAN

A five-year plan of assessment for the Educational Leadership program details the connection of each course with the program learning outcomes. The following are the direct measures based upon a signature assignment that covers each of the following Program Learning Outcomes (PLOs): PLO 1 – Social Justice Leadership Analysis, which involves comparing and contrasting usual leaders with social justice leaders; PLO 2 – Ethical and Legal Issues for School Multicultural Plan, which is a plan to indicate how the candidate will improve the success of a particular diverse group; PLO 3 – Empowerment Plan, which involves constructing an empowerment plan, involving students, teachers, administrators, and parents; PLO 4 – Communication Plan, which involves constructing a communication plan that would close the achievement gap at their school; PLO 5 – School Finance Project, which involves interpreting the social justice implications of contemporary school finance theory and policy; PLO 6 – School Accountability Plan, which demonstrates quantitative and qualitative elements of a multidimensional accountability system; PLO 7 – Resource Management Plan, which demonstrates accessing and altering the components of the school culture; PLO 8 – School Supervision Project, which involves constructing a plan for continual evaluation of all members of the school community; PLO 9 – Conflict Resolution Project, which involves constructing a plan for peaceful resolution of conflicts involving diverse families, schools, and classrooms; PLO 10 – School Anti-Bias Curriculum Plan, which involves constructing a plan based upon critically evaluating educational practices and societal obstacles; PLO 11 – Collaboration Plan, which establishes how diverse families can be included in the decision making in a social justice school; PLO 12 – Completed ePortfolio, which involves presenting for outside review of their completed ePortfolio; PLO 13 – Leadership Plan, which involves producing a leadership plan that balances leading social justice, equity, and instructional quality with professional growth and survival; and PLO 14 – Research Project, which uses an evidence-based decision-making process that demonstrates their becoming a social justice leader who can turn around struggling urban schools.

CONCLUSION

The Educational Leadership program offered by Pacific Oaks College more than meets the challenge to which Murphy (1999) presented Schools of Education more than a decade ago. The components of democratic community, social justice, and school improvement are embedded in most of the courses in this program. Moreover, this program also satisfies the CTC and NBCEL standards as well. It has been the intent of the author of both this program and this chapter to offer other educational leaders in higher education with a sample of how to meet Murphy's challenge. The section on the courses provides course descriptions and many of the sources for which the courses were built; the section on assessments provides a sample of signature assignments that measure the program learning outcomes. Finally, it is the hope of this author that other educational leaders will take up Murphy's challenge even if they do not utilize the work done by Pacific Oaks College. Through our combined efforts, we can change the direction of schools and school districts by preparing the next generation of social justice leaders who can foster democratic communities and bring about the school improvements necessary to ensure that all members of their school communities have a chance to reach their full potential as teachers and learners.

REFERENCES

Acculturation and intercultural identity in the post-modern world. (2011). Retrieved from http://www.wichert.org/icid.html. Accessed on November 29, 2011.

Akey, T. M. (2006). School context, student attitudes and behavior, and academic achievement. *MDRC.* Retrieved from http://www.mdrc.org/publications/419/full.pdf. Accessed on November 29, 2011.

Anderson, G. (2001). Promoting educational equity in a period of growing social inequity. *Education and Urban Society, 33*(3), 320–332.

Aneas, M. A., & Sandin, M. P. (2009). Intercultural and cross-cultural communication research. *Forum: Qualitative Social Research, 10*(1). Retrieved from http://www.qualitative-research.net/index.php/fqs/article/viewArticle/1251/2738. Accessed on November 29, 2011.

Angelo, T. A., & Cross, K. P. (2011). *Classroom assessment techniques.* Retrieved from http://honolulu.hawaii.edu/intranet/committees/FacDevCom/guidebk/teachtip/assess-1.htm. Accessed on June 1, 2011.

Aseltine, J. M., Faryniarz, J. O., & Rigazio-Digilio, A. J. (2011). *Reconceptualizing supervision and evaluation.* Association of Supervision and Curriculum Development. Retrieved from http://www.ascd.org/publications/books/106001/chapters/Reconceptualizing-Supervision-and-Evaluation.aspx. Accessed on July 22, 2011.

Assessing student learning. (2011). Retrieved from http://www.columbia.edu/cu/tat/pdfs/assessment.pdf. Accessed on June 1, 2011.

Baron, D. (2011). *Consensus building: A key to school transformation.* Retrieved from http://www.pkwy.k12.mo.us/CandD/CurriculumAreas/cte/documents/Article.Consensus.Bldg 0001.pdf. Accessed on July 13, 2011.

Barstow, C. (2008). The power differential and the power paradox: Avoiding the pitfalls. *Hakomi Forum, 19–21*(Summer). Retrieved from http://www.hakomiinstitute.com/Forum/Issue19-1/6Power%20DifferentialPowerParadoxyes.pdf. Accessed on November 29, 2011.

Beck, M., & Malley, J. (2011). *A pedagogy of belonging.* The International Child and Youth Care Network. Retrieved from http://www.cyc-net.org/cyc-online/cycol-0303-belonging.html. Accessed on July 20, 2011.

Besaw, A., Kalt, J. P., Lee, A., Sethi, J., Wilson, J. B., & Zemler, M. (2004). The context and meaning of family strengthening in Indian America. *ERIC Digest,* ED485942. Retrieved from http://www.eric.ed.gov/PDFS/ED485942.pdf. Accessed on July 21, 2011.

Beyer, D. (1997). School safety and the legal rights of students. *ERIC/CUE Digest,* ED414345(121). Retrieved from http://www.ericdigests.org/1998-2/safety.htm. Accessed on July 21, 2011.

Blackmore, J. (2002). Leadership for socially just schooling: More substance and less style in high-risk, low-trust times? *Journal of School Leadership, 12*(2), 198–222.

Blasé, J., & Blasé, J. (1999). Effective instructional leadership. Teachers perspectives on how principals promote teaching and learning in schools. *Journal of Educational*

Administrative, 38(2). Retrieved from http://peoplelearn.homestead.com/Instruc.Effective. pdf. Accessed on July 21, 2011.

Bolger, R., & Somech, A. (2004). *Teaching and Teacher Education, 20,* 277–289. Retrieved from http://www.units.muohio.edu/eduleadership/FACULTY/QUANTZ/bogler.pdf. Accessed on July 21, 2011.

Boyd, W., & Crowson, R. (2002). The quest for a new hierarchy in education: From loose coupling back to tight? *Journal of Educational Administration, 40*(6), 521–533.

Brahm, E. (2004). Benefits of intractable conflict. *Beyond Intractability.* Retrieved from http://www.beyondintractability.org/bi-essay/benefits. Accessed on July 21, 2011.

Bull, B. L., & McCarthy, M. M. (1995). Reflections on the knowledge base in law and ethics for educational leaders. *Educational Administration Quarterly, 31*(4), 613–631.

Bush, R. A., & Folger, J. P. (2005). *The promise of mediation: The transformative approach* (2nd ed.). San Francisco, CA: Jossey-Bass.

Cambron-McCabe, N. (2005). Educating school leaders for social justice. *Educational Policy, 19*(1), 201–222.

Cambron-McCabe, N., & Dantley, M. (2001). Administrative preparation and social justice concerns in Ohio. Paper presented at the American Educational Research Association annual meeting, Seattle, WA.

Cambron-McCabe, N., & McCarthy, M. (2011). *Challenges confronting the preparation and development of school leaders: Implications for social justice.* Retrieved from http://www.pacificoaks.edu/Our_Programs/Masters_Programs/MA_EducationCredential. Accessed on July 8, 2011.

Cameron, K. S., & Quinn, R. E. (2006). *Diagnosing and changing organizational culture.* San Francisco, CA: Jossey-Bass.

Carney, T. H. (2000). Beyond classroom walls: The rediscovery of the family and community as partners in education. *Educational Review, 52*(2). Retrieved from http://www.edc.uoc.gr/~didgram/ago1/p163_s.pdf. Accessed on July 21, 2011.

Caspe, M. (2003). How teachers come to understand families. *Family Involvement Research Digests.* Retrieved from http://www.hfrp.org/family-involvement/publications-resources/how-teachers-come-to-understand-families. Accessed on July 21, 2011.

Causes and solutions to family conflict. (2011). The Family Assistance and Parent Support Program. Retrieved from http://familyconflict.freeyellow.com/FAPSP/CausesOfConflict. html. Accessed on July 21, 2011.

Changing an organizational culture. (2011). Cognitivebehavior.com. Retrieved from http://www.cognitivebehavior.com/management/concepts/changing_org_culture.html. Accessed on July 15, 2011.

Clair, N., & Adger, C. T. (1999). *Professional development for teachers in culturally diverse schools.* Center for Applied Statistics. Retrieved from http://www.cal.org/resources/digest/profdvpt.html. Accessed on July 21, 2011.

Cohen, J. (2007). Evaluation and improving school climate. *School Culture and Climate.* Retrieved from http://www.nais.org/publications/ismagazinearticle.cfm?ItemNumber=150284

Collaborative skills. (2011). Learning forward. Retrieved from http://www.learningforward. org/standards/collaborationskills.cfm. Accessed on July 21, 2011.

Common denominators: Shared governance & work place advocacy. (2011). *Medscape Today.* Retrieved from http://www.medscape.com/viewarticle/490770_4. Accessed on November 29, 2011.

Communication models. (2011). Retrieved from http://www.shkaminski.com/Classes/Handouts/ Communication%20Models.htm. Accessed on November 29, 2011.

Conflict resolution education: Four approaches. (2011). *Education World.* Retrieved from http:// www.educationworld.com/a_curr/curr171.shtml. Accessed on November 30, 2011.

Critical issues: Constructing school partnerships. (2011). Learning Point Associates. Retrieved from http://www.ncrel.org/sdrs/areas/issues/envrnmnt/famncomm/pa400.htm. Accessed on June 3, 2011.

Critical race theory. (2011). A Justice Site. Retrieved from http://www.habermas.org/ critraceth01bk.htm. Accessed on July 21, 2011.

Cuevas De Caissie, R. M. (2011). The meaning of family. *Hispanic Culture Site.* Retrieved from http://www.bellaonline.com/articles/art29820.asp. Accessed on November 30, 2011.

Dearden, L., Ferri, J., & Meghir, C. (2002). *The effects of school quality on educational attainment and wages.* Retrieved from http://discovery.ucl.ac.uk/17052/1/17052.pdf. Accessed on July 21, 2011.

Developing cultural awareness in schools. (2011). Retrieved from http://www.edplus.canterbury. ac.nz/ESOL/documents/developing_cultural_awareness.pdf. Accessed on November 29, 2011.

Dialogue on learning. (2011). Retrieved from http://www.dialogueonlearning.tc3.edu/model/ environment/Emotional%20Safety-grp.htm. Accessed on November 29, 2011.

DuFour, R. (2004). What is a "Professional Learning Community"? *Schools as Learning Communities, 61*(8). Retrieved from http://pdonline.ascd.org/pd_online/secondary_ reading/el200405_dufour.html. Accessed on June 3, 2011.

Ellis, D., & Hughes, K. (2002). Connecting schools, families, and communities for youth success: Partnerships by design. *Creating Communities of Learning & Excellence.* Retrieved from http://educationnorthwest.org/webfm_send/127. Accessed on June 3, 2011.

Equal protection and fundamental rights. (2011). *Exploring Constitutional Conflicts.* Retrieved from http://law2.umkc.edu/faculty/projects/ftrials/conlaw/fundrights.html. Accessed on July 21, 2011.

Facts for teens: Conflict resolution. (2011). National Youth Violence Prevention Resource Center. Retrieved from http://herkimercounty.org/content/Departments/View/11:field = services;/content/DepartmentServices/View/68:field = documents;/content/Documents/ File/124.PDF. Accessed on July 21, 2011.

Finding the simple secrets of successful community groups. (2011). Ourcommunity.com. au. Retrieved from http://www.ourcommunity.com.au/marketplace/marketplace_article. jsp?articleId = 3483. Accessed on June 3, 2011.

Frattura, E. M., & Capper, C. A. (2007). *Leading for social justice: Transforming schools for all learners.* Thousand Oaks, CA: Corwin Press.

Free speech rights of students. (2011). *Exploring Constitutional Conflicts.* Retrieved from http:// law2.umkc.edu/faculty/projects/ftrials/conlaw/studentspeech.htm. Accessed on July 21, 2011.

Fullan, M. (2001a). *Leading in a culture of change.* San Francisco, CA: Jossey-Bass.

Fullan, M. (2001b). *The new meaning of educational change* (3rd ed.). New York, NY: Teachers College Press.

Fuller, E., & Johnson, J. (2001). Can state accountability systems drive improvements in school performance for children of color and children from low-income homes? *Education and Urban Society, 33*(3), 260–283.

Fuller, H. (1998). Transforming learning: The struggle to save urban education. *UCEA Review, 34*(1), 1.

Fuller, R. (2002). The power of context: Creating meaning in language and thought. *Home Educator's Family Times*. Retrieved from http://www.homeeducator.com/FamilyTimes/ articles/10-3article10.htm. Accessed on July 21, 2011.

Furman, G. C., & Shields, C. M. (2003). *How can educational leaders promote and support social justice and democratic community in schools?* Paper presented at the annual meeting of the American Educational Research Association, Chicago, IL.

Gaetane, J. (2008). Leadership for social justice: An agenda for 21st century schools. *Educational Forum, 72*(4), 340–354.

Gaetane, J., & Normore, A. H. (2009). Leadership for social justice: Preparing 21st century school leaders for a new social order. *Journal of Research on Leadership Education, 4*(1). Retrieved from http://www.ucea.org/storage/jrle/pdf/vol4_issue1_2009/Jean_Marie_ Normore%20_Brooks.pdf. Accessed on July 8, 2011.

Gordon, P. D. (2003). *Changing organizational culture: Unleashing creative energy.* Retrieved from http://users.rcn.com/pgordon/homeland/change_culture.pdf. Accessed on July 15, 2011.

Graue, M. E. (2011) Representing relationships between parents and schools: Making visible the force of theory. *Parenthood in America*. Retrieved from http://parenthood.library. wisc.edu/Graue/Graue.html. Accessed on July 15, 2011.

Guide for implementing the balanced and restorative justice model. (2011). Retrieved from http:// www.ojjdp.gov/pubs/implementing/safety.html. Accessed on July 15, 2011.

Gupta, A. (2009). Changing organizational culture. *Practical-Management.com –Transforming Theories into Practice*. Retrieved from http://practical-management.com/pdf/Organization-Development/Changing-Organizational-Culture.pdf?format = phocapdf. Accessed on July 15, 2011.

Hattie, J., & Timperley, H. (2007). The power of feedback. *Review of Educational Research, 77*(1), 81–112.

Haycock, K. (2001). Closing the achievement gap. *Educational Leadership, 58*(6), 6–12. Retrieved from http://www.ascd.org/readingroom/edlead/0103/haycock.html

Heathfield, S. H. (2010). *How to understand your current culture: Artifacts and interactions display your existing culture.* About.com guide. Retrieved from http://humanresources. about.com/od/organizationalculture/a/culture_create.htm. Accessed on July 15, 2011.

Heathfield, S. M. (2011a). *Culture: Your environment for people at work.* About.com guide. Retrieved from http://humanresources.about.com/od/organizationalculture/a/culture.htm. Accessed on July 15, 2011.

Heathfield, S. M. (2011b). *How to change your culture: Organizational culture change.* About.com guide. Retrieved from http://humanresources.about.com/od/organizational-culture/a/culture_change.htm. Accessed on July 15, 2011.

Hespe, D. (2011). *Valuing school diversity: Building ideas around the expectations of parents, students and policymakers.* Retrieved from http://www.aera.net/uploadedFiles/SIGs/ Leadership_for_Social_Justice_(165)/Collaborative_Policy_Papers/Hespe-Valuing_ School_Diversity.pdf. Accessed on November 29, 2011.

Hohensee, J. B., & Derman-Sparks, L. (1992). Implementing an anti-bias curriculum in early childhood classrooms. *ERIC Digest*, ED351146. Retrieved from http://www.ericdigests. org/1992-1/early.htm. Accessed on November 29, 2011.

Howard, G. (2007). As diversity grows, so must we. *Educational Leadership, 64*(6), 16–22. Retrieved from http://www.ascd.org/publications/educational-leadership/mar07/ vol64/num06/As-Diversity-Grows,-So-Must-We.aspx. Accessed on November 29, 2011.

Inger, M. (1991). Conflict resolution programs in school. (1992). *ERIC Clearinghouse,* ED338791. Retrieved from http://www.ericdigests.org/1992-5/conflict.htm. Accessed on November 29, 2011.

Intercultural communication. (2011). Retrieved from http://faculty.buffalostate.edu/smithrd/UAE%20Communication/Unit5.pdf. Accessed on November 29, 2011.

Johnson, D. W., Johnson, R. T., Dudley, B., & Burnett, R. (1992). Teaching students to be peer mediators. *Educational Leadership, 50*(1), 10–13. Retrieved from http://www.ascd.org/publications/educational-leadership/sept92/vol50/num01/Teaching-Students-to-Be-Peer-Mediators.aspx. Accessed on November 29, 2011.

Johnson, D. W., Johnson, R. T., Stevahn, L., & Hodne, P. (1997). The three Cs of safe schools. *Educational Leadership, 55*(2), 8–13. Retrieved from http://www.ascd.org/publications/educational-leadership/oct97/vol55/num02/The-Three-Cs-of-Safe-Schools.aspx. Accessed on November 29, 2011.

Jory, B., & Yodanis, C. L. (2011). *Power – Family relationships, marital relationships.* Retrieved from http://family.jrank.org/pages/1316/Power.html. Accessed on November 29, 2011.

Klassen, K. J., & Willoughby, K. A. (2011). In-class simulations games: Assessing student learning. *Journal of Information Technology, 2.* Retrieved from http://jite.org/documents/Vol2/v2p001-013-59.pdf. Accessed on June 1, 2011.

Krüger, W. (2011). *Change management iceberg.* Retrieved from http://www.valuebasedmanagement.net/methods_change_management_iceberg.html. Accessed on July 15, 2011.

Lamantia, J. (2008). Designing ethical experiences: Understanding juicy rationalizations. *UX Matters.* Retrieved from http://www.uxmatters.com/mt/archives/2008/06/designing-ethical-experiences-understanding-juicy-rationalizations.php. Accessed on July 13, 2011.

Larson, C. (2001, April). Rethinking leadership: New York's efforts to create skilled and knowledgeable leaders for our schools. Paper presented at the American Educational Research Association annual meeting, Seattle, WA.

Lawrence, L. (2007). Using narrative inquiry to explore school transformation: A principal's tale. *Journal of Education, 41.* Retrieved from http://dbnweb2.ukzn.ac.za/joe/JoEPDFs/joe%2041%20lawrence.pdf. Accessed on July 13, 2011.

Lewis, R. E. (2003). Parents, families, and communities in schools. *Harvard Family Research Project.* Retrieved from http://www.hfrp.org/publications-resources/browse-our-publications/parents-families-and-communities-in-schools. Accessed on July 13, 2011.

Lusthaus, M. A., Anderson, G., Carden, F., & Montalván, G. P. (2002). *Organization assessment: A framework for improving performance.* Ottawa, Canada: International Research Center. Retrieved from http://www.idrc.ca/openebooks/998-4/. Accessed on June 3, 2011.

MacFarlane, D. A. (2011). Social communication in a technology-driven society: A philosophical exploration of factor-impacts and consequences. *American Communication Journal* (Winter). Retrieved from http://ac-journal.org/journal/pubs/2010/McFarlane.pdf. Accessed on November 29, 2011.

Markewicz, A. (2005). "A balancing act": Resolving multiple stakeholders interests in program evaluation. *Evaluation Journal of Australasia, 4*(1 & 2), 13–21. Retrieved from http://www.aes.asn.au/publications/Vol4No1_2/balancing_act.pdf. Accessed on July 21, 2011.

Marx, G. (2002). *Preparing students and schools for a radically different future.* Society for the Advancement of Education. Retrieved from http://www.tntdevelopment.org/resources/preparing_students.pdf. Accessed on July 21, 2011.

Mattocks, T. C. (1985). Legal and ethical bases for educational leadership. *Phi Delta Kappa Fastbacks, 426,* 7–51.

Meeting the diverse needs of young children. (2011). *Critical Issues.* Retrieved from http://www.ncrel.org/sdrs/areas/issues/students/earlycld/ea400.htm. Accessed on November 29, 2011.

Mitra, D. (2011). *Student voice or empowerment? Examining the role of school-based youth-adult partnerships as an avenue toward focusing on social.* Retrieved from http://www.ucalgary.ca/iejll/vol10/mitra. Accessed on July 21, 2011.

Moore, C. W. (2003). *The mediation process: Practical strategies for resolving conflicts* (3rd ed.). San Francisco, CA: Jossey-Bass.

Murphy, J. (1999). *The quest for center: Notes on the state of the profession of educational leadership.* Columbia, MO: The University Council for Educational Administration.

National Board for Professional Teaching Standards Accomplished Principal Standards. (2010). Retrieved from http://www.dpi.state.nc.us/docs/recruitment/nationalboardcertification/principals/standards.pdf. Accessed on November 28, 2011.

Newbury, J. (2005). Our next big challenge: Genuine cultural SELF self awareness. *The International Child and Youth Care Network, 78.* Retrieved from http://www.cyc-net.org/cyc-online/cycol-0705-newbury.html. Accessed on November 28, 2011.

No Child Left Behind reform: What's the alternative? (2007). FairTest, October. Retrieved from http://fairtest.org/no-child-left-behind-reform-whats-alternative. Accessed on June 1, 2011.

Normore, A., & Blanco, R I. (2011). Leadership for social justice and morality: Collaborative partnerships, school-linked services and the plight of the poor. *International Electronic Journal for Leadership in Learning.* Retrieved from http://www.ucalgary.ca/iejll/vol10/blanco. Accessed on November 28, 2011.

Partnering for student success – The cradle to career framework. First edition. (2011). Retrieved from http://cradletocareer.files.wordpress.com/2010/10/community-report-nov-4.pdf. Accessed on July 21, 2011.

Prichard, D. C. (1996). Graduate school admissions: Writing an effective personal statement. *The New Social Worker, 3*(2). Retrieved from http://www.socialworker.com/admissio.htm. Accessed on July 21, 2011.

Principles and indicators for student assessment systems. (2007). FairTest. Retrieved from http://fairtest.org/principles-and-indicators-student-assessment-syste. Accessed on June 1, 2011.

9 Principles of good practice for assessing student learning. (2011). Center for Teaching, Learning and Assessment. Retrieved from http://www.iuk.edu/~koctla/assessment/9principles.shtml. Accessed on June 1, 2011.

Professional learning communities. (2011). Annenberg Institute. Retrieved from http://www.annenberginstitute.org/pdf/proflearning.pdf. Accessed on June 3, 2011.

Reamer, R. G. (2008). When ethics and law collide. *Social Work Today, 8*(5). Retrieved from http://www.hawaii.edu/powerkills/TJP.CHAP4.HTM. Accessed on July 13, 2011.

Schein, E. (1993). *Organizational culture and leadership.* Retrieved from http://www.tnellen.com/ted/tc/schein.html. Accessed on July 15, 2011.

School climate and learning. (2004). *Best Practice Briefs, 31*(December). Retrieved from http://outreach.msu.edu/bpbriefs/issues/brief31.pdf. Accessed on July 20, 2011.

School mission statements: Where is your school going? *Education World.* Retrieved from http://www.educationworld.com/a_admin/admin/admin229.shtml. Accessed on July 21, 2011.

Seahorn, A. (2011). *How to implement an anti-bias curriculum in preschool programs.* eHow. Retrieved from http://www.ehow.com/how_5125304_implement-antibias-curriculum-preschool-programs.html. Accessed on November 28, 2011.

Self, E. (2009). A school for peace and justice. *Educational Leadership, 66.* Retrieved from http://www.ascd.org/publications/educational-leadership/jul09/vol66/num10/A-School-for-Peace-and-Justice.aspx. Accessed on July 8, 2011.

Spagola, M., & Fiese, B. H. (2007). *Family routines and rituals: A context for development in the lives of young children.* Retrieved from http://depts.washington.edu/isei/iyc/20.4_spagnola.pdf. Accessed on November 28, 2011.

Spangler, B. (2003). Competitive and cooperative approaches to conflict. *Beyond Intractability.* Retrieved from http://www.beyondintractability.org/bi-essay/competitive-cooperative-frames. Accessed on November 28, 2011.

Standards of quality and effectiveness for administrative services credential. (2009). Commission on Teacher Credentialing. Retrieved from http://www.ctc.ca.gov/educator-prep/standards/SVC-Admin-Handbook.pdf.9. Accessed on July 7, 2011.

Stevahn, L. (1998). *Teaching all students constructive conflict resolution through academic coursework.* Professional Development Associates. Retrieved from http://www.creducation.org/resources/Teaching_All_Students_Constructive_Conflict_Resolution.pdf. Accessed on November 28, 2011.

Stevens, J., & Stevens, L. (2011). The nature of conflict and managing it effectively. *Online Newsletter.* Retrieved from http://www.itstime.com/feb2005.htm. Accessed on November 28, 2011.

Sullivan, A. M. (2011). *Pursuit of goals in partnerships: Empowerment in practice.* Retrieved from http://www.aare.edu.au/02pap/sul02098.htm. Accessed on November 28, 2011.

Tallinn, E. (1997). Nonviolence and conflict: Conditions for effective peaceful change. *UNPO international conference.* Retrieved from http://www.unpo.org/downloads/nonviolence report97.pdf. Accessed on November 30, 2011.

Taylor, E. (2011). Leadership for social justice: Envisioning an end to racial achievement gap. *New Horizons for Learning.* Retrieved from http://education.jhu.edu/newhorizons/Transforming%20Education/Leadership%20in%20Education/Leadership%20for%20Social%20Justice/index.html. Accessed on November 28, 2011.

Tetlock, P. E., & Mitchell, G. (2011). Unconscious prejudice and accountability systems: What must organizations do to prevent discrimination? Retrieved from http://www.law.virginia.edu/pdf/faculty/ImplicitBiasinOrganizationsandAdversarialCollaboration.pdf. Accessed on November 28, 2011.

Torres, A., & Burnett, J. (2011). *Student outcomes that measure the school's value-added.* National Association of Independent Schools. Retrieved from http://www.nais.org/sustainable/article.cfm?ItemNumber = 151607. Accessed on July 21, 2011.

Tracy, S. (1995). How historical concepts of supervision relate to supervisory practices today. *The Clearing House, 68*(5), 320–324.

Traditional teaching: Student relations, legal & ethical issues. (2011). Retrieved from http://cte.umdnj.edu/traditional_teaching/traditional_relations_legal.cfm. Accessed on July 21, 2011.

Transformational Leadership. (2011). Coalition of Essential Schools. Retrieved from http://www.essentialschools.org/benchmarks/3. Accessed on July 22, 2011.

Twadell, E. (2008). Win-win contract negotiation: Collective bargaining for student learning. In *The collaborative administrator: Working together as a professional learning community* (pp. 218–233). Bloomington, IN: Solution Tree Press.

Understanding conflict and conflict management. (2011). The Foundation Coalition. Retrieved from http://foundationcoalition.org/publications/brochures/conflict.pdf. Accessed on November 29, 2011.

Utt, R. D. (1999). *Is there a better way to finance and build new schools?* Education Report. Retrieved from http://www.educationreport.org/pubs/mer/article.aspx?id = 1693. Accessed on July 21, 2011.

101 ways you can beat prejudice. (2011). Close the Book on Hate. Retrieved from http://www.adl.org/prejudice/prejudice_school.html. Accessed on June 1, 2011.

What are promising ways to assess student learning? (1996). *Improving America's Schools: A Newsletter on Issues in School Reform* (Spring). Retrieved from http://www2.ed.gov/pubs/IASA/newsletters/assess/pt3.html. Accessed June 2011.

What is culture? (2011). Retrieved from http://anthro.palomar.edu/culture/culture_1.htm. Accessed on July 22, 2011.

What is "supervision"? What do supervisors do? (2011). Retrieved from http://managementhelp.org/management/guidebook.htm#anchor227239. Accessed on July 16, 2011.

Whelan, J. (2011). *Community engagement: Practical strategies for empowerment or a wishful narrative.* Retrieved from http://comm-org.wisc.edu/papers2006/whelan.htm. Accessed on November 30, 2011.

Who should students turn when they have trouble resolving conflict? (2011). *teAchnology.* Retrieved from http://www.teach-nology.com/litined/conflict_resolution/. Accessed on July 21, 2011.

Why school finance matters? (2011). EdSource. Retrieved from http://www.edsource.org/iss_fin_whyitmatters.html. Accessed on July 21, 2011.

Wilde, M. (2011). *The ins and outs of school finance.* Greatschools. Retrieved from http://www.greatschools.org/improvement/volunteering/101-the-ins-and-outs-of-school-finance.gs. Accessed on July 21, 2011.

Winslade, J., & Monk, G. D. (2000). *Narrative mediation: A new approach to conflict resolution.* San Francisco, CA: Jossey-Bass.

CHAPTER 5

PREPARING SCHOOL LEADERS FOR SOCIAL JUSTICE: EXAMINING THE EFFICACY OF PROGRAM PREPARATION

Karie Huchting and Jill Bickett

ABSTRACT

The purpose of this chapter is to describe the practices being implemented within the doctorate for Educational Leadership for Social Justice (Ed.D.) program at Loyola Marymount University. Furthermore, the chapter shares data from a qualitative method of inquiry to assess the program's efficacy. The goal of the program is to produce leaders who can advocate for social justice in educational settings, implement theory into practice, and lead to facilitate transformation in the field of education. The foundational elements of the program include a cohort model, a rigorous curriculum, supportive structures, and the culminating dissertation. Data from program graduates and their supervisors suggest that students are transformed in the program to respect, educate, advocate, and lead educational settings.

Global Leadership for Social Justice: Taking it from the Field to Practice
Advances in Educational Administration, Volume 14, 79–101
Copyright © 2012 by Emerald Group Publishing Limited
All rights of reproduction in any form reserved
ISSN: 1479-3660/doi:10.1108/S1479-3660(2012)0000014009

INTRODUCTION

The goal of the Ed.D. in Educational Leadership for Social Justice at Loyola Marymount University (LMU) in Los Angeles is to produce leaders who can advocate for social justice in educational settings, implement theory into practice, and lead to facilitate transformation in the field of education. The intent of this chapter is to explore the practices within the LMU doctoral program that purport to prepare school leaders to lead socially just schools, and through a qualitative inquiry, to assess graduate engagement in social justice practices in the field.

There is a clear need for research in this area, both in the arena of educational leadership and in its relationship to social justice. McCarthy (1999) suggests that "research on educational leadership preparation programs, faculty members, and students is needed to inform deliberations about how to better prepare school leaders" (p. 135). And Firestone and Riehl (2005) suggest that research on educational leadership "has been weakened by ... the frequent failure to articulate how a given instance of research addresses linkages among leadership, learning, and equity" (p. 1). However, in the last decade, a growing body of scholarship on leadership for social justice has emerged (Bogotch, 2002; Brooks, Jean-Marie, & Normore, 2007; Larson & Murtadha, 2002; McKenzie, Skrla, & Scheurich, 2006; Tillman, Brown, & Jones, 2006). This is key as leader preparation programs attempt to prepare school leaders to face the difficult issues of class, race, gender, and sexual orientation, among others, while leading in institutions that produce inherently unequal educational outcomes (Black & Murtadha, 2007). Yet, despite the growing body of research in this area, there is scant research which addresses the efficacy of these theoretical frameworks, or of programs that adopt these frames. Ed.D. programs that address the inequities in the educational system through a social justice lens must be evaluated to determine whether they can be efficacious in transforming practice for all students and families. Using a qualitative lens, this chapter promises to address this gap and measure the outcomes of an Ed.D. in Educational Leadership for Social Justice whose stated mission is "to prepare educational leaders with the tools, theories, and experiences they will need to succeed in transforming educational settings into inclusive and equitable learning environments." As professors in the program, we are not content with graduate students who have mastered the theories or learned the practices of successful leadership. It is not enough for us to graduate students who "know." We want to produce educational change agents, who can "act effectively on what they know" (Ball & Tyson, 2012) so that they can improve the lived experiences of students and their families, and be effectively prepared to lead socially just schools.

DEFINING LEADERSHIP FOR SOCIAL JUSTICE AND THE JESUIT INSTITUTION

The need for school leaders who are prepared to face the difficulties of the current educational landscape of a widening achievement gap (NAEP, 2011), and the necessity of providing access and care for all of the nation's students becomes more urgent daily. However, in order for school leaders to become the change agents necessary to transform inequitable systems, they must receive a broad and deep understanding of social justice in their leadership preparation programs (Marshall & Olivia, 2006). Bogotch (2000) asserts that "educational leadership must continuously confront the issue of social justice in all its guises, and deliberately make social justice a central part of educational leadership discourse and actions" (p. 3); yet, he also confirms that the term itself has "no fixed or predictable meanings" (2002, p. 153). In fact, the term social justice can be subject to a multitude of interpretations and may be politically charged, depending on the context (Shoho, Merchant, & Lugg, 2005).

Some scholars have addressed this definitional challenge by broadly characterizing social justice in education to include creating equity and access for all students (Jean-Marie, 2008; Marshall & Olivia, 2006). Ayers, Quinn, and Stovall (2009) provide a framework for this definition of social justice education by introducing the three principles of equity, activism, and social literacy. Equity is students' equal access to the most challenging and nurturing educational experiences; activism is the principle of agency, making sure that children can understand, and if necessary change what is before them; and social literacy, the principle of relevance, is the nourishing of our own identities and honoring the importance of context. Likewise, Chubbuck (2007) asserts that scholars have described a "cluster of outcomes" (p. 240) that make up socially just teaching, including teacher knowledge of their own and their students' cultural identity, equitable access to learning for all students, teacher activism around policy, and empowerment of students as engaged citizens.

Similarly, rooted in theology and the vision of the S.J.'s 16th century founder, St. Ignatius Loyola, the Jesuit definition of social justice calls for the need to challenge the established order which "supports, maintains, and perpetuates a real disorder, an institutionalized violence; that is to say, social and political structures which have injustice and oppression built into them" (Arrupe, 1980, p. 107). The systemized oppression and disenfranchisement of students based on race, color, gender, ability, or sexual orientation, and the widening gap between those students who have access to quality education and those who do not, is in fact an institutionalized violence. It is perpetuated by structures in our society, which the principles of social justice, and the Jesuit ideology, demand educators must challenge.

Jesuit institutions are explicit about their mission of social justice. The aim of a Jesuit education is to prepare leaders who will become conscionable citizens in a global context (Kolvenbach, 2000) and be formed as "men and women for others" (Arrupe, 1973). Further, characteristics of Jesuit education include "an attention to the formation of the whole person, an affirmation of the world, a dialogue across cultures, a lifelong openness to growth and reflection, and a willingness to analyze institutional structures" (Chubbuck, 2007, p. 240) and pursue action oriented solidarity with the poor (ICAJE, 1994). Programs for educational leadership for social justice are unique in their focus on this ideology. Andrews and Grogan (2002) assert that educational leadership programs are, in the main, characterized as "preparing aspiring principals for the role of principal as a top down building manager" (p. 4). But a Jesuit orientation requires a focus on social justice, and the Ed.D. program at LMU in Educational Leadership for Social Justice embraces this principle, where it is integrated in the program title, the mission, the curriculum, and the learning outcomes of the program.

Hernandez and McKenzie (2010) assert that the literature on leadership for social justice "provides no clear consensus on what an entire educational leadership program oriented toward social justice would include" (p. 49). The purpose of this chapter is to fill this gap by describing the characteristics of an Ed.D program in Educational Leadership for Social Justice and then measuring its efficacy in producing leaders for social justice as reflected in conversations with both graduates and their supervisors about alignment with program outcomes.

ASSESSMENT METHODS

Leadership programs should produce educational change agents, who can serve and improve their varied educational contexts. To this end, we examined graduate perspectives on leadership for social justice in terms of their knowledge and experiences in the field and examined the perspectives of the graduates' supervisors or colleagues in the field to assess the program efficacy of producing leaders who are able to implement theory into practice. A significant component of this program assessment is its exploration of the perspectives of the graduates' supervisors and colleagues, which provides an added measure of validity to the perspectives of the students themselves. By moving beyond an analysis of the coursework and programmatic experience to examine the daily practice in the K-20 settings of graduates from educational leadership programs, we can truly evaluate graduate preparedness to lead socially just schools.

DESIGN AND PROCEDURES

To assess leadership for social justice, we employed an empirical approach, using two sources of qualitative data to form our conclusions. In addition to analyzing student-level data for evidence of transformation, we also included another voice – interviews with supervisors or colleagues – who could speak to the daily practice of the graduate. While student-level data are important to document transformation, the field of educational leadership has been criticized for relying heavily on self-report data (Murphy & Vriesenga, 2006) to determine program success. Certainly, evidence of true transformation occurs on a daily basis where concepts of leadership and social justice are applied in the K-20 educational system. Therefore, we chose to document not only the student's perspective of his/her transformation but also how a colleague or supervisor views the efficacy of the graduate's leadership for social justice in the field.

Semi-structured interviews were conducted with recent graduates from the program, lasting approximately 60 minutes, and were audio recorded and transcribed. Both researchers conducted the interviews for quality assurance, and transcriptions were sent to all participants for member checking. Graduates were purposefully selected to participate in the study because they (1) had reached a satisfactory level of completion of the dissertation for prepublication review and (2) had worked in the K-20 educational system during their three years of doctoral studies.

Supervisors or colleagues were also selected because they (1) had worked with the graduate student during their doctoral studies and were comfortable speaking about the graduate's daily work in the field and (2) had the graduate's consent to be contacted for an interview, providing their contact information. Supervisors were then interviewed in a similar format. The study was reviewed and approved by the Institutional Review Board at the sponsoring University.

To assess the transformation of the graduate during the program in demonstrating mastery of the learning outcomes of the doctoral program, similar questions were asked of both the graduates and their supervisors or colleagues. For instance, participants were asked to define leadership and social justice; reflect on perspectives of leadership for social justice before the program and upon completion of the program; provide examples of leadership from a social justice perspective found in the graduate's daily work; and provide general reflections about the program. The interviews were then coded for evidence of the candidate's transformation in the area of each of the learning outcomes which will now be described.

PROGRAM DESIGN

The Ed.D. program at LMU is grounded in the University mission, and guided by the Ignatian tradition which supports the education of the whole person, the encouragement of learning, the service of faith and the promotion of justice. This mission informs the conceptual framework of the School of Education to produce candidates who can respect, educate, advocate, and lead (REAL). Specifically, the learning outcomes of the Ed.D. program align to the conceptual framework as illustrated below:

Conceptual Framework	Learning Outcomes
Respect	Offer a rigorous course of study that connects theory, practice, and advocacy in leadership, equity, and diversity
Educate	Prepare candidates who are knowledgeable in advanced research methodologies and able to design, implement, and evaluate educational policies, programs, and practices
Advocate	Prepare leaders to critically engage complex issues impacting education and student achievement and to demonstrate commitment to social justice
Lead	Help meet existing and projected needs for moral and ethical leaders throughout the preK-20 public and private system

LMU, founded in 1911, resides in the large urban metropolis of Los Angeles, which includes the vibrant but troubled LAUSD school district, close to 1,000 charter schools (National Charter School Directory, 2011), approximately 250 Catholic elementary and secondary schools in the Archdiocese of Los Angeles (2011) and a multitude of private and alternative educational settings, and nonprofit organizations. This provides a diverse educator population for the applicant pool.

The Ed.D program is a relatively new program, begun in 2004, that has graduated 5 cohorts of students, for a total of 53 degrees awarded. LMU serves all populations of educators in Los Angeles, from the public, Catholic, charter, private and nonprofit sectors. Students from each of these segments are enrolled each cohort. The application process includes a required personal statement and interview which asks students to describe their understanding of leadership for social justice and their commitment to research in this area. Students write individual, not group dissertations, which must address issues of social justice in education.

Specifically, the program is intentionally designed to promote leadership for social justice through four key foundational elements: (1) cohort model, (2) curriculum, (3) supportive structures, and (4) dissertation.

COHORT MODEL

The Ed.D. was designed to include a close cohort model, where students within a cohort progress through coursework together. Cohort sizes are kept small, at a maximum of 18 students in order to provide personalized attention to student growth. It is rare that new students are admitted once the cohort begins. Within the cohort model and over the course of the three-year program, students develop strong bonds of trust. The cohort model was one aspect of the program that several graduates spoke of during their exit interview. They talked about "the friendships and the camaraderie" and the importance of that support system to their success, but they also spoke of another added value of the cohort – the diversity of background within each group. LMU actively recruits public, charter, Catholic, private, and nonprofit interests in each cohort, and students felt enriched by the variety of opinion and the heterogeneity of voices in the classroom. One student talked about "seeing different perspectives."

I had a very narrow perspective [when first in the program] ... the biggest thing for me from day one was hearing the different perspectives of the different people in public,

private, and charter education ... [and] all the ways that we are the same in terms of
dealing with some of the same issues for our students was an eye opener.

Another graduate said "I felt like a better person every Tuesday morning
[after a Monday night class]. And part of it was because I was having
conversations with people I would have never had in the past."

A different type of diversity was discussed by a white male candidate who
appreciated the cohort model for another reason. He talked about having
been "broken open" by the experience of his cohort. As a white male, in a
diverse cohort of white, African American, Latino/a, differently abled,
female, and gay students, this candidate felt his male white privilege very
acutely. And through the discussions with his cohort he felt both "targeted"
and enriched by his association with his doctoral classmates. He noted that
by being part of the cohort his understanding of white privilege grew
beyond the readings of Peggy McIntosh (1989) and he indicated that
coming to this understanding was a "process oriented reality" that was able
to be achieved through trust in his cohort members and work in this
program.

CURRICULUM

The curriculum of the program focuses on the two strands that are featured
in the title: leadership and social justice. The program is committed to the
integration of theory and practice in the context of leadership for social
justice. Thus, *leadership* and *social justice* are integrated concepts. While
specific courses may emphasize one area more than the other, for the
purposes of the LMU program they are always viewed as interactive.
Therefore, courses in leadership will always include a meaningful reference
to social justice issues and courses in social justice will always have a focus
on leadership. In this way the two constructs are seamless and inform
each other.

Fig. 1 details the curricular offerings of the program, scaffolding research
skill building and dissertation writing over the course of the three years,
while integrating the theories and practices of leadership and social justice
throughout.

Students were impacted by the social justice curriculum in various ways.
One of the requirements of the program is that dissertation research connect
in some way to issues of social justice in education. Several students
mentioned that coursework helped them to make these connections. Others

Doctor of Education in Educational Leadership for Social Justice

Course Sequence and Program Benchmarks

Cohort 8 (2011 – 2014)

	Summer	Fall	Spring	Total Units
Year 1 2011-12	**Summer Session I** Orientation **Summer Session II** EDLA 7002 Moral and Ethical Leadership (3 units) EDLA 7020 Situated Inquiry in Education (3 units)	EDLA 7045 Transformational Leadership for Student Achievement (3 units) EDLA 7021 Quantitative Research in Education (3 units)	EDLA 7001 Leadership for Social Justice in Education (3 units) EDLA 7022 Qualitative Research in Education (3 units)	**18**
Year 2 2012-13	**Summer Session I** EDLA 7940 Preliminary Review (Benchmark #1) (1 units, Credit/No Credit) EDLA 7950 Dissertation Proposal Design (Chapter 1) (2 units) **Summer Session II** EDLA 7950 Dissertation Proposal Design (Chapter 1) (Cont'd 0 units) EDLA 7040 Contextualizing Leadership in Public Education (3 units) – OR – EDLA 7060 Contextualizing Leadership in Private Education (3 units)	EDLA 7004 Organizational Theory and Change (3 units) EDLA 7049 Research Seminar (Chapters 1-3) (2 units, Credit/No Credit)	EDLA 7005 Educational Change and Innovation (3 units) EDLA 7043 Legal and Policy Issues in Education (3 units) Dissertation Proposal Defense Advancement to Candidacy, & LMU Institutional Review Board (Benchmark #2)	**17**
Year 3 2013-14	**Summer Session II** EDLA 7951 Dissertation Seminar I (2 units) (Chapters 4-5) EDLA 7042 Management of Fiscal/Human Capital (3 units)	EDLA 7952 Dissertation Seminar II (Chapters 4-5) (2 units)	EDLA 7953 Doctoral Dissertation I (2 units, Credit/No Credit) EDLA 7023 Doctoral Colloquia (2 Unit, C/NC) Dissertation Defense (Benchmark #3)	**11**

Fig. 1. Course Sequence for Doctoral Program in Educational Leadership for Social Justice.

spoke of their interest in critical pedagogy and critical theory because of their introduction to these concepts in coursework. One graduate talked about how his critical lens was sharpened in this program.

> As the three years progressed, I felt much more comfortable reading literature with a critical eye. I don't think I would have done that at first … I would have felt a little uncomfortable because sometimes the literature was challenging the realities of everything that I held true … for example the theory of meritocracy, you work hard, you'll do fine, everybody's equal … and now because of the program I know that's not always true.

Finally, one student, who is a leader in the public school system, talked about how the curriculum helped him to see how social justice meant more than just equity and access. Because of his experience in the program he spoke about being able to deconstruct privilege in a way that he had not understood before. He indicated that he now asks questions about the origin of curriculum and the authorship of books, and thinks deeply about how privilege is not just about access – but about access to all structures and systems that shape the education of our children.

Students were also impacted by the leadership strand of the curriculum. One veteran Catholic school educator commented that the program gave her the confidence as a leader to voice her opinions about social justice at her school broadly and passionately. She said,

> Instead of being something that I might think about by myself in the office, I now speak it to the teachers, I speak it to the pastor, I speak it to the school board, I speak it to the PTA. And I think the program has given me the confidence and the voice to do that.

Another student talked about a definition of leadership as "something that moves things along." He spoke of "gaining a lot more tools that I can use to lead," and he mentioned learning the importance of being a collaborator and not an obstructionist in his leadership capacity. Further, one veteran female educator described her transformation this way: "Now I am not just the leader [at her school site], I am the educational leader." She described how she is now able to speak confidently to her staff about current educational trends, and is planning in-services for her district. Additionally, students spoke of leadership skills in change management that were acquired in the program. A public school leader discussed the change in perspective that the program had precipitated. He said, "I think about it now from a landscape perspective rather than a district perspective. So I think about Los Angeles as a whole, rather than just Los Angeles Unified," concluding:

> The program is not only about the conversation about educational change and leadership in Los Angeles, but its part of the work, and in my opinion, that's what a school of education does. It gets into the mix, rather than just talks about or studies the mix.

SUPPORTIVE STRUCTURES

LMU embeds several features in its program that attempt to provide student support for research, writing, and learning. First, as part of the coursework, the doctoral program has initiated a "doctoral colloquium" which provides a series of seminars and speakers open to all cohorts over the course of their three years. Students are required to attend 9 seminars over 3 years, and the program offers approximately 15 seminars per year. Recent topics have included "theoretical frameworks," "new topics in education law," "dissertation mapping," "leveraging your degree," and tutorials on research software such as SPSS and NVivo. Students have indicated satisfaction with the recent offerings, and though only a minimal number of seminars are required over the course of three years, some have indicated that they feel they would benefit by attending "all of them" because of their relevance to the doctoral work.

Another feature of the program is the guest speakers who are invited to campus to speak to the doctoral students. Because of the practice orientation of the Ed.D., it is part of the program philosophy to expose the doctoral candidates to a variety of practitioners from the field. Students have heard from current superintendent John Deasy, previous superintendent Ray Cortines, Catholic school law expert Sr. Mary Angela Shaughnessy, and various other veteran practitioners in the field who spoke to current issues in education where social justice was at the core. After hearing these speakers, students were inspired to hold in-class discussions about transforming their own educational contexts to be more socially just.

Further, the program, again focused on theory into practice, sponsors a trip to Sacramento for each cohort in the second year of classes. This is a daylong experience where candidates are able to speak to legislators and lobbyists individually and in group settings about education reform initiatives currently under consideration, and future planned reforms. It takes place in the context of a policy class that deals with large-scale school reform. One student commented, "those classes [on policy] gave me a different prism to look at the origination of policy," which he then said were applied to his job requiring policy analysis and creation.

One of the most supportive structures embedded in the program is the faculty–student relationship. Because the dissertation is a one to one process, students develop deep, transformative relationships with their professors, both through the classroom experience and in the dissertation enterprise. Faculty are chosen by the student after the first year of classes, and after the second year, candidates' "dissertation classes," as detailed in the curriculum matrix, are completely dissertation-chair driven, so that students are receiving program credit for year-long faculty tutorials. This feature, individual student attention coupled with embedded dissertation writing coursework, aims to keep students on track to meet the three year program completion goal. One student reflected that "I was pleasantly surprised that the professors here at LMU are genuinely interested in making things happen [promoting social justice initiatives] and want to help other people learn about that. There was a strong modeling that this is possible."

DISSERTATION

In the LMU program, the dissertation is defined by a set of required elements. In 2010, a doctoral task force was convened to reconstruct LMU's notion of the dissertation. There was a concern that the dissertation not be locked into the five chapter Ph.D. formula – and thus, instead of a dissertation defined by chapters, the task force approved a reconstruction of the dissertation as defined by elements. Key elements of the LMU dissertation were determined as follows: Use of leadership for social justice as a focusing lens; literature review/knowledge base; research question(s); acknowledgment of lens/theoretical framework; methodology; rationale/contextual analysis; findings/evidence; and implications for practice. While these elements may closely mirror a traditional dissertation, it is made clear to candidates that should they desire to pursue an alternative dissertation model, they are welcome to do so. Some of the alternative dissertations recently produced include program reviews and policy analyses.

One of the unique features of the LMU program is the requirement that the dissertation include leadership for social justice as a focusing lens. Students understand this from the first course, when they are asked to write a literature review based on a topic of their choice which is linked to social justice.

One veteran educational leader commented that her dissertation topic and research encouraged her advocacy for persons of color. "I think the dissertation has given me a greater responsibility to use this doctorate to be an advocate, or to have a platform and voice for underserved communities." Thus, the focusing lens of leadership for social justice can provide the impetus for dissertations that can make a difference to educational communities in need.

While the four foundational elements – the cohort model, the curriculum, the supportive structures, and the dissertation – which compose the essence of the Ed.D. in Educational Leadership for Social Justice at LMU are structured intentionally to transform educational leaders to lead from a social justice perspective, how do we know whether the program is producing such leaders? The purpose of this next section is to share findings, highlighting qualitative data from two sources: graduates and their supervisors from the field.

FINDINGS

Based on the qualitative data from interviews with the graduates and their supervisors from the field, evidence of the graduates' transformation was coded by the four learning outcomes of the program. These learning outcomes align with the School of Education's conceptual framework of REAL.

Respect

The program defines *respect* by encouraging students to develop the ability to connect theory and practice through rigorous course content, integrating leadership and social justice, to produce leaders who advocate for equity and diversity. Certainly the notion of praxis is at the heart of leadership for social justice, moving beyond knowledge to a commitment to action. Most graduates interviewed in this study shared that they were attracted to this doctoral program because of its emphasis on social justice. Even though students self-selected to apply to this program, evidence emerged from the interviews suggesting that candidates were transformed in the area of developing a theoretical foundation to deepen their understanding of social justice and apply it to their daily practice. For instance, several students commented on theories they had never heard of before the program but were now comfortable applying to their daily practice, such as funds of knowledge, liberation theology, and critical race theory, to name a few.

A female graduate student, who is a principal of a Catholic elementary school, commented that the courses gave her a foundation and a voice from which to speak, describing herself as moving from a philosophy of doing *for* others to doing *with* others. She shared an example of implementing social justice theory into practice at her school site by encouraging the students to be integrated into lives of the people they are trying to help:

> When I started, I thought, oh, we do social justice all the time. That was like raising money and giving money and helping charities and things like that. I came in very naïve ... I see [social justice] more broadly now. We are very good at raising money ... but it's one thing to raise the money and to write a check and send the check off. We are trying to bring it closer to the kids ... every classroom now has to have a social justice project. It might be sponsoring a family at Christmas, and then you take what you have to the family. So you see the family and you see the need. Many of the classes write letters to the soldiers. We have [military] bases close by ... and we have different people from the community with sons over there, and then they write letters back and forth to us. Sometimes the soldiers, when they come back to the states, will

come and visit ... and they'll show us pictures where they hung up all the kids' cards in Afghanistan, in the war zone and how much it meant to them ... so it's more personal.

Her work demonstrates her commitment to praxis which was informed by her participation in the doctoral program. And this commitment is recognized by her colleagues who stated that social justice at their school site now goes "beyond the little coin box that we used to pass out ... it's way beyond that ... there's a face behind it now."

Moreover, during the interviews, graduates frequently commented on the rigorous coursework of the program. Unanimously, all graduates described the doctoral coursework as deeply focused on social justice. One graduate commented about the coursework contributing to his transformation:

I think it's accurate to say that it is incremental ... without a doubt, every class taught me something about [social justice] ... if it didn't happen as a direct result of the curriculum, it happened as a direct result of conversations that happened during that class.

He went on to describe specific courses in the program that focused on social justice theory and shared his connection to practice:

Probably seminal to all of that was what happened in the qualitative methodology class ... the social justice theory that was covered started to become very strongly applied to methodology and pedagogy.

He continued with an example of how social justice theory from the program informed his own teaching:

I teach a book ... it's the story of a guy hitting an immigrant from Mexico. And the book actually satirizes both sides of the story. And I thought I was teaching and bringing up issues of race and issues of class already. But as I looked at this, I realized – the book is a joke. So the book may bring up those ideas but it does not go nearly deep. And it is satirizing from a place of strong white privilege where I think the writer doesn't even get it. So I augmented the [curriculum] ... . The program helped me to understand this.

These examples suggest that the coursework in the program provided a foundation for social justice which students applied in their educational context to transform their environments into socially just schools.

Several supervisors also shared that graduates were always committed to social justice but observed how the coursework contributed to the graduates' abilities to implement theory into practice. One supervisor stated, "the LMU program is empowering ... where the program itself walks the [social justice] path, if you will."

Educate

The program defines *educate* by preparing candidates who can design, implement, and evaluate educational policies, programs, and practices through advanced research methodology. Graduates and their supervisors offered examples of how the program helped them to be informed as they led their school sites. For example, one graduate shared that at his school site, he would "mention a few things about race and class that the school won't always recognize or will put to one side" but that due to the program, he was able to work with faculty in a way that brought research to their daily practice:

> When I saw something, rather than just commenting on it, I attached a research article. So I started doing research for the faculty members and when I reported back to them on their class visit, it might have been something very good that I saw or something that needed some growth. I said, I have attached this research article that would help you address this ... and in my end of the year evaluation, I got a number of teachers saying that they liked the research articles because it got them thinking a little bit. So what I have is a whole library of research articles now that I can share with them and [I'm] subscribing to a number of publications, not only for school leadership but also education research that I have in my office available to faculty too. Just opening up a world to them that hasn't been available ...

His colleague commented about her observation of his transformation by stating that "he is dedicated to getting new information to especially young faculty, sharing current research, keeping them abreast of things that he thinks will inform – whether it is pedagogy or simply content information" and that she sees that "his confidence has grown as a researcher and as someone who has much to contribute to the field." Thanks to his efforts in the school, she commented that related to department organization and teaching practices "there are certainly new conversations that are emerging."

Advocate

The program defines *advocacy* by preparing leaders to critically engage in complex issues, demonstrating a commitment to social justice. Graduates and their supervisors offered examples of transformation during the Ed.D. program in advocating for social justice through critical engagement with complex issues. Such evidence suggests a disposition on the part of the graduate that includes both awareness of social justice and the tendency to act on that awareness. For example, one graduate commented about his view of leadership for social justice:

> Leadership for social justice means that you are trying to create an environment where many things can happen. One is where people can feel comfortable with who they are in the world and where they are in the world and at the same time feel that they can make a change in that world. The other side of it is educational ... you want to help people along the way to understand that the world isn't perfect and that they are agents of change. That you, yourself, as a leader, are an agent of change.

His definition of leadership for social justice echoes Ayers et al. (2009) who discuss this aspect of social literacy, the nourishing of our own identities and honoring the importance of context. He continued to reflect about his own transformation during the Ed.D. program, stating:

> There was a part of me that had to get very humbled and very much aware that what I thought about things was not so ... an awareness that you think you see things a certain way, but you come to understand that you're not able to see things or haven't seen things and now you can. The humbling part is that I feel like I have only half started, that there's so much more to learn, especially in the areas of race, gender, and socioeconomic status ... I really believe that the program in a very strong way broke that open for me on many, many levels.

In this section, the graduate described his own transformation as eye-opening and reveals his level of commitment to the work of social justice as ongoing. The graduate's supervisor confirmed this observation of leadership for social justice by commenting on the graduate's behavior in the field as a high school teacher. She shared:

> His behavior has changed significantly. He is less likely to jump in and try to fix things. He tends to stop and think it through. He still gets upset by things that happen and he still advocates for the things he cares about, but he does it in a way that allows people to feel that he's approaching them with a reasonableness, rather than just emotion ... He is a better leader as a result of that, because when he does approach people, he does it in a way that is less accusatory, that's more accepting of the fact that we all face difficulties and therefore maybe there are reasons for why things happen the way they do ... I think he listens more.

These examples indicate the graduate's awareness of social justice and transformation as a result of the program to lead from the perspective of a change agent. The graduate's own transformation was confirmed by his supervisor who has witnessed this in action in his daily practice as a high school teacher. Similarly, another candidate, when asked about his view of social justice upon conclusion of the Ed.D. program, commented:

> It's a call to challenge the status quo ... making education a vehicle for change and a vehicle for advancement for everybody ... it doesn't matter their economic background,

it doesn't matter their racial [*sic*] or ethnicity, everyone deserves an equal chance and it's an educator's responsibility, especially a leader, to make sure that that is available to all students.

This is reminiscent of the Jesuit definition of social justice as defined by Arrupe (1980), which advocates challenging a status quo that perpetuates injustice. This graduate's colleague commented that, prior to the program, the candidate in his role as administrator may not have realized that school policies offered preferential treatment to some. She went on to describe:

He really looks at the individual in the context of the whole, in a more just way, recognizing that if [he's] going to give a student a particular privilege, then really all students should have access to that particular privilege.

Such evidence suggests that the graduate transformed his views and practice of social justice, demonstrating critical engagement with the complexity of justice – that even when educators might believe they are doing the right thing for a student, social justice occurs when all students have access to privilege.

Another candidate, who works at the district level, shared that due to the program:

I feel like I'm advocating with the knowledge that I have around leadership, but also around instruction, so that children in the school can really have great teaching and learning happening every day. Sometimes people want to do kind of a managed instruction, and everything looked alike in every classroom, and that's not necessarily what's best for all children. So I feel like I am an advocate, and I provide a social justice platform to make sure that these kids are getting a really great curriculum, a very rigorous curriculum, and one that's not like a cookie-cutter structure.

Her supervisor confirmed that his observation of her transformation during the program went from seeing "one way of fixing schools, fixing systems ... one way of doing the work" to now:

The opposite of one way. I really believe that she has a tremendous insight and tolerance, for lack of a better word, for different approaches, different ways to fix the system, to fix schools ... that there's more inclusivity that she sees. So whereas before, just an example would be that she really felt that a traditional school district on its own could reform schools; as a result of this program, I think she realizes that there are many different partners and ways of approaching reform that may be even more lasting because they're rooted in community solutions or diverse solutions.

Thus, graduates emerge from the program with a deeper connection to social justice and a commitment to advocacy.

Lead

The program defines *leadership* by encouraging the development of moral and ethical leaders who can help meet existing and projected needs throughout the preK-20 public and private education system. The goal is to produce educational change agents who can improve the lived experiences of students and their families and lead socially just schools. For instance, one graduate shared his perspective:

> I think leadership for social justice – is understanding that ... social justice is about so many different things. It's about race. It's about creed. It's about gender. It's about socioeconomics. It's so broad. So many things need to be changed. At the same time you've got to be positive and even though there is so much that needs to change, that you help people come to realize that they can do something. And you can do something. It's important that you have to own that first before you can teach it.

Further, several students discussed a transformation to lead from a social justice perspective by no longer staying quiet when issues at their school site emerge.

> I feel like I'm at a school where there's not yet permission to talk about race. So that's very difficult but at the same time, when it popped up, we talked about it. I didn't avoid it. I tried to work through some of this stuff at the administrative level and on a pedagogical level.

Similarly, a student reflected, "I've learned through this program that I can't be quiet." Another student reflected that he feels more "assertive" commenting that, "it's irresponsible to have gone through a program like this and then not call someone to the carpet when something is unfair." Graduates students' awareness of unjust practices at school sites also seems to have been impacted by the program. One student reflected, "we think we have a multicultural curriculum. And I think we're not even close anymore. I think we're fooling ourselves." Graduates also reflected about the questions they now ask of their educational system, such as, "what should go into [the curriculum] to make sure that the experience is rich, is rigorous, really approaches the urban and racial issues that are impacting our underserved communities?" Such comments provide evidence of program efficacy, illustrating how graduates have transformed to lead from the lens of social justice.

Supervisors also commented on graduates by stating that they have seen the candidates become more "collaborative" in their leadership approach, and have found them to be more "strong" and "confident" and willing to "take responsibility" for decisions. One supervisor stated that after the program, a graduate truly demonstrated that:

> She wants to know you first before diving into questions about practices or questions about structures. The reason why I connect that to social justice is because the notion is there's a belief that people are doing the best with what they know and what they have, but the only way to understand where they're coming from is to get to know them better. So rather than making a quick judgment ... it's starting with the individual and asking about ... their own journey to the work that they do.

Finally, the notion of being a true leader changed for many graduates. Many stated that their reasons for pursuing the Ed.D. degree originally included greater potential for upward career movement. For instance, students said that there was an "initial allure" to having the degree but this notion changed to a sense of greater connection and responsibility for others:

> I wanted to get this degree to be the principal at this school. I don't know that I want to do that anymore. I want to have bigger impact, and I think ... the bigger impact would be not just one school but a bigger impact on education as a whole. So I'm questioning my own priorities. I think what this program did, it changed my thinking and my priorities in terms of what I want. I don't just want things for the sake of a title, even though with a title you can do great things, but I don't think I'd want the title without the foundation of what it is that I'd like to change.

He continued to say that his focus originally was "on how much work [the degree] was going to take, not so much the benefit afterward – I take that back, not the benefit, the responsibility afterward."

PROGRAM EFFICACY

With this evidence, we conclude that the program is successful in accomplishing its learning outcomes, producing quality educational leaders who lead from a social justice perspective, but we recommend further and more comprehensive review of graduate exit interviews and supervisor responses to provide a more robust understanding of program efficacy. For instance, while graduates had mostly positive responses about the program, not all comments shared about the program were positive. Some of the negative reflections about the program included frustration with some courses or policies which felt unsatisfactory. Others found the intensity of the program to be overwhelming at times. As such, this feedback shared by students provides us with a sense of how to rework aspects of the curriculum to better meet student needs.

While our conclusions are aligned to the program's learning goals and offer great insight to our own program development, we hope they also provide a model to other programs for evaluating the efficacy of the preparation of leaders for social justice. But generalization is cautioned as our program is unique in its design, its Ignatian tradition, and its social justice focus. Some limitations of the findings include the fact that students self-select to apply to the program, mainly because social justice is in the title of the degree. As such, students are naturally motivated to embrace issues of leadership preparation for social justice. Yet, evidence from the graduates and their supervisors often captured the before and after picture of the candidate with several comments tying the transformation of the candidate to the program itself, rather than a dispositional trait or prior skill. Still, these perspectives came from graduates who were able to meet the three-year deadline to complete the degree. Other students who had difficulty completing the degree within the program's three years may have different perspectives not captured here. Furthermore, the insights shared by the supervisors came from people selected by the graduate who felt comfortable with that supervisor discussing their work. It is likely that candidates selected individuals with whom they have a favorable relationship already, limiting the perspective of the supervisors. These limitations raise the question of whether the assessment methods used to assess program efficacy are socially just. Still, a key strength of this program assessment is the fact that we did not rely solely on the perspective of the student's self-reported data to determine success – something that has become the standard in the field of educational leadership preparation to determine success. As such, other programs are encouraged to also connect with their graduate students' educational communities to measure actual impact in the field.

IMPLICATIONS

Implications from this research are varied and have significant impact on programs for educational leadership in social justice. First, the efficacy of leadership programs in social justice is a much under-researched phenomenon. While this study aims to begin to fill that gap, much more must be done to measure the success of programs that purport to train leaders for the complex educational challenges that they will face. Further, exploring the graduates' practice in the field via supervisor interviews is one innovative way to measure this success, as utilized in this research. By interviewing supervisors we were able to capture graduates' transformation that occurred beyond dispositions or prior skills which may have initially attracted them to our program. However, the limitations to this method are not inconsequential, and though the findings are more credible because they move beyond self-reported data, a longitudinal study of this nature would provide more conclusive evidence that this method is sound and socially just. A longitudinal study, for example, could examine the social justice actions of graduates, such as curricular reform. Other implications point to the question of what happens to leaders when social justice is at the core of the academic and curricular experience. In this study, it is clear that the exposure to concepts of social justice, and the ability to operationalize those concepts through a leadership lens, was highly impactful for leaders as they earned their doctoral degree. Thus, when educational leaders are exposed to social justice issues and practices, they can and do become agents of change in their classrooms, their schools, and their world. In addition, graduates from this program understood that while social justice must be lived locally, it can also have a global impact, much like the philosophy of the Jesuit Universities the world over. In fact, the unique context of an Ed.D. program for educational leadership in social justice at a Jesuit university provides fertile ground and an encouraging atmosphere for concepts of social justice to take root. In sum, programs that teach with leadership for social justice as a focusing lens provide a necessary contribution to an educational field in search of equity and access for all the world's children.

REFERENCES

Andrews, R., & Grogan, M. (2002). Defining preparation and professional development for the Future. Paper presented at the Annual Meeting of the National Commission for the Advancement of Educational Leadership Preparation. Retrieved from http://www. eric.ed.gov/ERICWebPortal/search/detailmini.jsp?_nfpb=true&_&ERICExtSearch_ SearchValue_0=ED459534&ERICExtSearch_SearchType_0=no&accno=ED459534

Archdiocese of Los Angeles. (2011). Retrieved from http://www.archdiocese.la/learning/ schools/index.php

Arrupe, P., S.J. (1973). Men for others. In C. E. Meirose, SJ (Compiler) (1994). *Foundations* (pp. 31–40). Washington, DC: Jesuit Secondary Education Association.

Arrupe, P., S.J. (1980). *Justice with faith today* (2nd ed.). St Louis, MO: The Institute of Jesuit Sources.

Ayers, W., Quinn, T., & Stovall, D. (2009). *Handbook for social justice in education.* New York, NY: Routeledge.

Ball, A., & Tyson, C. (2012). *Non satis scire: To know is not enough*. Retrieved from http://www.aera.net

Black, W., & Murtadha, K. (2007). Toward a signature pedagogy in educational leadership preparation and program assessment. *Journal of Research on Leadership Education, 2*(1), 1–29. Retrieved from http://scholar.google.com/scholar_url?hl=en&q=http://www.ucea.org/storage/JRLE/pdf/vol2_issue1_2007/Black_Murtadha%2520PDF.pdf&sa=X&scisig=AAGBfm3-Itn7VW56nuUDgWxgglROkIA5zA&oi=scholarr

Bogotch, I. (2000). Educational leadership and social justice: Theory into practice. Paper presented at the Annual Meeting of the University Council for Edcuational Administration, UCEA), Albuquerque, New Mexico. Retrieved from http://www.eric.ed.gov/ERICWebPortal/contentdelivery/servlet/ERICServlet?accno=ED452585

Bogotch, I. (2002). Educational leadership and social justice: Practice into theory. *Journal of School Leadership, 12*(2), 138–156.

Brooks, J., Jean-Marie, G., & Normore, H. (2007). Distributed leadership for social justice: Exploring how influence and equity are stretched over an urban high school. *Journal of School Leadership, 17*(4), 378–408.

Chubbuck, S. (2007). Socially just teaching and the complementarity of Ignatian pedagogy and critical pedagogy. *Christian Higher Education, 6*, 239–265. doi:10.1080/153637 40701268145

Firestone, W. A., & Riehl, C. (Eds.). (2005). *A new agenda for research in educational leadership*. New York, NY: Teacher's College Press.

Hernandez, F., & McKenzie, K. B. (2010). Resisting social justice leadership preparation programs: Mechanisms that subvert. *Journal of Research on Leadership Education, 5*(3.2), 48–72. Special Edition.

International Commission on the Apostolate of Jesuit Education. (ICAJE). (1994). Go forth and teach: The characteristics of a Jesuit education. In C. E. Meirose, SJ (Compiler), *Foundations* (pp. 129–153). Washington DC: Jesuit Secondary Education.

Jean-Marie, G. (2008). Leadership for social justice: An agenda for the 21st century schools. *The Educational Forum, 72*, 340–354.

Kolvenbach, P.-H., S.J. (2000). The service of faith and the promotion of justice in American Jesuit higher education. Address presented at the Commitment to Justice in Jesuit Higher Education Conference, Santa Clara University, Santa Clara, CA. Retrieved from http://www.sjweb.info/resources/searchList.cfm

Larson, C., & Murtadha, K. (2002). Leadership for social justice. In J. Murphy (Ed.), *The educational leadership challenge: Redefining leadership for the 21st century* (pp. 134–151). Chicago, IL: National Society for the Study of Education.

Marshall, C., & Olivia, M. (2006). *Leadership for social justice: Making revolutions in education*. Boston, MA: Pearson Education.

McCarthy, M. M. (1999). The evolution of educational leadership preparation programs. In J. Murphy & K. S. Louis (Eds.), *Handbook of research on educational administration* (2nd ed., pp. 119–139). San Francisco, CA: Jossey-Bass.

McIntosh, P. (1989). White privilege: Unpacking the invisible knapsack. *Peace and Freedom Magazine*, July/August, pp. 10–12. Retrieved from http://www.google.com/url?sa=t&rct=j&q=&esrc=s&source=web&cd=3&ved=0CEQQFjAC&url=http%3A%2F%2Fnymbp.org%2Freference%2FWhitePrivilege.pdf&ei=bP7Tr72EcHZiQK92t XGDg&usg=AFQjCNG7iYdhtNJq5z7gZf-NkAdnRaZ3JA&sig2=OiN5XwKtUd NhouZun03Oqw

McKenzie, K., Skrla, L., & Scheurich, J. (2006). Preparing instructional leaders for social justice. *Journal of School Leadership, 16*(2), 158–170.

Murphy, J., & Vriesenga, M. (2006). Research on school leadership preparation in the United States: An analysis. *School Leadership and Management, 26*, 183–195. doi: 126342306600589758

National Assessment of Educational Progress (NAEP). (2011). *The nation's report card: Findings in brief reading and mathematics 2011*. Retrieved from http://nces.ed.gov/pubsearch/pubsinfo.asp?pubid=2012459

National Charter School Directory. (2011). Retrieved from http://www.charterschoolsearch.com/stateprofile.cfm?&state_id=5

Shoho, A., Merchant, B., & Lugg, C. (2005). Social justice: Seeking a common language. In F. W. English (Ed.), *The sage handbook of educational leadership: Advances in theory, research and practice* (pp. 47–67). Thousand Oaks, CA: Sage.

Tillman, L., Brown, K., & Jones, F. C. (2006). Transformative leadership for social justice: Concluding thoughts. *Journal of School Leadership, 16*(2), 207–209.

CHAPTER 6

RACIAL IDENTITY DEVELOPMENT IN PRINCIPAL PREPARATION PROGRAMS: LINKING THEORY TO PRACTICE

Frank Hernandez

ABSTRACT

This conceptual chapter argues that an understanding of racial identity development theory should be a fundamental element of school principals' preparation and practice. The chapter includes a brief examination of the related research that merges school leadership and racial identity, and a description of three racial identity development theoretical models (Black, White, and Latino); after suggesting questions that still exist regarding racial identity development theory, the author highlights specific ways in which racial identity development can be incorporated in principal preparation programs.

Based on the overall theme of the book *Global Leadership for Social Justice: Taking it from the Field to Practice*, this conceptual chapter argues that an understanding of racial identity development theory should be a fundamental element of school principals' preparation and practice (Young & Laible,

Global Leadership for Social Justice: Taking it from the Field to Practice
Advances in Educational Administration, Volume 14, 103–118
Copyright © 2012 by Emerald Group Publishing Limited
All rights of reproduction in any form reserved
ISSN: 1479-3660/doi:10.1108/S1479-3660(2012)0000014010

2000). However, many of our principal preparation programs continue to avoid both discussions and direct teaching about issues related to race and racial identity (Young & Brooks, 2008). This void in preparation programs proves to be even graver when one considers the changes occurring in student demographics. North Carolina, for instance, experienced a Latino-population increase of 394% from 1990 to 2000. Many of these Latinos in North Carolina and elsewhere in the United States fall below the age of 18 and will continue to enroll in U.S. schools (Hornor, 2002). Furthermore, racially diverse students continue to lag behind in achievement when compared to their White counterparts and are both segregated during the school day from their school peers and disproportionately represented in special-education and other remedial-education programs (Capper, Frattura, & Keyes, 2000). These challenges, coupled with the fact that most aspiring principals are White, require us in principal preparation programs to make racial identity development theory a fundamental element of school principals' preparation.

In order to examine racial identity development theory and to suggest ways in which these theories could be linked to practice in principal preparation programs, I first briefly examine the related research that merges school leadership and racial identity; I then highlight theoretical models of racial identity development (regarding such racial categories as Black, White, and Latino groups); after posing persistently relevant questions regarding racial identity development theory, I highlight specific ways in which racial identity development can be incorporated into principal preparation programs; I conclude the chapter by identifying implications for practice, preparation programs, and theory.

RELATED LITERATURE AND RACIAL IDENTITY DEVELOPMENT THEORETICAL MODELS

It is important to note, before discussing the related literature, that conversations and research on racial identity development in teacher education have had a long-standing presence in educational research (see Ladson-Billings, 1995; Lawrence & Bunche, 1997; Tatum, 1997). Although leadership research on the integration of racial identity development and leadership preparation has lagged behind other leadership-research topics, some researchers have confirmed that an important aspect of principal preparation programs involves diversity self-awareness and self-reflection;

these researchers argue that programs should facilitate discussions on privilege, inequity, and racism (Brown, 2004; Hackman, 2005; Hafner, 2005; Scheurich & Skrla, 2003), and should raise expectations for all students while advocating for – and endeavoring to understand the backgrounds of – traditionally marginalized students (Dantley & Tillman, 2006; Kose, 2007; Theoharis, 2007). In order for aspiring principals to have a rigorous understanding of equity and racism, principal preparation programs should cover racial identity development theory and its application to leadership practice. The leadership literature gives us several examples of attempts to integrate racial identity into leadership-preparation programs.

For example, Brown's (2004) work on transformative learning practices examines both the teaching in principal preparation programs and participants' approaches to social-justice work. While this chapter does not explicitly address racial identity development, it does call for faculty in educational leadership programs to implement teaching practices that encourage the programs' students to reflect on their own cultural identity. In particular, Brown (2004) suggests eight distinct learning experiences (e.g., cultural autobiography, reflective analysis journals, and educational plunges) that can help future school leaders who examine their own values, beliefs, and identities, be "better equipped to work with and guide themselves and others in translating their perspectives, perceptions, and goals into agendas for social change" (p. 101).

Hafner (2006) uses the film *The Color of Fear* (1995) to help aspiring leaders understand the impact of "racism and privilege on the lived experiences of individuals from different racial and ethnic groups" (p. 178). Before her students watch this highly emotional film, Hafner has them reflect on issues related to racism and White privilege. During particular segments of the film, Hafner (2006) provides students an opportunity to reflect on three key questions: (1) What emotional experiences are you having as you watch the film? (b) Where do you think these emotions are coming from? (c) What aspects of your personal experiences with race and your own racial identity might account for the feelings you may be experiencing?

Young and Laible (2000) suggest that in order to prepare leaders who lead for antiracist ends, and who specifically work against oppression in K-12 schools, principal preparation programs must provide opportunities for future leaders to examine their own racial identity development and to learn how personal, group, and institutional racisms influence the experience of students. Specifically, Young and Laible (2000) use individual reflection to help students think about their own racial identity development: in one instance, students read several articles related to White and Black racial identity development models, and then Young and Liable asked the students to reflect on their own racial identity development, to describe their current self-perceptions of identity development on the basis of the readings, and to answer the following questions: (1) What life experiences have powerfully affected your development process? (2) How have racial identity development models helped you reflect on your development?

The current chapter represents an intentional effort to discuss racial identity development outside of some unpublished dissertations addressing the matter relative to schools leaders. The current chapter builds on the work of the aforementioned scholars and provides a concrete link between racial identity theory in general and racial identity practices in principal preparation programs.

BACKGROUND OF RACIAL IDENTITY AND RACIAL IDENTITY THEORETICAL MODELS

It's important to note that racial identity is generally described as "one's identification with a particular racial group" (Reynolds & Baluch, 2001) and has historically included elements associated with ancestry, ethnicity, physical appearance, early socialization, and personal experiences (Wijeyesinghe, 2001). Other scholars have asserted that racial identity is also defined as one's racial category, for instance Black and White, and is often referenced as a collective identity based on individual perceptions that one belongs to a specific racial group (e.g., Helms, 1995).

Racial identity development constitutes the processes or experiences that, over time, contribute to an individual's identification with a racial group and the cultural aspects of that racial group, and is usually described by models using typologies (Cross, Parham, & Helms, 1991; Helms, 1990; Parham & Williams, 1993) or a linear path characterized by stages in racial identity development (Cross, 1991; Helms, 1995). For example, Helms (1984, 1990, 1993, 1995) proposed that White racial identity development is based on the attitudes, behaviors, and feelings that White people have developed as a result of their being raised to embrace and to perpetuate White racist attitudes. Helms' (1995) model is divided into six stages (later called statuses) that, in many cases, are "expressed according to level of dominance within the individual's personality structure" (p. 184).

Individuals raised in the United States and in other Western countries are often aware of racial identity from an early age, whether fully consciously or semiconsciously, and are bombarded with racial depictions of different groups that are often embedded with stereotypes and misinformation about particular racial groups.

In the section to follow, I highlight racial identity development theories that focus on racial groups, such as Whites (Helms, 1990; Hardiman, 1994, 2001), African Americans (Cross, 1991; Jackson, 2001), and Latinos (Ferdman & Gallegos, 2001; Hernandez, 2005).

BLACK RACIAL IDENTITY DEVELOPMENT THEORY

Since the Civil Rights Movement of the 1950s and the 1960s, Black racial identity development models have appeared mostly within the field of counseling psychology and psychotherapy (e.g., Helms, 1990). Some authors argue that Blacks in the United States have "been deprived of the means to develop a self-respecting, independently affirmed identity and, instead, have been conditioned to conform to White superiority/Black inferiority beliefs that apply, without exception, to every aspect of social life" (Jenkins, 1994, pp. 63–64). With this in mind, scholars have developed several models to illuminate Black racial identity development. One study in particular is *The Psychology of Nigrescence* (Cross, 1991, 1995), the French word "nigrescence" meaning the process of becoming Black. In other words, as Thompson (1994) argues in Torres, Howard-Hamilton, and Cooper (2003), "[The psychology of nigrescence is] the gradual transcendence of Black individuals from a worldview in which African Americans are devalued and Whites are reified to a worldview characterized by an inner confidence in and appreciation of self and others as racial beings" (p. 18).

Cross' (1995) model consists of five stages: *pre-encounter, encounter, immersion–emersion, internalization,* and *internalization–commitment. Pre-encounter* is the first stage of the model and is defined by its low salience attitude toward being Black. Blacks in this stage do not deny being Black but do argue that their Blackness is in no way connected to how others interact with them. Cross (1995) argues that "pre-encounter persons place value in things other than their Blackness, such as their religion, their lifestyle, their social status, or their profession" (p. 98). Stage two, called *encounter,* is where Blacks begin to seek identification with Black culture. This stage is also characterized by a crisis that causes people to question their worldview and that brings them closer to nigrescence (Cross, 1995). Plummer (1995) argues that this crisis is a "critical incident in one's life that leads the individual to reconceptualize issues of race in society and to reorganize racial feelings in one's personal life" (p. 169).

Stage three is characterized as the most critical stage: the one in which dichotomous feelings – pro-Black and anti-White sentiments – create substantial conflicts. This stage is grounded in feelings of guilt and shame that arise from Blacks' perception that they have bought into dominant White attitudes; consequently, a sense of pride surfaces among Blacks when they learn about Black heritage and its role in the lives of Black individuals. Plummer (1995) argues that, during this stage, a "person makes a conscious effort to become Black" and that this person's immersion attitude manifests itself when he or she begins "wearing ethnic clothing and hairstyles, choosing African American entertainment forms and associating primarily with other African Americans" (p. 169). At the fourth stage, called *internalization*, Blacks begin to experience a comfort level with being Black and to acknowledge their African American background. This is the stage when the person internalizes the new identity, "which now evidences itself in naturalistic ways in the everyday psychology of the person" (Cross, 1995, p. 113). Finally, the *internalization–commitment* stage is a repeat of the activities, behaviors, and attributes of what was shown in stage four (Torres et al., 2003). Cross (1995) describes this stage by comparing Blacks who "fail to sustain a long-term interest in Black affairs" to those who "devote an extended period of time, if not a lifetime, to finding ways to translate their personal sense of Blackness into a plan of action or general sense of commitment" (p. 121).

LATINO RACIAL IDENTITY DEVELOPMENT THEORY

Latinos in the United States have had a long history with racial categories and have not easily fit either the labels that have been developed for them (Chicanos, Hispanics, Latinos, and Illegals) or the boxes they have been required to check (Latino and White; Latino and non-White; Hispanic). As the growing population of Latinos increases, a properly complex understanding of their racial identity development is critical to families, schools, and business organizations across the country. Ferdman and Gallegos (2001) explore the topic of racial identity development and Latinos in the United States and propose a framework for looking at Latino racial identity.

The authors argue that their model captures the intricate nature of Latino identity development and state that "the difficulty in understanding Latinos is caused primarily by attempts to impose models from other racial groups onto Latinos," models that generally do not address the array of identities that Latinos display (p. 48). To this end, any model that is intended to facilitate an understanding of Latino racial identity development must take into account the complexities of these Latino identities. Ferdman and Gallegos (2001) argue that Latinos' varied historical experiences of the social construction of race "make it difficult to describe the racial identity of Latinos in conventional ways" (p. 42).

The model proposed by Ferdman and Gallegos (2001) is not a stage-development theoretical model, but a systematic conceptualization illuminating patterns and orientations found within Latino identity. According to the authors, this model identifies several dimensions – individuals' identities as Latinos, individuals' perceptions of identity, how Latinos identify themselves, how Latinos as a group are perceived, how Latinos perceive Whites, and how race fits into the equation – as the most important dimensions in any rigorous understanding of Latinos' orientation.

The first orientation in the model is called *Latino-integrated*, and individuals in this orientation can deal with the complexity of their Latino identity and are closely connected to their national origin and other social identities, such as gender, profession, and class. This orientation accepts both the positive and the negative attributes associated with Latinos, as well as the importance of Latinos' group membership. The second orientation, called *Latino-identified*, is characterized by individuals that define themselves as *La Raza* because they consider their culture, history, and other ethnic indicators to be important in their lives. Their view of others is less rigid and "their notion of race is a uniquely Latino one, which means they do not accept the either/or nature of U.S. racial constructs," argue Ferdman and Gallegos (2001, p. 51).

Subgroup-identified Latinos are closely connected to their identity within the subgroup and not to the broader Latino community. For example, one might identify oneself as Puerto Rican and not Latino on the basis of this model. Subgroup-identified Latinos see themselves neither as White nor as Latinos, but are "aware of discrimination against themselves and other Latinos" and "join coalitions across subgroups, not so much from a sense of shared history or culture but more from necessity and the practical reality of greater numbers leading to increased societal power" (Ferdman & Gallegos, 2001, p. 52). Hernandez (2008) found that in his study with Spanish-speaking assistant principals, overwhelmingly the participants indentified with their subgroup (or nationality) more often than with the signified object of the term "Latino." The fourth orientation is *Latino as "Other,"* that is, individuals who are not connected to their specific Latino background, including history and culture, and who identify themselves as a person of color without identifying themselves as members of a Latino subgroup. These are the individuals who most often identify themselves as having a "minority" status. As Ferdman and Gallegos (2001) argue, these individuals use an external lens "and focus on the way the group is viewed by others outside the group" but do not see themselves as White or Latino and view race as "White or not White" (p. 53).

The orientation of *Undifferentiated* describes Latinos who have closed lenses and "prefer to identify themselves and others as 'just people' often claiming to be color-blind and promoting this orientation to others of all groups" (Ferdman & Gallegos, 2001, p. 53). Individuals in this orientation are not aware of differences and adhere to the dominant values and norms of society. When they encounter barriers, they attribute them to behavior rather than to race, racism, or their Latinoness. The final orientation is called *White-identified*, which describes Latinos who see themselves racially as White and consider themselves superior to people of color. These individuals value Whiteness over all other systems of values, assimilate to mainstream society, and are disconnected from Latino culture. The authors of this model argue that these individuals "recognize, either consciously or unconsciously, that they are different in some way from Whites as defined in the U.S., but they continue to prefer all that is connected to Whiteness, and to emphasize that for themselves and/or their children" (p. 54). These Latinos do not question the U.S. racial order and, if they happen to be biracial, identify with their Whiteness over anything else.

WHITE RACIAL IDENTITY DEVELOPMENT THEORY

Hardiman (2001) argues that the study of White racial identity development theory is a result of Black scholars "urging Whites to turn their lens of analysis about race around and look at themselves in the mirror" rather than focus on Blacks and other marginalized groups (p. 108). Hardiman (2001) developed a model of White identity to help her bring to light how race and racism affect Whites in the United States. In addition, Hardiman also wanted to "understand whether and how Whites could escape from the effects of their racist programming" and whether becoming unprejudiced or antiracist is possible for Whites (p. 109). The White identity development (WID) model has five stages that depict the racial identity development of White Americans (Hardiman, 1994, 2001; Hardiman & Jackson, 1992).

No social consciousness of race – which is to say, naïveté about race – characterizes the first stage, in the WID model. Whites in this stage lack a social perspective on the meaning of one's race. Whites may be aware of physical and cultural differences but do not feel superior or normal when differences are identified. This stage generally ends in early childhood and is followed by the *Acceptance stage*. It is at this stage that Whites begin to "receive and accept the messages about racial group membership and believe in the superiority or normalcy of Whiteness and White culture and the inferiority of people of color" (Hardiman, 1994, p. 125). Hardiman (2001) argues that it is "impossible in this society to escape racist socialization in some form because of its pervasive, systemic, and interlocking nature" (p. 111).

The third stage is called *Resistance* and involves people questioning the dominant structures that are in place and that perpetuate racism. These individuals also begin to reject their own racist learning. Whites in this stage may also begin to recognize their Whiteness and their own racist attitudes, a recognition that can result in anger, hurt, and frustration. The fourth stage is called *Redefinition* and "occurs when the White person begins to clarify his own self-interest in working against racism, and begins to accept and take responsibility for his Whiteness" (Hardiman, 2001, p. 111). Terry (1977) cited in Hardiman (2001) argues that Whites in this stage "redefine themselves as 'new Whites'" and "take ownership of their Whiteness rather than deny it" (p. 110). Finally, the fifth stage is called *Internalization*, which refers to a person's efforts to eradicate racism – efforts that "increase consciousness regarding race and racism" and incorporate one's "new White identity into all aspects of one's life" (Hardiman, 2001, p. 112).

Hardiman (2001) posits that her model describes the experiences of only a small number of White people, mostly "those who were activists in the struggle against racism" (p. 112). This model, which has not been empirically studied, is limited in its usefulness for counseling psychology but has been adopted by practitioners who have studied White racial identity development and conflict resolution.

Other White racial identity development models are worth noting here. Helms (1984, 1990, 1993, 1995) proposed a theory based on the attitudes, behaviors, and feelings that White people have developed as a result of their being raised to embrace and to perpetuate White racist attitudes. Helms' (1995) model is divided into six stages (later called statuses) and are "assumed to develop or mature sequentially," but in many cases are "expressed according to level of dominance within the individual's personality structure" (p. 184).

The following section includes a description of four ways in which racial identity theory can be linked to the practice and preparation of school

leaders and then ends with a brief critique of the theoretical models and
questions that persist in this area of study.

RACIAL IDENTITY DEVELOPMENT THEORY AND WAYS TO EMBED IT IN THE PRACTICE AND PREPARATION OF SCHOOL LEADERS

A point stated earlier but worth repeating is that racial identity development
theory and issues related to race and racism are rarely found in the
preparation of school leaders. More importantly, as racially diverse students
continue to make their way into PK-12 schools, it is imperative that
preparation programs find ways to address issues related to racial identity
development for the benefit of both the individuals training to become
school leaders and the students whom the aspiring leaders will be interacting
with at their school buildings. The instructional assignments that follow are
just a few of the ways in which racial identity theory can be infused into the
practice of working with aspiring school administrators. By no means is this
meant to be an exhaustive list of assignments that would integrate racial
identity theoretical models into leadership preparation. Rather, the assignments that are explained in this chapter are pedagogical methods that
I have used myself with aspiring principals. These assignments contribute
to a more authentic understanding of racial identity development for
both students and instructors. In line with Young and Laible (2000), these
assignments help students reflect on their own racial identity; however, in
contrast to Young and Laible (2000), several assignments here are used to
support the scaffolding that is needed in order for aspiring students to reflect
more authentically when asked to place themselves on a racial identity
development model. The assignments are presented sequentially and build
on one another to help students become more aware of their identities. The
first assignment is called "What's in a Name?"

The first assignment that I often use and one that has paid dividends in
allowing students to address issues of identity involves Sandra Cisneros' *The
House on Mango Street* (1991). Before the first class, I ask students to read a
short chapter, entitled "My Name," about Cisneros' name. I then ask
students to reflect and write on their own names (first and last) and to
answer the following questions: (1) What is you name? (2) Who named you
and are you named after someone in your family? (3) What does your name
mean? (4) What is your name's ethnic/cultural background? (5) What would

you like for your classmates to call you here in class? Though some may view this as a petty activity that is more about introductions (which it is) than identity, I have found this assignment to provide insights into the students in the class. It affords me, as the professor, both an opportunity to develop a safe space in the classroom where students can feel comfortable about sharing personal information and an opportunity for students to ask their classmates various questions.

Another instructional assignment that I have found to be very useful for engaging students in discussions about racial identity development is an activity called "Becoming Aware of Difference." This activity links the theory of racial identity to principal preparation practices by giving students an opportunity to reflect on when they first became aware of racial differences – and on the particular subject of whether they have ever either been targeted for being racially different or targeted someone else for being racially different. The students are asked to reflect on their childhood or adolescent years and write about their first encounter with racial difference, that is, when they came to learn about racial difference. This moment could be a personal encounter or an encounter that they witnessed. Several questions guide this assignment and include the following:

– What do you remember about the specific context in which this experience took place?
– Which emblem of identity were you (or some other person) being targeted for?
– What emotions, if any, do you remember experiencing during this encounter?
– Do you recall whether anyone intervened as your (or some other person's) ally?

After students have had an opportunity to reflect on and write answers to the questions listed above, I have students share their findings with the large classroom group. Since almost all of the students whom I have worked with in principal preparation programs have been White, I typically proceed with the next step: after completing the aforementioned activity, students are introduced to the White racial identity theoretical model. For example, I share with the students Helms' (1995) White racial identity statuses (*contact, disintegration, reintegration, pseudo-independence, immersion–emersion,* and *autonomy*) and provide an explanation of each status. The students are then asked to consider their answers to the questions listed above. And on the basis of their past experiences at that time, the students should try to place themselves on the racial identity development model. I take this approach for several reasons. First, it allows the students an opportunity to place themselves on the White racial identity development model according to an early experience in their lives. It also captures a baseline for the students in terms of racial identity development and allows them to be more conscious of the types of experiences that have influenced their initial placement on the continuum of racial identity development and how they think about issues related to race or racial identity. My experience in asking students to place themselves on the White racial identity model without scaffolding early racial identity experiences is that more often than not, students tend to perceive themselves as being much further along the racial identity developmental continuum than they actually are.

An additional assignment that allows students to consider their movement on the racial identity development continuum has them make assertions about present-day U.S. race relations. At the beginning of this assignment, I ask students to consider race relations in the United States and how freedom and equality for all individuals were and continue to be national ideals. I then ask the students to list words that describe the ideals that people aspire to in the United States in regards to race relations. Some of the words that often appear are "equity," "multicultural," "access," "pluralism," and "social justice." The next step in this assignment is to ask the students to consider how far the United States has come toward realizing the ideals just listed in the class. Rather than ask students to share their initial impression with the group, I ask them first to think deeply about their answer and to compose a written reflection on the question. I then ask the students to stand up and visualize one end of the classroom as 0 (representing no progress) and the other end as 100 (representing a completely realized ideal), and to place themselves somewhere between these numbers according to how well they think the United States meets the ideals that listed earlier in the lesson. Next, I ask the students to explain why they have positioned themselves where they did and which of their personal experiences have influenced where they currently stand on the continuum.

The dialogue that occurs during the debriefing of this assignment is informative, as it provides knowledge of the students' worldviews of race and racial identity. For instance, I have had White students place themselves between 95 and 100 in this activity and declare that – because "slavery is no longer used," "the Civil Rights Movement has passed," "many individuals of color are very successful," and "I don't see racism that often" – the United States has made either complete or almost complete progress in the pursuit of these original ideals of equity and social justice. The point here is not that the professor is trying to interrogate the students. Rather, it is to highlight the differences in experiences and worldviews that often inform our values and beliefs around racial identity specifically – and differences in general. After a lengthy discussion, the students are then asked to revisit the issue of racial identity development and to consider where they would place themselves on the theoretical model. Written reflections and then discussions about school-leadership implications follow.

DISCUSSION AND IMPLICATIONS

Racial identity is fluid and constantly changing. Thus, any theoretical model that examines racial identity should be revisited often as the theory develops. Several questions pose themselves as we discuss current racial identity theoretical models. I consider the most important question to be the one inquiring into the factors that lead to each stage, typology, or orientation found within a given racial identity model. Each stage is well defined and easy to understand; however, in order to understand how fluid racial identity is, a thorough understanding of how an individual moves from one stage to another needs to be available. Cross (1995) has provided one explanation of how individuals move from one stage to the next. He suggests that for Blacks, a crisis (critical incident) requiring them to question their own worldviews allows them to move to a more complex racial identity development stage.

The second question that continues to resist definitive answers concerns how fluid racial identity development is and whether individuals move in and out of stages and orientations on the basis of context and experience. The research suggests that racial identity is not stagnant. Rather, as Tatum (1997) suggests, "The process of racial identity development, often beginning in adolescence and continuing into adulthood, is not so much linear as circular" (p. 83). She compares it to moving up spiral staircases where steps are often revisited but often with a new perspective. That is, although one may revisit a particular step (stage) in Black racial identity development, one is "not exactly in the same spot" (Tatum, 1997, p. 83).

The third question addresses the unique challenges and strengths that are associated with each stage or orientation. The theories themselves suggest that attitudes and values are associated with each stage, but we know very little about challenges that may exist depending on where individuals would place themselves on the racial identity continuum. The final two questions that I find most challenging as a professor who trains both teachers and school leaders concern how individuals, according to where they are in a racial identity development model, fit into an organization or into institutions such as namely PK-12 schools or higher-education institutions; and what the best way is to assess an individual's location on different racial identity continuums or orientations. These questions continue to be explored in my teaching and in my reading about race and racial identity development. I have often contemplated whether placement in a particular stage in a racial identity development model results in a particular teaching or leadership style. I do not have the answers to the above questions and often find myself coming across more questions than possible answers.

The understanding of racial identity development theory has implications for leadership practice. For example, students who attend our K-12 schools vary regarding the level that they occupy in their own racial identity development, a fact that presents both opportunities and challenges to administrators who try to provide a safe place where students can explore these racial identity issues with others. For instance, if our school administrators have an understanding of Black racial identity development relative to their student body, perhaps there will be less mystery as to why "Black kids are sitting together" (Tatum, 2003) and more inquiry into the possibility of creating spaces where students can interact with members of their own racial group as they move through their own racial identity development. Second, this understanding of racial identity development theory can assist school leaders in their multicultural competency and help them better understand how Black students specifically, and people of color generally, process and perceive the world around them. Finally, having an understanding of racial identity development theory can help leaders grasp the nuances found among different racial groups and the conditions that may affect the lives of the school leaders' students.

REFERENCES

Brown, K. M. (2004). Leadership for social justice and equity: Weaving a transformative framework and pedagogy. *Educational Administration Quarterly, 40*(1), 77–108.

Capper, C. A., Frattura, E., & Keyes, M. (2000). *Meeting the needs of students of all abilities: How leaders go beyond inclusion.* Newbury Park, CA: Corwin Press.

Cross, W. E. (1991). *Shades of Black: Diversity in African American identity.* Philadelphia, PA: Temple University Press.

Cross, W. E., Jr. (1995). The psychology of nigrescence: Revising the cross model. In J. G. Ponterotto, M. J. Casas, L. A. Suzuki & C. M. Alexander (Eds.), *Handbook of multicultural counseling.* Thousand Oaks, CA: Sage.

Cross, W. E., Parham, T. A., & Helms, J. E. (1991). The stages of black identity development: Nigrescence models. In R. E. Jones (Ed.), *Black psychology* (3rd ed., pp. 319–339). New York, NY: Harper & Row.

Dantley, M., & Tillman, L. C. (2006). Social justice and moral transformative leadership. In C. Marshall & M. Oliva (Eds.), *Leadership for social justice: Making revolutions in education*. Boston, MA: Pearson.

Ferdman, B. M., & Gallegos, P. I. (2001). Racial identity development and Latinos in the United States. In C. L. Wijeyesinghe & B. W. Jackson, III (Eds.), *New perspectives on racial identity development: A theoretical and practical anthology* (pp. 32–66). New York, NY: New York University Press.

Hackman, H. W. (2005). Five essential components for social justice education. *Equity and Excellence in Education, 38*(2), 103–109.

Hafner, M. (2005). Preparing school leaders to ensure equity and work toward social justice: An exploratory study of leadership dispositions. Paper presented at the American Educational Research Association, Montreal, Quebec.

Hafner, M. (2006). Teaching strategies for developing leaders for social justice. In C. Marshall & M. Oliva (Eds.), *Leadership for social justice: Making revolutions in education*. Boston, MA: Pearson.

Hardiman, R. (1994). White racial identity development in the United States. In E. P. Salett & D. R. Koslow (Eds.), *Race, ethnicity, and self: Identity in multicultural perspective*. Washington, DC: NMCI Publications.

Hardiman, R. (2001). Reflections on white identity development theory. In C. L. Wijeyesinghe & B. W. Jackson (Eds.), *New perspectives on racial identity development: A theoretical and practical anthology*. New York, NY: New York University Press.

Hardiman, R., & Jackson, B. W. (1992). Racial identity development: Understanding racial dynamics in college classrooms and on campus. *New Directions for Teaching and Learning, 52*, 21–37.

Helms, J. E. (1984). Toward a theoretical explanation of the effects of race on counseling: A black and white model. *The Counseling Psychologist, 13*, 695–710.

Helms, J. E. (1990). Toward a model of white racial identity development. In J. E. Helms (Ed.), *Black and white racial identity: Theory, research, and practice*. New York, NY: Greenwood Press.

Helms, J. E. (1993). I also said, "White racial identity influences white researchers". *The Counseling Psychologist, 21*(2), 240–243.

Helms, J. E. (1995). An update of Helm's white and people of color racial identity models. In J. G. Ponterotto, M. J. Casas, L. A. Suzuki & C. M. Alexander (Eds.), *Handbook of multicultural counseling*. Thousand Oaks, CA: Sage.

Hernandez, F. (2005). *The racial identity development of selected Latino school principals and its relation to their leadership practices*. Unpublished dissertation, University of Wisconsin-Madison, Madison.

Hernandez, F. (November, 2008). Latina/o assistant principals: Early findings from a national study. Paper presented at the University Council for Educational Administration Conference. Orlando, FL.

Hornor, L. L. (Ed.). (2002). *Hispanic Americans: A statistical sourcebook*. Palo Alto, CA: Information Publications.

Jackson, B. W. (2001). Black identity development: Further analysis and elaboration. In C. L. Wijeyesinghe & B. W. Jackson (Eds.), *New perspectives on racial identity development: A theoretical and practical anthology*. New York, NY: New York University Press.

Jenkins, R. (1994). *Social identity*. London: Routledge.

Kose, B. W. (2007). Principal leadership for social justice: Uncovering the content of teacher professional development. *Journal of School Leadership, 17,* 276–312.

Ladson-Billings, G. (1995). *The dreamkeepers: Successful teachers of African American children*. San Francisco, CA: Jossey-Bass.

Lawrence, S. M., & Bunche, T. (1997). Feeling and dealing: Teaching White students about racial privilege. *Teaching and Teacher Education, 12*(5), 531–542.

Parham, T. A., & Williams, P. (1993). The relationship of demographic and background factors to racial identity attitudes. *Journal of Black Psychology, 19,* 7–24.

Plummer, D. L. (1995). Patterns of racial identity development of African American adolescent males and females. *The Journal of Black Psychology, 21*(2), 168–180.

Reynolds, A., & Baluch, S. (2001). Racial identity theories in counseling: A literature review and evaluation. In C. L. Wijeyesinghe & B. W. Jackson (Eds.), *New perspectives on racial identity development: A theoretical and practical anthology*. New York, NY: New York University Press.

Scheurich, J. J., & Skrla, L. (2003). *Leadership for equity and excellence: Creating high-achievement classrooms, schools, and districts*. Thousand Oaks, CA: Corwin Press.

Tatum, B. D. (1997). *Why are all the black kids sitting together in the cafeteria? And other conversations about race*. New York, NY: Basic Books.

Tatum, B. D. (2003). *Why are all the Black kids sitting together in the cafeteria? And other conversations about race*. New York, NY: Basic Books.

Terry, R. W. (1977). *For whites only*. Grand Rapids, MI: William B. Eerdmans.

Theoharis, G. (2007). Social justice educational leaders and resistance: Toward a theory of social justice leadership. *Educational Administration Quarterly, 43,* 221–258.

Thompson, C. E. (1994). Helms's white racial identity development (WRID) theory: Another look. *The Counseling Psychologist, 22*(4), 645–649.

Torres, V., Howard-Hamilton, M. F., & Cooper, D. L. (2003). *Identity development of diverse populations: Implications for teaching and administration in higher education* (Vol. 29). Washington, DC: ERIC Clearinghouse on Higher Education.

Wah, L. M. (Producer/Director). (1995). *The Color of Fear* [Flim]. Los Angeles.

Wijeyesinghe, C. L. (2001). Racial identity in multiracial people: An alternative paradigm. In C. L. Wijeyesinghe & B. W. Jackson (Eds.), *New perspectives on racial identity development: A theoretical and practical anthology*. New York, NY: New York University Press.

Young, M., & Brooks, J. (2008). Supporting graduate students of color in educational administration preparation programs: Faculty perspectives on best practices, possibilities, and problems. *Educational Administration Quarterly, 44*(3), 391–423.

Young, M., & Laible, J. (2000). White racism, antiracism, and school leadership preparation. *Journal of School Leadership, 10,* 374–415.

PART 3
ENGAGING PRACTITIONERS IN SOCIAL JUSTICE AND EQUITY-ORIENTED WORK IN SCHOOLS

CHAPTER 7

DAVIS K-8 SCHOOL: UTILIZING TRANSFORMATIONAL LEADERSHIP TO DRIVE INCLUSIVE PRACTICE

Thad Dugan

ABSTRACT

Scholars have been calling for educational leadership that emphasizes socially just practices to restructure school policies and practices to create an equitable schooling experience for all *students. The case of Davis K-8 exemplifies how a more traditional model of leadership (transformational leadership) coupled with a professional learning community model has created socially just practices that fully include the school's deaf and hearing-impaired students. Davis has recreated the school environment to truly value participation from all students. Utilizing a mixed-methods approach, data were gathered that highlight the practices that drive the inclusive culture of the school. Implications for practice include the impact that a socially just vision can have in more traditional leadership models and provides a model for including students with disabilities into the school culture.*

Global Leadership for Social Justice: Taking it from the Field to Practice
Advances in Educational Administration, Volume 14, 121–137
Copyright © 2012 by Emerald Group Publishing Limited
All rights of reproduction in any form reserved
ISSN: 1479-3660/doi:10.1108/S1479-3660(2012)0000014011

"Unless school professionals see themselves as advocates for more equitable placement of children, they are colluding in a tracking system that is unjust" (Anderson, 2009, p. 24). This quote lies at the heart of this chapter. Presented in this chapter is the case of Davis K-8 School, a real-life example how transformational leadership can be utilized to promote socially just practices (inclusion of students with disabilities in mainstream classes with nondisabled peers). The Davis case is an exemplar of how social justice leadership "moves beyond present day definitions of school leadership" (Theoharis, 2008) and responds to criticisms (i.e., Theoharis & Causton-Theoharis, 2008) that there is minimal literature linking leadership for social justice and inclusive schooling.

The chapter begins with an overview of literature on social justice leadership and inclusion. This is followed by contextual information about Davis K-8 School and the methods used to gather data. Next, transformational leadership is defined and this provides the framework for presenting Davis' development of inclusive practices. The chapter concludes with a brief discussion of implications for practitioners and scholars promoting social justice leadership in preparation programs.

SOCIAL JUSTICE LEADERSHIP

Over the past decade, educational leadership scholars have moved beyond an emphasis on school management to emphasize the need to transform society through schools (e.g., Otunga, 2010). These scholars have called for leadership that confronts inequitable structures and practices that marginalize portions of the student population while privileging others (e.g., Goldfarb & Grinberg, 2002; Marshall & Oliva, 2006). While it is not uncommon for some leaders to effect change by encouraging instructional leadership, distributed leadership, or transformational leadership models to support effective instruction, some leaders adopt other approaches to explicitly address inequities. Often at the forefront of transformative discourse is the call for leadership for social justice.

Bogotch (2002) noted, "there are no fixed or predictable meanings of social justice prior to engaging in educational leadership practices"; however, scholars have presented various conceptions of social justice leadership that link leadership practices with the transformation of school structures and practices. While social justice leadership is at the core of transformative educational change, an agreed upon definition remains elusive.

For example, McKenzie, Sklra, and Scheurich (2006) viewed the role of the leader for social justice as a change agent who confronts issues of inequity and transforms traditional, marginalizing practices to more just practices. Similarly, Theoharis (2007) argued that leaders for social justice guide schools to transform the culture, pedagogical practices, and school-wide priorities to benefit marginalized populations. Others have defined social justice leadership in terms of advocacy leadership (Anderson, 2009), moral transformative leadership (Foster, 1986), culturally responsive leadership (Johnson, Møller, Pashiardis, Vedøy, & Savvides, 2011), and inclusive leadership (Doyle, 2004; Sapon-Shevin, 2003). Despite the differences in approaches presented by each of these scholars, a common thread among them is the focus on leaders promoting equitable schooling that addresses issues of race, gender, diversity, marginalization, gender, religion, sexual orientation, language, ability, and identity. While equitable schooling is essential, social justice, for the purpose of this chapter, is about inclusion, especially inclusion of students with disabilities.

Inclusion is premised on a belief that inclusive practices "assist all individual students while improving society by fostering care, adaptability, and inclusiveness" (Doyle, 2004, p. 12). For Doyle, inclusion is a school-wide reform that eliminates tracking and integrates programs and blends resources for the benefit of all children. While inclusion seems straightforward, it cannot simply be approached as the opposite of exclusion. Rather, inclusion is a mindset and a part of the school culture (Zepeda & Langenbach, 1999). According to Ainscow et al. (2006), inclusion can be understood from two premises, narrow definitions and broad definitions. Narrow definitions promote the inclusion of specific groups of students into mainstream classes while broad definitions refer to how school staff and members of the school community react to the needs of diverse student groups. It is imperative, for this chapter, that inclusion be defined in broad terms to emphasize the positive effects on all students, not just deaf and hearing-impaired students.

Sapon-Shevin (2003) argued that social justice is about inclusion and the two cannot be separated. Leaders for social justice promote inclusive practices. These practices are not to be confused with integrating students. Integrating students is simply placing students with disabilities in proximity of nondisabled peers while inclusion is more than proximity. Inclusion is the process of changing values, policies, and practices to create a school culture that values all students (Polat, 2011). The purpose of this chapter is to present how Davis K-8 School created such a structure.

While discussions of social justice and inclusive practices have moved focus away from more traditional models of leadership, Davis K-8 provides an understanding of how more traditional models of leadership (i.e., transformational leadership) and adopted structures such as Professional

Learning Communities (PLCs) can be used to operationalize social justice in practice. By embedding a vision that all students can learn and be active members in the school community, Davis K-8 has leveraged their PLC practices to implement inclusive structures and practices into the daily lives of their deaf and hearing-impaired students, as well as nondisabled students. This is their journey.

WHO IS DAVIS?

Davis K-8 School is a "Highly Performing" school located in the Southwestern United States and is one of over 100 schools in the Southwest Valley Unified School District. Southwest Valley Unified is a large, urban district that is comprised of schools varying from elementary and intermediate schools, middle schools, high schools, alternative education schools, and combination K-8 schools. Davis is the only school that has been identified as an exploratory learning center in the district.

Davis K-8 School has an enrollment of 305 students ranging from preschool aged to eighth grade. The school is comprised of 26 teachers and 1 principal. There is also a large number of exceptional education staff specializing in working with hearing-impaired student populations as many of the students have diagnoses of deaf and hard of hearing and are included in the classrooms with nondisabled peers.[1] While Davis is one of many schools in the district, they have adopted inclusive practices that differentiate them from other schools in the district. These practices, including multiaged classrooms, inclusion of students with disabilities (co-convened classes), and transformation of the way the school community views dual language instruction, will be discussed in the framework of transformational leadership. By adopting a strong sense of transformational leadership, the school has pushed the boundaries of what it is meant to be socially just regarding students with disabilities.

To provide context for the case, the next section discusses the original impetus for the study and outlines methods used to gather data.

METHODOLOGY AND DATA COLLECTION

The case presented in this chapter was studied as part of the International Successful School Principal Project (ISSPP) and included piloting adaptations made to existing surveys. ISSPP is a vast project spanning more than eight countries. The project utilizes a mixed-methods approach including principal and teacher surveys, semi-structured qualitative interviews, document analysis, and participant observations. While the study emphasized the knowledge, disposition, and skills principals have used in successful schools across national and international contexts, other findings have emerged that extend beyond capacity building. It is these findings that will be presented later in the chapter.

Surveys

Piloted teacher and principal surveys were based on modifications to previous surveys developed by ISSPP (Day & Leithwood, 2005). The modified teacher surveys contained seven sections that assessed teacher perceptions of student learning, school capacity, curriculum and instruction, priorities, systems for evaluation and accountability, leadership tensions and dilemmas, and perceptions of student background and attainment and how they perceived that the principal contributed to these. All items ($N = 155$) were ranked according to a five-point Likert scale.

Principal surveys contained an additional section that assessed the extent to which the principal perceived that they demonstrate successful leadership characteristics in 12 areas (e.g., reflection, relationship-building, planning, and professionalism). Principal responses were compared with teacher responses with particular attention paid to patterns of similarities and gaps. These patterns were used to develop qualitative interview protocols.

Qualitative Semi-Structured Interviews

Based on survey results, interview protocols were developed to gain a deeper understanding of leadership and capacity building at the school. Results from surveys indicated that there was a high level of capacity and significant differences were noticed on only four items (collaboration between school and outside partners, principal contributes to collaboration with outside community, receipt of resources from outside the school, and principal contributes to receipt of resources from outside the school). Survey results also indicated that the teacher and principal prioritized democratic citizenship, valued teacher collaboration and decision-making, were accountable to stakeholders, and were ethically responsible for student success. Similarly, teacher initiative and risk-taking were rewarded and the school's vision and results were clearly communicated to all stakeholders. Surveys additionally indicated that students and parents were valued and participate in school decisions.

Interview protocols focused on trends identified in the data consisted of nine teacher questions and nine principal questions. Teachers were asked to narrate the school's philosophy and how it has changed, how curriculum is developed and implemented, how teacher leadership is developed, ways that teachers collaborate with each other, ways in which they feel supported, how accountability has impacted practice, and how professional development aligns with school goals. Principal questions were similar with the addition of describing the process for involving parents and the community in school decisions and how she communicated the school's vision and results to stakeholders.

Additional Data Sources

Additional data sources were used to both garner additional information and triangulate findings from the quantitative and qualitative components of the study. These sources included nonparticipant observations, document reviews (e.g., lesson plans and mission statement), review of the school's website, and survey results from district satisfaction surveys given to staff, parents, students, and the larger community. The review of additional data sources indicated that responses given during the initial survey and interviews were trustworthy. Additional insights were gained from the satisfaction survey and pertinent results are presented in Table 1.

Participants

Survey data were gathered during a professional development block that is regularly scheduled on Wednesday afternoons. The principal arranged for the survey to be given and the study was placed on the agenda. Through the support of the principal and face-to-face administration, there was a 100% return rate on the surveys (teachers and principal). Qualitative interviews comprised of four teachers (ranging from primary to middle grades) and the principal. The small number of interviews could be conceived as a limitation. Another limitation is that students and parents were not interviewed. However, the use of multiple data sources including the satisfaction surveys mitigated this. Additionally, the interviewing of parents and students was not a component of the pilot study.

Table 1. Staff, Parent, and Student Satisfaction Survey Results.

Category	N	Agree/Strongly Agree (%)
I reflect on my own cultural background and biases related to race and culture that may influence my behavior	4,047	93.7
Students respect the special needs of others	4,128	89.6
Students participate in a school program and activities that represents the diversity of the school	3,941	92.2
Are satisfied with the school	4,161	90.1

Note: Survey is distributed online by district each year.

BEYOND INITIAL FINDINGS: INCLUSION AND SOCIAL JUSTICE

While initial findings identified that Davis K-8 School is a high capacity Learning Community school (Mitchell & Sackney, 2009), it was how the school used transformational leadership and leveraged a PLC model to operationalize socially just practices for the inclusion of students with disabilities, specifically students identified as deaf and hearing impaired, that was most intriguing. Davis provides a real-life example of how a social justice agenda can be achieved through the use of transformational leadership structures. More specifically, the school has used a transformational leadership model coupled with PLC practices to not only include students with disabilities but also to change the school's culture to bring forward the strengths and cultural aspects of their deaf and hearing-impaired students. Davis K-8 School practices will be discussed in the framework of transformational leadership and the adoption of the tenets of a PLC school in the upcoming section.

TRANSFORMATIONAL LEADERSHIP: PRACTICES FOR SOCIAL JUSTICE

When one thinks of transformational leadership in the context of education and educational leadership literature, social justice is not explicitly thought of as a goal. Rather, one thinks of a leadership model that addresses change and meeting adopted standards brought forth by No Child Left Behind

(NCLB, 2002). However, Davis K-8 School has utilized the various aspects of transformational leadership and created a school culture where social justice practices are behind every aspect of principal, staff, student, and parent action. Social justice, for the Davis community, lives through the inclusion of its deaf and hearing-impaired students and mission of learning for all students.

Schools and their leaders must be flexible and open to change, as well as knowledgeable about how to do so. One such way was the contextual change in the role of the principal as a transformational leader. Transformational leadership has been defined in a variety of ways. Leithwood (1994) identified three categories of leadership in the area of transformational leadership. Utilizing the concepts of setting directions, developing people, and redesigning the organization, Leithwood and Jantzi (2006) developed a framework based on two generalizations: transformational leadership directly affects teacher perceptions in the areas of student achievement and student grades. It also indirectly affects student outcomes by influencing perceptions of organizational learning, teacher commitment, and school characteristics.

According to Marks and Printy (2003), transformational leadership is needed to lead schools through reform efforts. Changes are developed through ideas, influence, and consideration for the individual in the process. Similarly, Bass and Avolio (1994) categorized transformational leadership into four I's: idealized influence which is defined as building trust and respect, inspirational motivation which is defined as setting the vision, intellectual stimulation, and individualized consideration, building on people's strengths.

Transformational leadership has had significant and large impact on perceived organizational effectiveness and independent indicators of organizational effectiveness. It has impacted independently measured student outcomes and has displayed a modest positive impact on student engagement in school (Leithwood, Jantzi, & Steinbach, 1999). This case study depicts a transformational leadership model that has driven a social justice agenda, one focused on inclusion of students with disabilities.

For the purpose of this investigation and discussion, transformational leadership will be defined as setting directions, redesigning the organization, and developing people (Leithwood & Jantzi, 2006). Each of these areas will be discussed regarding specific actions undertaken by Davis K-8 School to transform the school into a real-life model of inclusion. While many schools have utilized a transformational leadership model to produce change, Davis is unique in the way that transformational leadership practices have transformed school structures and practices to meet the needs of all students through inclusion.

Setting Directions

Leadership from principals is essential in creating inclusive schools (Capper, Frattura, & Keyes, 2000; Theoharis & Causton-Theoharis, 2008). Principals that lead schools set directions that drive school practices and policies. Leithwood (1994) defined setting directions as creating a vision, developing school-wide goals, and having high expectations. Through setting directions, leaders create opportunities to define social justice and develop empowering environments (Bogotch, 2002). Davis' principal created such an empowering environment framed in a vision for inclusion, collaboration, and engaging the entire school community. Davis' vision emphasizes high achievement, inclusion, and responsibility for the success of all children. At Davis, this vision extended beyond integration of deaf and hearing-impaired students to full inclusion of all students in the school community. Rather than emphasize students adapting to existing school structures, the mission and vision were driven by the need for restructuring and reculturing the school to emphasize the needs and participation of all students.

The vision of Davis K-8 involves several key components: the education of all students, staff collaboration for inclusive practices regarding their deaf and hearing-impaired students, and engaging the school community. According to the school's mission statement, each individual is valued and involved and teachers, students, and parents work together as active engaged readers, writers, researchers, mathematicians, scientists, artists, athletes, and historians. The emphasis is on the creation of an inclusive, collaborative culture whereas students develop skills in inquiry and research, face real problems, and construct solutions while developing self-confidence. When asked to summarize the school's mission, the principal responded with statements such as "noncompetitive spirit" and the "whole child." She noted that putting kids first is the right thing to do. She also emphasized the school's focus on inclusion of their deaf and hearing-impaired students and providing a quality education for all students. "What you do is try to take care of the kids. We have that mentality here which is a good thing because I believe in that." Teachers also responded that the school's mission is linked to developing students' self-esteem and educating students as individuals, paying particular attention to their individual needs. This was highlighted by responses such as "What's best for kids trumps particular curriculum or personally held philosophy."

The school's mission has become a working philosophy to which all staff, students, and parents adhere. The school's philosophy is child-centered and is based on inclusion, individual needs, and high levels of achievement of all students. There is also an emphasis on community. However, community was not defined in terms of the broader community. Rather, community was defined within the school walls and was seen as the parents, *all* students, and staff. There was no mention of the district or community partnerships regarding the definition of community. The school's instructional coach stated that the school's philosophy "has to do with the community."

The last tenet of the schools mission is collaborative practices for inclusion. This tenet is explained in more detail in the following section. Collaborative practices at Davis are directly linked to their PLC model and the ways that community is fostered. Through the development of people, Davis K-8 School's philosophy has taken hold and socially just, inclusive practices have been developed.

Developing People

Kose (2009) conceptualized social justice leadership as a leadership model where principal practice is guided by visions of teaching and learning for social justice. Principals enact this vision through staff professional development that increases content expertise and emphasizes a social justice perspective. Kose (2009) indicated that the goal of professional development must develop socially just organizational capacity that aligns the school culture, structure, curricula, and assessments with sustained development and promotion of socially just learning and classrooms. Doyle (2004), in agreement with Kose, identified that a focus on building capacity and reflection leads to reculturing for inclusive practice.

A vital component to the successful incorporation of the Davis mission into practice has been the use of a PLC model. According to Graham and Ferriter (2008), a key role of administrators is to support the development of PLCs and to emphasize the distribution of leadership. Thus, the role of principal changes with the initiation of PLCs. "Principals of PLCs are called upon to consider themselves as leaders of leaders, rather than leaders of followers, and broadening teacher leadership becomes one of their priorities" (Dufour, Eaker, & Dufour, 2005, p. 23). The principal creates structures for participation in discussions and builds consensus about school goals (Leithwood & Jantzi, 2006). Hoy and Miskel (2008) stated that "followers become leaders, and leaders become change agents and ultimately transform the organization" (p. 448). In this section, an overview of PLC practices at Davis K-8 School will be discussed.

Capacity building was evident in the school's practices. Davis K-8 School utilizes an early release schedule each Wednesday to foster professional development and staff collaboration. According to the principal, professional development "depends on what the needs are each week" and professional development activities and collaboration time is based upon projects that the staff develops at the beginning of each school year to support inclusive practices. School teams, comprised of grade level groups (primary, intermediate, and middle), determine the course of action necessary for success of all students. The principal noted:

> We all have a brainstorming session at the beginning of the year, come up with different topics we are interested in, network with each other to figure out what other people are in and figure out how we can collaborate, how we can learn together, and form teams. Those teams take on certain goals with their professional development, what they are interested in, and we have sheets that we report what we've been doing, what the next goal is, where we're going with professional development, and what we've learned.

Additionally, she mentioned that the brainstorming generally revolves around developing student-centered curriculum, identifying individual goals, and promoting inclusive practices for students with disabilities. Through this process, teams develop priorities, identify specific goals, and schedule focused collaborative time. Teachers identified that the use of collaboration time allowed for them to develop curriculum and build upon their leadership skills. Pam, a middle-school science teacher, responded that professional development and collaboration time was the area she got the most support from the principal. "A huge part of it [principal support] is allowing us to have professional development time, not necessarily to do lessons, but to allow us to collaborate together." She also stated that the principal gives time to work together as a team and encourages outside professional development, including scheduling summer workshops such as *Skillful Teacher, Understanding by Design,* and *Professional Learning Communities.*

While the collaboration time was most important to Pam, Sally, an elementary teacher viewed the opportunity to collaborate as an opportunity for teachers to take on leadership responsibilities. She felt that the principal supported teacher leadership and the teacher projects were a way for them to take a larger responsibility in the school. For her, the most important supports from the principal were that she [principal] "treats us like professionals" and "encourages teacher leadership." While teacher leadership and collaboration were emphasized, teachers also responded that the collaboration time allowed them to develop curriculum that reflected their philosophy and mission, "what's best for kids" and "promoting inclusion."

Although each of the teachers discussed curriculum in terms of standards, they did not lose focus of the individual needs of students. Standards and curriculum were discussed in terms beyond them. As an intermediate teacher mentioned, curriculum is developed with standards in mind and "we justify how we meet objectives"; however, curriculum is developed around problem-solving skills, team goals, and meeting the needs of all students. Elements of the curriculum that "don't work for us" are reworked and sometimes discarded. Sally noted, that "curriculum is more student led than in a lot of schools and pacing is definitely guided by the students." The principal responded that few teachers at the school use the adopted textbooks, opting for student-centered learning experiences and hands-on activities. In fact, the school "got rid of a lot of unused, brand new textbooks." Several teachers and the principal responded that the curriculum choices were led by school structures such as multiaged classrooms and students' current levels of mastery in the specific content areas. Rather than follow district curriculum guides, collaboration time is devoted to work together, with other teachers, to develop units on a three-year cycle. This allows for the development of deeper knowledge. There is a "more narrow, deep focus; as opposed to an inch deep, mile wide focus," and students, especially the school's deaf and hearing-impaired students are able to excel in areas of strength and receive additional time in areas that need improvement.

The PLC process at Davis extends beyond the school staff and integrates parents, staff, students, and community members into the decision-making process. The school has adopted a shared decision-making process where decisions are made through a consensus process with the school's vision "making decisions that are in the best interests of students' academic achievement and personal growth" at the forefront of all decisions. Coordinating Council members work in collaboration with staff and students to facilitate practices that are in the best interest of students and the school community. In the next section, processes that have been achieved through the implementation of PLCs and the shared decision-making process will be discussed.

The most important aspect of the school's PLC model is that it fosters discussion around school policies and structures that run counter to the school's philosophy of inclusion. Eleweke and Rodda (2002) stated that inclusion redefines a school's culture and changes policies and practices to meet the learning needs of all students. Through dialogue and collaboration, the school has transformed its practices to become inclusive and foster the culture of its deaf and hearing-impaired students. Not only are these students present in the classroom, their needs are placed at the forefront of many of the schools practices including a multiaged approach, co-convened classes, and American Sign Language as the school's second language program. Through the implementation of these practices, the school has been re-designed to become more socially just.

Redesigning the Organization

PLCs have been implemented to encourage collaboration and shared leadership among faculty in schools. This shift in focus has had significant effects on improving schools (CCSO, 2002). While PLCs are based on three core ideas: ensuring that students learn, a focus on results, and a shift in culture from individual to collaborative work (Dufour, 2004), they also provide an opportunity for staff to dialogue, question existing practices, and develop organizational structures that best benefit students and their learning. In the case of Davis K-8 School, PLCs have been the driving force for instructional practices and structures that have moved beyond mere integration of deaf and hearing-impaired students and students with disabilities, to reculturing practices that value and build upon the strengths of students with disabilities. At Davis, the school has adopted practices that adopt the culture of these students and promote inclusion for all students. In this section, Davis K-8 School's co-convened and multiage programs will be discussed along with a differentiated view of second language learning.

Davis has adopted the practice of co-convened/co-enrolled classrooms where students work alongside students with disabilities. The co-convened model allows for students with disabilities to be fully integrated into the school's classrooms. The co-convened model integrates both deaf and hearing-impaired students and their hearing peers in a classroom setting where a general education teacher and a teacher of the deaf and hard of hearing work together educating students in curriculum developed in PLCs. Each of the classrooms is staffed with two additional support staff (sign language interpreters) and an instructional aide. Classrooms have also been modified with sound field systems that amplify teacher's voices and instruction is presented in both spoken form and sign language. The expectation at Davis is that all students and staff become proficient in sign language.

Besides being able to participate with nondisabled peers, the co-convened classes also support deaf and hearing-impaired students by providing a forum of supportive peers who can communicate with each other. According to

Sally, this social support allows for students to "develop friendships and participate in the education process as equals, without any of the negatives sometimes attached to students who are different." Thus, all students are valued and the signing skills of deaf and hearing-impaired students are seen as an asset.

Another aspect of the Davis K-8 program is an adapted grade level structure where students engage in multiage classrooms. This structure, coupled with the co-convened nature of the program, allows for students to develop skills over a three-year period with the same teachers. The program structure includes Primary grades (K-1-2), Intermediate grades (3-4-5), and Middle School (6-7-8). According to the teachers and principal, the multiaged component of the school leads to students' sense of belonging, encourages community, and allows for students to work on mastery of skills without time lapses getting to know students at the beginning of each year. Students are also able to develop leadership skills and help each other learn to support each individual student's growth. According to the teachers, the multiaged format "allows kids to work at the level they are really at." The multiaged concept allows for students to be role models for other students including younger students and disabled students role modeling for older and non-disabled students. It also promotes a cooperative learning environment where students' individual needs are met.

Meeting students' individual needs and developing a sense of community has also led to the development of Davis' second language program. Since courses are co-convened and multiaged, students are able to develop second language skills in American Sign Language. Besides the benefit of promoting peer interaction and support, the development of sign language skills provides both disabled and nondisabled students with a tangible skill and the ability to communicate with members of the deaf community who often participate in school activities. By taking a perceived deficit and incorporating it into school practice, deaf and hearing-impaired students are placed on a level playing field with hearing peers and they are able to model for students struggling with learning a "new language."

SUMMARY

The Davis K-8 School is a model of excellence and social justice regarding deaf and hearing-impaired students. Driven by a philosophy of inclusion, community, and collaboration, the school has transformed itself into an exemplar of inclusive practices that promote the strengths and individual needs of all students. Through the use of a Professional Learning Community model, collaboration has fostered transformation and has displayed how traditional school practices can be used to push forward a social justice agenda. Not only are students learning at a high level, they are encouraged to develop self-esteem, take leadership roles, and learning for all remains the focus of efforts at the school. Davis shows us that perceived deficits in students could be utilized to build a sense of community and belonging. The school also provides a real-life example that creates a "sense that social justice in schools is not just educational theory or rhetoric but actually practiced by leaders" (in the case of Davis, all stakeholders) and indeed possible (Theoharis, 2008, p. 4).

IMPLICATIONS FOR PRACTICE

Scholars have called for leadership that is inclusive (Doyle, 2004; Theoharis & Causton-Theoharis, 2008), transformative (Foster, 1986), advocates for marginalized students (Anderson, 2009), is democratically accountable (Mullen, Harris, Pryor, & Browne-Ferrigno, 2008), and socially just (Marshall & Oliva, 2006; McKenzie et al., 2008). The common theme is a more socially just practice of schooling. Often overlooked in discussions are the ways that other models of leadership can be used in concert with a social justice agenda to promote inclusive practices that benefit all students. While social justice is a term that is abstract and conceptual, more traditional, accepted leadership structures can be included into the discourse around social justice. Davis K-8 School is an example of how social justice practices can be derived through the use of a leadership model based on transformational practices and provides a model for making inclusion work.

NOTE

1. The city where Davis is located also has a school specifically for deaf and blind students from around the state.

REFERENCES

Ainscow, M., Booth, A., Dyson, P., Farrell, J., Frankham, F., Gallannaugh, A., ... Smith, R. (2006). *Improving schools, developing inclusion*. London: Routledge.
Anderson, G. (2009). *Advocacy leadership: Toward a post-reform agenda in education*. London: Routledge.

Bass, B., & Avolio, B. (1994). *Improving organizational effectiveness through transformational leadership.* Thousand Oaks, CA: Sage.

Bogotch, I. (2002). Educational leadership and social justice: Practice into theory. *Journal of School Leadership, 12,* 138–156.

Capper, C., Frattura, E., & Keyes, M. (2000). *Meeting the need of students of all abilities: How leaders go beyond inclusion.* Thousand Oaks, CA: Corwin.

Council of Chief School Officers. (2002). *Expecting success: A study of five high performing, high poverty schools.* Washington, DC: Author.

Day, C., & Leithwood, K. (2005, September). International successful school principals project survey. *European conference of educational research,* Dublin, Ireland.

Doyle, L. (2004). Inclusion: The unifying thread for fragmented metaphors. *Journal of School Leadership, 14*(4), 352–377.

Dufour, R. (2004). What is a professional learning community. *Education Leadership, 11*(8), 6–11.

Dufour, R., Eaker, R., & Dufour, R. (2005). *On common ground: The power of professional learning communities.* Bloomington, IN: Solution Tree.

Eleweke, C., & Rodda, M. (2002). The challenge of enhancing inclusive education in developing countries. *International Journal of Inclusive Education, 6*(2), 113–126.

Foster, W. (1986). *Paradigms and promises: New approaches to educational administration.* Amherst, NY: Prometheus Books.

Goldfarb, K., & Grinberg, J. (2002). Leadership for social justice: Authentic participation in the case of a community center in Caracas, Venezuela. *Journal of School Leadership, 12,* 157–173.

Graham, P., & Ferriter, B. (2008). One step at a time. *National Staff Development Council, 29*(3), 38–42.

Hoy, W., & Miskel, C. (2008). *Educational administration: Theory, research and practice* (8th ed). New York, NY: McGraw Hill.

Johnson, L., Møller, J., Pashiardis, P., Vedøy, G., & Savvides, V. (2011). Culturally responsive practices. In R. Ylimaki, & S. Jacobson (Eds.), *US and cross-national policies, practices and preparation: Implications for successful instructional leadership, organizational learning, and culturally responsive practices.* Netherlands: Springer-Kluwer.

Kose, B. (2009). The principal's role in professional development for social justice: An empirically based transformative framework. *Urban Education, 44*(6), 628–663.

Leithwood, K. (1994). Leadership for school restructuring. *Educational Administration Quarterly, 30*(4), 498–518.

Leithwood, K., & Jantzi, D. (2006). A review of transformational school leadership research 1996–2005. *Leadership and Policy in Schools, 4*(3), 177–199.

Leithwood, K., Jantzi, D., & Steinbach, R. (1999). *Changing leadership for changing times.* Buckingham: Open University Press.

Marks, H., & Printy, S. (2003). Principal leadership and school performance: An integration of transformational and instructional leadership. *Educational Administration Quarterly, 39*(3), 370–397.

Marshall, C., & Oliva, M. (2006). *Leadership for social justice: Making revolutions in education.* Boston, MA: Pearson.

McKenzie, K., Christman, D., Hernandez, F., Fierro, E., Capper, C., Dantley, M., ... Scheurich, J. (2008). From the field: A proposal for educating leaders for social justice. *Educational Administration Quarterly, 44*(1), 111–138.

McKenzie, K., Sklra, L., & Scheurich, J. (2006). Preparing instructional leaders for social justice. *Journal of School Leadership, 16*, 158–170.

Mitchell, C., & Sackney, L. (2009). *Sustainable improvement: Building learning communities that endure.* Rotterdam, Netherlands: Sense Publishers.

Mullen, C., Harris, S., Pryor, C., & Browne-Ferrigno, T. (2008). Democratically accountable leadership: Tensions, actions, and principals in action. *Journal of School Leadership, 18*, 224–248.

NCLB. (2002). No Child Left Behind Act of 2001, 20 U.S.C. § 6319 (2008).

Otunga, R. (2010). A response to leadership for social justice: A transnational dialogue. *Journal of Research on Educational Leadership, 4*(1), 1–5.

Polat, F. (2011). Inclusion in education: A step towards social justice. *International Journal of Educational Development, 31*, 50–58.

Sapon-Shevin, M. (2003). Inclusion a matter of social justice. *Educational Leadership, 61*(2), 25–28.

Theoharis, G. (2007). Social justice educational leaders and resistance: Toward a theory of social justice leadership. *Educational Administration Quarterly, 43*(2), 228–251.

Theoharis, G. (2008). Woven deeply: Identity and leadership of urban social justice principals. *Education and Urban Society, 41*(1), 3–25.

Theoharis, G., & Causton-Theoharis, J. (2008). Oppressors or emancipators: Critical dispositions for preparing school leaders. *Equity and Excellence in Education, 41*(2), 230–246.

Zepeda, S., & Langenbach, M. (1999). *Special programs in regular schools: Historical foundations, standards, and contemporary issues.* Boston, MA: Allyn & Bacon.

CHAPTER 8

TEACHER LEADERSHIP: LEADING FOR SOCIAL JUSTICE IN TEACHER EDUCATION

Walter S. Gershon

ABSTRACT

In spite of the abundance of literature on teaching for social justice and a recent increase in discussions of the construction of teacher leadership, there is a dearth of studies that address the intersection of teacher leadership and social justice. Additionally, scholarship focused on teacher leadership tends to focus on teaching as measurable efficiency, a mainstream orientation toward teaching that can serve to reify the very kinds of inequities such reforms are designed to interrupt. Drawing from his own experiences as a teacher educator, the author argues that strong teaching is teaching for social justice and, similarly, that a teacher cannot be a leader unless she or he explicitly attends to questions of equity, access, and justice.

INTRODUCTION

What does teaching for social justice mean in practice? How can this be conveyed to future secondary school teachers in ways that are explicit yet

Global Leadership for Social Justice: Taking it from the Field to Practice
Advances in Educational Administration, Volume 14, 139–157
Copyright © 2012 by Emerald Group Publishing Limited
All rights of reproduction in any form reserved
ISSN: 1479-3660/doi:10.1108/S1479-3660(2012)0000014012

not pedantic? What is the relationship between teaching and leading? How can preservice teachers come to understand themselves as future leaders for social justice?

This chapter is one set of theoretical and practical answers to these questions that reside at the intersection of teaching, leadership, and social justice. Such questions are significant as they in many ways lie at the heart of definitions of what teaching means and the ways in which those meanings are enacted in the daily life of classrooms. They are similarly important as they address some of the possible ways for preparing future teachers to understand that their sociocultural role as "teacher" is necessarily related to questions of leading for social justice.

Although leadership is most often considered the domain of school leaders, namely, principals and assistant principals, there is also a strain of literature in teacher education that similarly constructs teachers as leaders (e.g., Hiltey, 2011; Lieberman & Miller, 2004; Reeves, 2008). While somewhat varied in their construction, what these discussions of such possibilities tend to share is (1) an understanding of the centrality of effectiveness and efficiency as tools toward improving schools and teaching and (2) a relatively linear and sequentially prescriptive stance toward the ways in which teacher leadership should be either taught or practiced (Crowther, Ferguson, & Hann, 2008; Farr & Teach for America, 2010; Reeves, 2008; Stone & Cuper, 2006).

Given that the measurement of teachers' and administrators' effectiveness according to students' scores on annual standardized assessments and the tendency to borrow business terminology such as "best practices" have become *de rigeur* in conversations of contemporary schooling, these tendencies are perhaps not surprising. However, as other scholars have noted, it is precisely this mainstream orientation toward leading, teaching, and learning that has helped foster many of the very injustices that such teacher leadership practices have been implemented to disrupt (e.g., Alonso, Anderson, Su, & Theoharis, 2009; Anderson, 2009; Taubman, 2009; Valenzuela, 2005; Watkins, 2011). Further complicating matters are the depth and breadth of what social justice means – a wide variety of discussions and histories that are not necessarily in agreement (see Ayers, Quinn, & Stovall, 2007).

While there are discussions of teaching for social justice (e.g., Adams, Bell, & Griffin, 2007; Ayers et al., 2007; Kumashiro, 2009) and leadership for social justice (e.g., Boske, 2011; Brown, 2004; Marshall & Oliva, 2010), there is little, if any, talk about the nexus of teacher leadership and social justice.[1] It is as if efforts to assert that teachers are leaders largely ignored contemporary discussions about teaching and leading for social justice and, instead, worked emulate outdated constructions of both fields that largely ignore the sociocultural and economic contexts that strongly inform all aspects of schooling.

Of the many meaningful ways to construct a teacher's classroom role, one is as a leader. Defining what students are to do in classrooms and the ways in which these educational interactions are to be conducted is a central aspect of what it means to be a teacher (Page, 1991, p. 33). Here, I wish to separate constructions of leadership that are linked to questions of efficiency, standardized measurement, and effectiveness. This is not because efficiency, standardized measurement, or questions of effectiveness are either unimportant or not part of leadership, for they are most certainly central to many leadership conversations. However, similar to the point raised above about the ways in which many contemporary school reform practices are unjust in spite of their stated purposes, notions of measurement against a standard, questions of efficiency, and understandings of effectiveness in schooling have a strong tendency to reify social and economic inequities in US education (Anyon, 2005; Kliebard, 2004; Valli, Croninger, Chambliss, Graeber, & Buese, 2008; Watkins, 2011; Winfield, 2007).

Thus, my understanding of what it means to be a leader in schools reflects literature that notes the necessity of addressing questions of inequity in all its forms, constructions of leading that might include but are not prerequisites for questions of efficiency, management, and measurement in schooling (e.g., Boske, 2011; Boske & Tooms, 2010; Brown, 2004, 2006; Marshall & Oliva, 2010). Along similar lines, it is also of equal importance to note that just as being a leader is not only about teaching, being a teacher is not only about leadership. In this way, talk of teachers leading for social justice here is meant somewhat literally. Here I refer to both my own acts of facilitating preservice teachers' constructions of teaching as part and parcel of social justice and, in turn, how these interactions can serve as an example of the ways in which students can be teacher leaders for social justice in their future lives as high school teachers.

What follows, then, are some of the ways that I engender and enact the notion of teacher leadership for social justice for a class I teach for future secondary school teachers. It is important to note that these practices are meant to be indicative of some of the kinds of ways that one might consider teaching for social justice with future teacher leaders and, as such, are in no way meant to be either exhaustive or prescriptive. I begin by presenting the context in which I teach including the course requirements and components, then provide my own understandings and definitions of social justice. The third section addresses the ways of knowing and being that inform how I approach leading for social justice and an example of how this is put into practice for future high school teachers within these contexts.

CONTEXTS

Each fall I teach either two or three sections of a course called Principles of Teaching. This is the first of the education-centric courses preservice teachers are required to take as part of a process through which undergraduates are screened, then officially admitted to our adolescent education program, most often in their third year. I often think of this as a kitchen sink course. Over the 16-week semester, Principles is designed to cover the following: provide students with the nuts and bolts of teaching such as classroom management and teaching strategies; teach them how to create lesson plans; and consider the relationship between school and society as it applies to daily classroom lessons. It has a 5-week urban field placement, students' only mandatory time in a city school; is writing intensive; and has increased in numbers of students from just under 20 to just under 30 students since my arrival in the fall of 2006.

As one of four state schools within an hour's drive and the only school not located in a city, the student population for Principles is overwhelmingly, Anglo, middle class, and Christian. This past fall (2011) I had 2 female students of color out of 54 students, 1 woman in each of the two sections of the course I taught. Perhaps the greatest diversity in the students I encounter is in their location between suburban and rural contexts. It has been my experience that just over a third of students come from rural schooling contexts with a student or two in each class who attended high school in a city, most often in Ohio. Although largely from middle class families, most of the undergraduates I teach hold one, if not two, jobs in addition to taking a relatively large number of credits each semester – it is not unusual to hear students say they are working 20 hours on top of taking four or five courses.

Students' middle classness tends to manifest in having familial help in paying for tuition but often does not transcend to living and other associated expenses. This is further buttressed by a generally Midwestern work ethic; I have had many students share with me that their parents could pay for additional expenses but want them to have a sense of what it means to work for a living. However, the opposite also tends to hold true. Students from working class to poor families are more likely to work more and longer hours in order to pay for both tuition and living expenses, a difficulty further compounded by the fact that in each semester several students often come from families where annual income does not quite qualify them for the amount of financial aid they need. Many students also receive some kind of financial aid and are therefore doubly driven to keep their grades up as their aid is often contingent on keeping a particular GPA. Students also need to maintain their GPA to stay in good standing with our adolescent education program.

Most students have also lived their lives within the confines of their home communities. It is not unusual to have students who have never left the state of Ohio, although the state border with Pennsylvania is under an hour east, or have rarely, if ever, been to a major metropolitan area, although there are four cities in Northeast Ohio (Canton, Cleveland, Akron, and Youngstown).

As briefly noted above, Principles has a 5-week urban field placement for which students spend a minimum of 30 hours in middle and high schools with majority students of color student populations. Half of their time is spent tutoring students who need further help to pass the Ohio Graduation Test (OGT) and the other half of their time they observe a teacher or teachers in their particular content area, language arts, math, science, or social studies. It means that in a 16-week semester, I have 5 weeks to encourage students to think about teacher and student roles as well as the sociocultural contexts of schooling prior to their urban field placements.

DEFINING SOCIAL JUSTICE

How, then, does one fit social justice into such a jam-packed teaching schedule? What can truly be done in the name of social justice "on the ground" in the "real world" of schools and classrooms in light of the pressures teachers face for students to pass their high school graduation tests, gain access to college, and other such local and less local contexts that strongly inform what teachers do in classrooms?

In short, I reject the additive framing of social justice in such questions. Given the broad range of definitions of social justice in education, my purpose here is not to arrive upon a single, bounded definition but instead to make explicit the kinds of ideas and ideals that constitute my own understanding of this term. For me, social justice in education is the intentional ways in which educators (broadly concieved) actively work to enact and engender equity, access, respect, and awareness across all educational contexts, from national policies to daily classroom interactions (e.g., Delpit, 2006; DuBois, 1903; Friere, 2000 [1970]; Greene, 1995; Hooks, 1994;

Quinn & Meiners, 2009; Rist, 1970; Weiss & Fine, 2005). Similarly, I understand teaching for social justice in teacher education as helping students to (1) see the broader contexts that inform daily classroom lessons, (2) understand the ways in which their expectations and practices carry both explicit and implicit messages about students and society, (3) their roles in actively reifying or interrupting education as a tool for marginalization and inequity, and (4) the centrality of such matters as educators.

These thoughts are neither new nor radical. They are endemic to United States education, as central to the work of educators such as W. E. B. DuBois, George Counts, John Dewey, Booker T. Washington, and Harold Rugg[2] (cf. Kliebard, 2004; Kridel & Bullough, 2007) at the turn of the previous century as it is to contemporary scholars concerned with social justice (e.g., Ayers et al., 2007; Darling-Hammond, French, & Garcia-Lopez, 2002; Ladson-Billings & Tate, 2006). From another perspective, *Brown versus the Board of Education* is not only a lynchpin for civil rights, but also, as importantly, an educational issue of equity and access. Furthermore, teachers are mandatory reporters for child abuse and are therefore legally mandated advocates for student/child safety and well-being. In addition, should not one of a teacher's central roles and responsibilities be to advocate for her students?

Similarly, one cannot begin to be a teacher leader, a person who facilitates learning with students and advocates for children, without teaching for social justice. This is because social justice is not a series of steps or practices but is instead a way of knowing and being. From this perspective, teaching for social justice does not only address the broader and more local inequities in schooling, although expressly addressing such injustices is of utmost importance. Teaching for social justice is also how you greet students as they enter the room, asking a student how she or he is when you pass one another in the hall, and listening to students and taking their ideas seriously – the seemingly little things that can and do impact students' daily lives.

Social justice should therefore be an integral part of teaching. It should similarly be part and parcel of what it means to be a teacher leader, a person whose role is to enact and engender equity, access, respect, and inquiry for students and colleagues alike. In other words, I understand being a teacher leader for social justice as a question of both epistemology and ontology, inclusive of not only the ideas about what might be socially just but also the ways of being that enact those ideas and ideals.

While these constructions can certainly include standards and improvement, they are the concepts and constructs that should be the foundations for those standards and means of improvement rather than being conceptualized as a tool in service to such possibilities. Social justice does not need to be justified by its ability to help schools improve test scores or teachers to be more effective leaders. The following section details how I approach leading for social justice in the context of thinking with future secondary school teachers and the ways in which I work with them to adopt similar practices in their own future lives as teachers.

TEACHING, LEADING FOR SOCIAL JUSTICE WITH FUTURE SECONDARY TEACHERS

Because all academic content is both academic and social – a choice of this idea over that according to particular sets of sociocultural norms and values – all curriculum is necessarily political, not *the* curriculum but *a* curricular set of choices among many possibilities. The processes of education that are schooling are the result of similar set of sociocultural, socio-economic, and sociohistorical decisions – not *the* school but *a* school, one set of choices among a sea of possibilities. My construction of leading for social justice as a teacher educator is therefore rather straightforward. Because all aspects of education are choices and contextually dependent, then there is no reason not to make choices as an educator that are inclusive and respectful, consider the multitude of sociocultural contexts that inform daily classroom lessons and interactions, and other such factors in ways that are intentionally made to foster greater equity, access, and justice. In sum, as I detail below, there is no difference between strong teaching and leading for social justice.

This understanding applies to the content I teach, how I frame that content, and my ways of being as a teacher educator. Each of these aspects of leading for social justice deeply influences the other – the way I act and embody teaching, the lens through which I consider ideas, and the ideas I present all in some way both determine and are determined by one another. In light of these interwoven relationships, rather than try to separate them overly, I begin by articulating how I conceptualize these ways of knowing and being and then provide a few examples of these ideas and ideals function in practice as means of leading for social justice with future high school teachers.

Ontology: Embodying Social Justice

Because I understand social justice as a way of being, a means of interacting with people and ecologies, part of my approach to leading for social justice involves *not* delineating between daily teaching practices and the intentional action of teaching for equity, access, and movement toward such socio-cultural possibilities. One way to understand this approach is as performative, the ways in which the act of doing something is simultaneously an instance of that idea or ideal. The difficulty in expressing this approach lies not in the idea but in the deficiency of language to describe such events (on the importance of affect and ontology, see Gregg & Seigworth, 2010). Perhaps, the closest I can get to the point I wish to make here is to say that my teaching embodies social justice and/or that I intend to embody social justice in my teaching. I make an effort to walk my talk. I do not raise my voice during class, I approach concerns as questions, I make boundaries for appropriate discourse clear and maintain them, work hard to ensure that all voices are heard and respected, and other such manifestations of social justice.

Yet these too are not quite what I mean. The closest I can come to my intended explanation is a paradox: social justice is a way I move through the world and is a complex set of ideas and ideals that I intentionally try to enact in daily interactions regardless of their context. This also means that my body is impacted by the contexts in which I move, something that can be as uncomfortable (stomach in a knot, teeth on edge) as it can be opening (shoulders relaxing, sudden grin), and that, conversely, what I carry in my body can impact others and myself, for help or harm.

Other times, leading for social justice requires calling attention to how I approach my ways of being as a teacher. Although this may seem to be contrary or hypocritical, it is not. Just as Delpit (2006) argues that traditionally marginalized students can gain cultural capital by being shown the rules and practices of the powerful, engendering leading for social justice in future secondary teachers occasionally requires calling direct attention to a particular mode of being or way of interacting – making the everyday extraordinary.

Did everyone see how respectfully she disagreed with him? Have you noticed that every answer provided gets written on the board? Taking a student aside after class, letting her know that, if she's comfortable doing so, she has great ideas that would be most welcome during class. "What about our time together?" This made it seem as though that kind of language would be appropriate here. How do you think it sounds when you say "those people who live in that scary place," to whom is that respectful, and what are you not talking about? Stopping a student from talking over his peers yet again in ways that are closer to browbeating or a jeremiad than a conversation or discourse.

Although both processes can be understood as a way of modeling social justice, it does not align with common practices for modeling in teacher education, processes that are often presented as a kind of direct instruction. In the first instance, being with social justice as a means of leadership is neither discreet nor explicit. With the latter, calling attention to ways of being that foster or hinder equity, access, and respect is a means of stopping the flow of the ordinary to demonstrate its impact rather than stepping outside of the ordinary to demonstrate a discreet set of knowledge.

Finally, there is no singular way to *be* as a leader for social justice. However, given the ways in which sociocultural norms and values are imbedded in commonplace interactions and therefore often hidden in plain sight, embodying social justice requires operating in the paradox noted above. One must work in ways that are affective and cognitive as part of one's movement and orientation to the world; that attend to the complex web of local and less local contexts that inform any single (educational) interaction; and work intentionally toward serving as a catalyst for more just possibilities for others and one's self. As Wolcott (1990) noted about the nature of interpretive research, while it is not possible to get it all right, one must go to great lengths "not to get it all wrong" (p. 127).

Epistemology: Framing Social Justice

Frames are an apt metaphor for conceptualizing ideas and ideals. The understanding of frames as static, linear, and sequential is one of the central ways in which privilege is maintained, marginalization is reified, and injustices are perpetrated (see Butler, 2009; Handelman, 2001). Additionally, frames can be understood as part of a longstanding tradition of valuing sight over other senses, aspects of affect that are essential to conceptualizing equity, access, and possibility (Gershon, 2011). However, when conceptualized as nuanced, complex, and fluid, frames can be a powerful tool for both unpacking injustice and working toward social justice. If a framing can be noted as unjust, a double meaning that Judith Butler (2009) brings home solidly in the introduction to her recent book about framing, then it can be documented as an exemplar of what *not* to do. Similarly, frames can demonstrate ideas and ideals that foster social justice.

As some of the ways in which I frame social justice have already been enunciated above, I turn my attention here to a few examples of this framing that I have either not yet presented or done so in a rather cursory fashion. First, justice and fairness are not necessarily synonymous. This is particularly the case in education. For example, all students in the state need to pass the OGT to graduate high school and all students who take the assessment in any given year are presented with a few variations from the same pool of questions. However, if you are a high school math whiz who has recently immigrated from Vietnam, unless you had extensive English classes before moving to Ohio, you are likely to fail the math portion of the OGT. This is because the OGT, as with most standardized assessments, uses language in subtle ways to try and trick the test taker into selecting the wrong answer to a question (i.e., "which of the following is not") an because the test has a large number of "word problems" in which students need to be able to understand English well enough to decipher the math problems such questions contain, something that a fair percentage of high school students who grew up in Ohio have difficulty with.

From this perspective, although the test is fair, it is unjust. The OGT and all other standardized assessments of their kind privilege both those with money (a Vietnamese family who can afford private English lessons or those who can afford tutors) and students who are more proficient in English. If the standardized assessments were just, they would offer the mathematics portions, and perhaps the science portions as well, in a variety of languages; there is a literacy portion of the examination that focuses on the English language.

Second, social justice is social. It is therefore interactional and, as such, locates the self in relation to others. Whether it's yourself or someone else's self, groups of individuals, their ways of moving through and thinking about the world shape individuals' and groups' possibilities and limitations. This is why the choices made are important; not only they contribute to how one is understood or how one understands others but also they literally work to create and recreate how people are treated and the choices they have.

Third, social justice requires action. Justice can be something metered out, a condition in which things occur, or sets of ideas and ideals. Social justice is justice in relation to the social in action, how people interact, think, feel, and relate. Talking about social justice is one form of this action, like writing a chapter in a book, so is standing up for a child who often treats others poorly but is having a rough day herself or working with a student to grasp an idea. It is in the small things and the big things.

Finally, social justice requires an awareness not only of justice but also of the social, an awareness of others. The possibility that what is comfortable for one's self might be harmful for someone else or what seems unnatural to you is someone else's habit. This points to another paradox. On one hand, people are people, we laugh, we cry, we eat, we sleep, we live, and we die.

On the other hand, how people think, move, and exist in the world is a seemingly endless multitude of possible norms and values. It is the paradox of not being color blind, of noticing that a person is of a different race, ethnicity, gender, sexual orientation, age, height, smell (and on it goes), and treating them with dignity in a way that allows those differences not to be deficits. Social justice must therefore involve both awareness and reflexivity, changes made in light of reflection.

A strong example of how these ways of being and knowing manifest in one's daily life is a series of texts I received from a friend and doctoral student who has worked with students to establish a Gay–Straight Alliance at the suburban/rural, Anglo, conservative high school where she teaches. The Thursday I received this text was the second week she has been back teaching after taking time off for maternity leave with her first child. These are the initial text messages I received from her and a text clarifying the student's consequence.

> Text 1: After being told that I was indoctrinating students into a sexual orientation (from a staff member), that I'm wasting school resources on an irrelevant topic (staff), that Jews need to go back to San Francisco where the rest of them live (from a student), that gays need a special place in the room so nobody needs to [breathe] air near them (from a student) ... I had enough. Some people got a very large part of my mind this week.
> Clarifying Text: Well either way, he's been educated...and my classroom & 2 of my colleagues [sic] rooms are nicely cleaned as a result. I decided, while too late, that the next time he will be writing a page of research about any community he decides to target.

Here, all of the aspects of social justice presented in this section are present. Social justice is embodied and understood, explicit and implicit, interactional, action taken in the face of injustice, and reflexivity. It is simultaneously strong teaching and being a teacher leader in contexts that were originally intended to marginalize her perspectives. As this instance clearly enunciates, being a teacher leader for social justice is not always an easy task, but it is not necessarily always an uphill battle either. The following section presents an example of the ways in which I enact my role as a leader for social justice as a teacher educator.

Teaching as Social Justice

Classroom management is often the aspect of teaching that both most concerns future (and many current) teachers and is the topic to which we return over and again in Principles. It also serves as a good example of how I approach strong teaching as leading for social justice. As the ideas and ideals I present here are ones that I share with students in multiple ways over time, this discussion is necessarily incomplete (as is all teaching). It is my hope, however, that it will provide a concrete example of the talk presented in the previous sections of this chapter.

Ideas About Classroom Management
Strong classroom management begins with an understanding that teachers have much of the authority but almost none of the control over the students they teach. Socially, students decide they don't care about the consequences, lowering grades for example, they could walk out en masse and never return. Academically, no one person can make another learn. This is because, in spite of over 100 years of working to demonstrate otherwise in US education, the learner learns and the teacher teaches. While a teacher's teaching can and often does facilitate a student's learning, it is by no means a guarantee. Even if someone wants to learn something, building knowledge takes time and does not necessarily operate on a particular timetable, even if both the teacher and the student want it to! This is even further complicated by the fact that it is very difficult, if not impossible, to determine where learning occurs. A teacher can teach something during 1 day's lesson that one student learned 3 years ago, another student heard but didn't understand until his mother explained it to him after work, and a third student disregarded until she woke up the next morning thinking about and understanding that idea without having consciously considered it.

As a result, authority is negotiated in classrooms (Metz, 1978; Pace & Hemmings, 2006). This means that, in order to have some kind of meaningful learning interaction in classrooms, the teacher and students must agree on explicit and implicit sets of understandings about how classroom interactions are to function. One way to foster such interactional possibilities for learning is by providing a space for students to voice their thoughts and listening to their ideas. Another is to expressly come up with classroom codes of conduct together so that both teacher and students play an active role in deciding how they agree to interact with one another. A third way is to encourage discourse over debate, the idea that the purpose of discussion in a learning environment is to consider ideas and ideals in a manner that differing perspectives are respected and there does not need to be a winner and a loser.

Teaching Future Teachers About Classroom Management
Here are some of the ways in which I approach thinking with future classroom teachers about classroom management in Principles. First, we read several articles about how teacher expectations impact students' academic and

behavioral possibilities and its inverse, how student expectations and interactional choices impact what and how teachers teach. As we read them, I don't talk explicitly about classroom management. Instead, I use these moments to note how sociocultural contexts impact the classroom environment, thinking explicitly about social justice to implicitly consider classroom management. Then, when students are in the field during their urban field placements, they regularly post to an online discussion group about their experiences and write two reports, a study of a student whom they shadow for a portion of that student's daily school schedule and a field study report in which they consider multiple aspects of schooling, from the instructional strategies they saw or used themselves to the people they met walking through the hallways.

After students return from being in urban schools for at least 30 hours over 5 weeks, we expressly talk about classroom management. In these lessons students often work in groups, creating lists of the kinds of student behaviors that concern them and ways they think they might adapt their teaching to accommodate those concerns for example. We think together about the many ways that classroom authority is negotiated.

Throughout the course students are asked to use the visual and performing arts to consider what it means to be a teacher in general and about classroom management in specific. Students write songs about what teachers do and think; they put on skits in which they act out their concerns and possible means to respectfully address those concerns with students.

Then there are the questions. Discussions of classroom management, like all discussions in the classes I teach, tend to be led by open-ended questions. These are not known information questions (Mehan, 1979) but genuine inquiries into what students think and feel. When they don't answer, I wait. At the beginning of the course and occasionally throughout the semester, the silence after a question stretches. Although I do sometimes break the silence with either a clarifying statement or to ask if I was somehow unclear, these are questions I can't answer because I am not the student. I know the answers for myself, but the purpose of the questions is for these future teachers to consider what these questions mean to them as educators.

There are many other aspects to strong classroom management – giving students room to unwind while they work, attending to the feeling of the room to see if it's time for a brief break or change in activities, letting students know the timing of a lesson, not jumping on students whispering to one another as it is often about content (did you get that?) and it is not about the task at hand. These are not only topics of conversation but also how I approach teaching the future teachers in Principles. Occasionally, I do what I call "dropping the pedagogical screen," a term I made up to note a moment in class when I have just enacted a particular aspect of teaching, as it pertains to classroom management for example. While I do use the term in a somewhat self-mocking tone, the disjuncture between my own relatively informal talk about myself and my use of this term serves as a strong marker for such moments.

Social Justice Is Strong Teaching
This example of classroom management practices, a paradigm in teacher education that should be further explored and unpacked in light of its controlling history, also documents how strong teaching is social justice in action. For example, asking open-ended questions and taking students' answers seriously not only creates a space where students are more likely to learn but also helps engender classrooms as safe spaces. The kinds of questions used to find out what students know or ask after their ideas are the very questions often used to inquire about a students' well-being and safety: How are you, what's going on, you don't seem yourself today what's up, what's another way you might approach that?

Similarly, working from a perspective that authority in classrooms is negotiated creates the space for student agency, their ability to enact their available wiggle room in ways that help them maintain their dignity and be aware of others. This can also be seen in the ways in which reading texts about classroom management can serve as a springboard for critical discourse about how student and teacher perception of sociocultural precepts impacts daily classroom interactions.

Additionally, artful assignments not only provide an opportunity for students to otherwise consider questions, concerns, and possibilities of class-room management but also can be understood as a means to accommodate students' needs, a nontraditional queering of a rather traditional topic. Concretely, the arts can be a means in which students who are less inclined toward text-based schooling or have difficulty expressing themselves in reading and writing can express their ideas and feelings.

Furthermore, at least twice in our discussions of classroom management, I drop the pedagogical screen to explicitly note these connections between strong teaching, creating an environment conducive to learning, and social justice. The idea that strong classroom management is not an authoritarian space where students are controlled out of learning but is instead a safe space for ideas and feelings fosters the very same kind of safe space for students to be themselves and treated with dignity.

Finally, each of the lessons shared in this section is performative. Class discussions about respectful talk are led utilizing the parameters being presented; group work about how to use inquiry as a tool for classroom management is conducted using open-ended questions about the inquiry process. The discussion of classroom management as creating safe spaces is the process of creating a strong learning environment to create a safe space for the undergraduates who are thinking about these aspects of their lives as future teachers. They are leading for social justice in teacher education.

Students' Perspectives on Teacher Leadership as Social Justice
Principles is not only the first class in the sequence of education-centric courses taught by the core faculty of our Adolescent and Young Adult Program, but it is the only course that all students take across their various academic specializations. After the end of the semester, students then spend the majority of their time with others who share their particular academic discipline, integrated social studies students with integrated social studies students and integrated mathematics students with their peers in integrated mathematics. As a result, unlike my colleagues who spend the next year and a half with students in their academic domain, I am not scheduled to see undergraduates after I work with them each fall.

Because of this role, the information I have is a combination of student comments on formal course evaluations and anecdotal evidence in the form of comments from colleagues and students. For example, on her or his formal evaluation this past fall one student commented, "The instructor was able to motivate me to be passionate about my opinions by sharing his in a non discriminatory way" and another wrote, "Dr. Gershon was amazing and helped me see education in many new ways. He always made me think." Three additional comments were, "The discussion setting in which we worked allowed me to be more open and learn more than any class I've ever had;" "Dr. Gershon has a very helpful and respectful demeanor. His support in the class has really made so much difference;" and "He is respectful to us as students, motivational, knows his content and is always open after class for questions." Although these comments are not directly naming social justice, they speak to the ways I seek to integrate perspectives, possibilities, inquiry, and justice into everyday teaching.

What has perhaps surprised me most is that the more explicit I have made connections between social justice and strong teaching, the more appreciative students have become of the course and the centrality of questions of equity and access to strong secondary teaching practice. I regularly now have students who wish to meet with me to talk about everything from what it means to teach in an urban school to how they might address homophobia or class inequities with their future students. My colleagues have similarly noted a change in students' perspectives toward questions of equity, access, and justice – not that all students have made such a marked change but that there has been a general increase in openness toward the ideas and ideals that form the foundation of teaching for social justice.

To be clear, I am not claiming that all students who are in the sections I teach gain a social justice perspective in the short 16 weeks we spend together one fall. Nor am I claiming that this is necessarily enough time to foment deep-seated change. It is, however, more than enough time to begin to plant the seeds for the importance of social justice, its relationship to strong teaching, and its inexorable connection to teacher leadership.

CONCLUSION

The iterative, recursive, and open-ended nature of strong teaching and social justice cuts both ways. On one hand, in both teaching and social justice, the consideration of contexts and individuals, the attention to one's actions and choices, and other such aspects are never ending – there is no resting place, no finish line to cross, no laurels to rest on. On the other hand, that social justice and strong teaching require continual action and attention means that there is always possibility, always hope in their engaged enactment.

Teaching, social justice, and leadership are not separate interactions. One does not have to think about questions of ontology and epistemology for each but rather how one's educational ways of being and knowing impact the transfer of knowledge, its interpretations and the consequences of that knowledge as well as its means of transmission and translation. Along similar lines, strong teaching, regardless of academic content or social context, is social justice. For it is impossible to be a strong teacher without taking into account the sociocultural contexts in which one teaches, and leadership with attention to broader sociocultural norms and values is not leadership but some other managerial task.

In these ways, teacher leadership is social justice in action. Similarly, teacher education is inherently leading for social justice. It is my hope that in some small way this chapter is performative as well, a step toward further enunciating the mutually exclusive and codependent nature of teacher leadership/social justice.

NOTES

1. For example, even Eleanor Blair Hilty's (2011) recent edited book, *Teacher Leadership: A Reader*, a well-written socially minded volume, has only one mention of social justice (p. 285) outside of Nelda Cambron-McCabe & Martha M. McCarthy's (2005) chapter about education school leaders, not teacher leaders, for social justice.

2. Although as Winfield (2007, 2011) suggests, progressive educators like Counts and Rugg did not escape the grasp of eugenics, the vestiges of which we still grapple with today (Dewey is largely the exception) this also does not remove the significance of their work toward social justice – as African-American who actively sought access and justice, DuBois and Washington were not eugenicists.

REFERENCES

Adams, M., Bell, L. A., & Griffin, P. (Eds.). (2007). *Teaching for diversity and social justice* (2nd ed.). New York, NY: Routledge.

Alonso, G., Anderson, N., Su, C., & Theoharis, J. (2009). *Our schools suck: Students talk back to a segregated nation on the failures of urban education*. New York, NY: NYU Press.

Anderson, K. S. (2009). *War or common cause? A critical ethnography of language education policy, race, and cultural citizenship*. Charlotte, NC: Information Age Press.

Anyon, J. (2005). *Radical possibilities: Public policy, urban education and a new social movement*. New York, NY: Routledge.

Ayers, W. C., Quinn, T., & Stovall, D. (2007). *Handbook for social justice in education*. New York, NY: Routledge.

Boske, C. (2011). Using the senses in reflective practice: Preparing school leaders for non-text-based understandings. *Journal of Curriculum Theorizing, 27*(2). Retrieved from http://journal.jctonline.org/index.php/jct/issue/view/13/showToc. Accessed on January 9, 2012.

Boske, C., & Tooms, A. K. (2010). Social justice and doing "being ordinary". In A. K. Tooms & C. Boske (Eds.), *Building bridges: Connecting educational leadership and social justice to improve schools* (pp. xvii–xxviii). Charlotte, NC: Information Age Publishing.

Brown, K. (2004). Leadership for social justice and equity: Weaving a transformative framework and pedagogy. *Educational Administration Quarterly, 40*(1), 79–110.

Brown, K. (2006). Leadership for social justice and equity: Evaluating a transformative framework and andragogy. *Educational Administration Quarterly, 42*(5), 700–745.

Butler, J. (2009). *Frames of war: When is life grievable?* London: Verso.

Cambron-McCabe, N., & McCarthy, M. M. (2005). Educating school leaders for social justice. *Educational Policy, 19*(1), 201–222.

Crowther, F. A., Ferguson, & Hann, L. (2008). *Developing teacher leaders: How teacher leadership enhances school success* (2nd ed.). Thousand Oaks, CA: Corwin Press.

Darling-Hammond, L., French, J., & Garcia-Lopez, S. P. (Eds.). (2002). *Learning to teach for social justice*. New York, NY: Teachers College Press.

Delpit, L. D. (2006). *Other people's children: Cultural conflict in the classroom*. New York, NY: New Press.

DuBois, W. E. B. (1903). *The souls of black folk.* No copyright, for resources, see http:// www.webdubois.org/wdb-souls.html

Farr, S., & Teach for America. (2010). *Teaching as leadership: The highly effective teacher's guide to closing the achievement gap.* San Francisco, CA: Joseey-Bass.

Freire, P. (2000/1970). *Pedagogy of the oppressed* (Myra Bergman Ramos, Trans.). New York, NY: Herder & Herder.

Gershon, W. S. (2011). Sound curriculum: Recognizing the field. In R. Navqi & H. Schmidt (Eds.), *Thinking about and enacting curriculum in "frames of war"* (pp. 89–120). Lanham, MD: Lexington Books.

Greene, M. (1995). *Releasing the imagination: Essays on education, art, and social change.* San Francisco, CA: Jossey-Bass.

Gregg, M., & Seigworth, G. J. (Eds.). (2010). *The affect theory reader.* Durham, NC: Duke University Press.

Handelman, D. (2001). Framing, braiding, and killing play. *Focaal, 37,* 145–158.

Hiltey, E. B. (Ed.). (2011). *Teacher leadership: The "new" foundations of teacher education. A reader.* New York, NY: Peter Lang.

Hooks, B. (1994). *Teaching to transgress: Education as the practice of the freedom.* New York, NY: Routledge.

Kliebard, H. M. (2004). *The struggle for the American curriculum, 1893–1958* (3rd ed.). New York, NY: Routledge.

Kridel, C., & Bullough, R. V. (2007). *Stories of the eight-year study: Reexamining secondary education in America.* Albany, NY: SUNY Press.

Kumashiro, K. K. (2009). *Against common sense: Teaching and learning towards social justice.* New York, NY: Routledge.

Ladson-Billings, G., & Tate, W. F. (Eds.). (2006). *Education research in the public interest: Social justice, action, and policy.* New York, NY: Teachers College Press.

Lieberman, A., & Miller, L. M. (2004). *Teacher leadership.* San Francisco, CA: Jossey-Bass.

Marshall, C., & Oliva, M. (2010). *Leadership for social justice: Making revolutions in education* (2nd ed.). Boston, MA: Allyn & Bacon.

Mehan, H. (1979). "What time is it Denise?": Asking known information questions in classroom discourse. *Theory into Practice, 18,* 285–294.

Metz, M. H. (1978). *Classrooms and corridors: The crisis of authority in desegregated secondary schools.* Berkeley, CA: University of California Press.

Pace, J. L., & Hemmings, A. (Eds.). (2006). *Classroom authority: Theory, research, and practice.* Mahwah, NJ: Lawrence Erlbaum Associates.

Page, R. N. (1991). *Lower-track classrooms: A curricular and cultural perspective.* New York, NY: Teachers College Press.

Quinn, T., & Meiners, E. R. (2009). *Flaunt it! Queers organizing for public education and justice.* New York, NY: Peter Lang.

Reeves, D. B. (2008). *Reframing teacher leadership: To improve your school.* Alexandria, VA: Association for Supervision and Curriculum Development.

Rist, R. C. (1970). Student social class and teacher expectations: The self-fulfilling prophecy in ghetto education. *Harvard Educational Review, 40*(1), 411–451.

Stone, R., & Cuper, P. H. (2006). *Best practices for teacher leadership: What award-winning teachers do for their professional learning communities.* Thousand Oaks, CA: Corwin Press.

Taubman, P. M. (2009). *Teaching by numbers: Deconstructing the discourse of standards and accountability in education.* New York, NY: Routledge.

Valenzuela, A. (Ed.). (2005). *Leaving children behind: How "Texas-style" accountability fails Latino youth.* New York, NY: State University of New York Press.

Valli, L., Croninger, R., Chambliss, M. H., Graeber, A. O., & Buese, D. (2008). *Test driven: High-stakes accountability in elementary schools.* New York, NY: Teachers College.

Watkins, W. H. (Ed.). (2011). *The assault on public education: Confronting the politics of corporate school reform.* New York, NY: Teachers College Press.

Weiss, L., & Fine, M. (2005). *Beyond silenced voices: Class, race, and gender in United States schools* (3rd ed.). Albany, NY: State University of New York.

Winfield, A. (2007). *Eugenics and education in America: Institutionalized racism and the implications of history, ideology, and memory.* New York, NY: Peter Lang.

Winfield, A. (2011). Resuscitating bad science: Eugenics past and present. In W. H. Watkins (Ed.), *The assult on public education: Confronting the politics of corporate school reform.* New York, NY: Teachers College Press.

Wolcott, H. F. (1990). On seeking- and rejecting-validity in qualitative research. In E. W. Eisner & A. Pushkin (Eds.), *Qualitative inquiry in education: The continuing debate* (pp. 121–152). New York, NY: Teacher's College Press.

CHAPTER 9

STANDING STILL IS NO LONGER AN OPTION: UNDERSTANDING HOW TO PREPARE SCHOOL LEADERS TO INTERRUPT OPPRESSIVE PRACTICES

Christa Boske

ABSTRACT

The author examines how school leaders understood issues of social justice. Despite rising standards for excellence and equity, increasing demands on teachers and school leaders to raise standardized test scores, and the push for schools to achieve equal educational outcomes, many US public schools have not eliminated long-standing achievement gaps for those who live on the margins (i.e., race, class, gender, immigration status, ability (both mental and physical), and native language). The study, based in grounded theory, examined how 72 aspiring school leaders understood what was meant by leading for social justice in US public schools. Participants were more successful when they internalized an increased critical consciousness that encouraged a dialogue around issues of social justice work in schools in order to utilize their new understanding as a platform to promote this work.

Global Leadership for Social Justice: Taking it from the Field to Practice
Advances in Educational Administration, Volume 14, 159–172
Copyright © 2012 by Emerald Group Publishing Limited
All rights of reproduction in any form reserved
ISSN: 1479-3660/doi:10.1108/S1479-3660(2012)0000014013

In the United States, public school leadership is at the center of unprecedented attention. School leaders are often perceived as pivotal players in making systemic changes to schools in the pursuit of equity and social justice (see Boske, 2012; Boske & McEnery, 2010; Marshall & Oliva, 2010; Tooms & Boske, 2010). They are held accountable to local school communities to mobilize and sustain reform that promotes student learning for all children, especially those who do not meet federal mandates for annual yearly progress on standardized testing.

Addressing concerns centered on improving student achievement, specifically standardized test scores, create spaces for school leaders to reconsider how to improve learning environments for all children. These challenges encourage teachers and school leaders to deepen their understanding of self in relation to others (e.g., Boske & McEnery, 2010) as well as discover ways to utilize schools as spaces for new thinking and growth (Hooks, 1994; Alston, 2004). Therefore, this type of work emphasizes the word *public*, which supports school leaders in rethinking about ways to improve the life chances and experiences of those they serve as well as their role throughout the process. This consciousness raising is imperative to school leaders recognizing, valuing, and acting on behalf of those who live on the margins. The goal, therefore, is to respond collectively in authentic, meaningful ways to specific situations for particular individuals and groups of people in an effort to hold great promise for the welfare of those they serve. This chapter examines how public school educators understood what was meant by leading for social justice in US public schools.

I begin by referring to a brief review of extant literature. Next, I discuss the methodology, which is based in grounded theory. Emerging themes suggest school leaders begin by looking within, make meaning from their learning and utilize their new understandings as a springboard to promote social justice work in schools.

LITERATURE REVIEW

Despite rising standards for excellence and equity, increasing demands on teachers and school leaders to raise standardized test scores, and the push for schools to achieve equal educational outcomes, many US public schools have not eliminated long-standing achievement gaps for those who live on the margins (i.e., race, class, gender, immigration status, ability (both mental and physical), and native language) (Delpit, 1995; Kozol, 2006; Marshall & Oliva, 2010). Because those who serve in US schools will continue to serve increasing culturally diverse populations, school leaders will need the knowledge, skill set and courage to engage in culturally responsive practices that reject color-blind and oppressive ideologies (i.e., Boske, 2011; Cooper, 2009; Furman & Shields, 2005; Gay, 2010; Shields, 2003; Sleeter, 1996; Tooms & Boske, 2010).

The notion of social justice is a relevant area of discussion, especially when considering the lived realities of children and families from disenfranchised populations. Discussions on social justice range from promoting assimilation models (Ladson-Billings, 1994), to school policies that fail to serve marginalized student populations (Marshall & Gerstyl-Pipen), to understanding which students benefit from school practices (Delpit, 1995), to long-standing achievement gap between mainstream and marginalized children in US public schools (Apple, 1993; Darling-Hammond, 1997; Delpit, 1995; Marshall & Oliva, 2010; Valenzuela, 1999). Those who prepare school leaders will need to continuously negotiate and renegotiate, as well as construct, deconstruct, and reconstruct ways of knowing about community, political ideals, history, leadership, and what is meant by the social justice within specific contexts. For the purpose of this chapter, I refer to Bogotch (2002), who contends social justice is "a deliberate intervention that requires the moral use of power." Therefore, those leading schools should reconsider how they will challenge institutional structures and systems that perpetuate oppressive practices (Bourdieu & Passeron, 1977).

METHODOLOGY

I employed grounded theory. The methodology provided me with an opportunity to examine how aspiring school leaders understand what is meant by leading for social justice in US public schools (Strauss & Corbin, 1998). This was the preferred methodology because grounded theory was responsive to the situation in which the research was conducted. Grounded theory provided the researcher with rich, multidimensional data for a deepened appreciation of diverse perspectives regarding how aspiring school leaders understood what was meant by leading for social justice (Lincoln & Guba, 1985), which has its limitations in the field of educational leadership research (see Bogotch, 2002; Brown, 2004, 2006). Because grounded theory placed priority on the phenomena of study, the methodology afforded the researcher to see both data and analysis as created from shared experiences and relationships with participants and other sources of data (Charmaz, 2006). The method also provided the researcher with a focus on one context, namely that of how participants understood what it meant to lead for social justice.

Research Question

The following research question guided the researcher's choice of methodology, research design, data collection, and analysis. The question also furthered the researcher's understanding of the phenomena under examination. The research question was as follows: What does it mean to lead for social justice?

Participants

Seventy-two graduate students at a northeastern university participated in the course titled, "Leading for Social Justice." All of the students gave permission to participate in this study after final grades were submitted to the university. At the time of the study, all of the participants were employed in schools as teachers and 3 of the 72 students were employed as principals. Thirty-nine women and 33 men ranged in age from 23 to 52 years. All of the participants identified as heterosexual. Seven Black, 6 Asian, 6 Middle Eastern and 53 White students participated in the study.

Data Collection and Analysis

Data collection included 553 audio and video reflections (15–45 minutes), 475 written narratives, 72 artmaking exhibits, 64 equity audits, and field notes. Each reflection (i.e., audio, video, and/or written) was comprised of responses to 15–25 predetermined written prompts centered on how participants understood identity formation, power and privilege, social justice, and equity and cultural competency (e.g., Terrell & Lindsey, 2009). All of the reflections were transcribed and shared with participants for accuracy.

Audio/video reflections and written narratives were coded, because "coding is the pivotal link between collecting data and developing an emergent theory to explain these data" (Charmaz, 2006, p. 46). Open coding was used to break down, analyze, compare, and categorize data (Strauss & Corbin, 1998). I used the constant comparative method of data analysis (Bogdan & Biklen, 1998; Glaser & Strauss, 1967; Strauss & Corbin, 1998) using both inductive and deductive components (Strauss & Corbin, 1998). In the first phase, I named the data (Charmaz, 2006). Next, I focused on the most frequently recurring codes (Charmaz, 2006) by using the process of constant comparison. I identified conceptual categories that reflected emerging themes (Harry, Sturges, & Klinger, 2005). I used analytic memos to track data and establish patterns (Charmaz, 2003; Maxwell, 2005). As I coded, certain theoretical propositions occurred. Links made between categories or about a core category were central to the study. Open codes combined with other conceptually similar open codes formed axial codes. The researcher collected axial codes, placed them into categories, which developed themes presented in this study.

The methods support the study's credibility and trustworthiness (Fielding & Fielding, 1986; Maxwell, 1992). Theoretical saturation was achieved when no new data about the categories emerged from the data (Strauss & Corbin, 1998). The following themes emerged from the analyses: (a) increased critical consciousness; (b) developing effective dialogue; (c) deepened empathic responses, and (d) self-transformation. These emergent themes translated into meaning making for significant change, which I describe in the "Discussion" section.

Limitation

A limitation to the study is that the researcher explored one northeastern university with an overrepresentation of White participants; however, the number of Graduates of Color is often limited in educational leadership programs across the United States (Young & Brooks, 2008). Despite the noted limitation, this study is significant to the field of educational leadership because it contributes academic knowledge about developing empathic responses. The study also encourages those who prepare school leaders to reconsider how pedagogical practices may affect a school leader's perspectives about self, social justice and her/his role in addressing such issues in US public schools.

INCREASED CRITICAL CONSCIOUSNESS

Participants emphasized the paradox of undermining the promise of education in US education. They realized the "power of language" such as the term "United States." Several participants noted the name "United States" suggests children and families lives in nation that is "united."

However, several participants noted after inquiring about issues of race, class, gender, and sexual identity, they came to understand how often they assumed their discriminatory beliefs and values were actually perpetuated and supported by members of the dominant culture. Sarah, Nicole, and Samantha emphasized their responsibility as "White people" to look beyond and act upon "racist, classist and sexist, homophobic conversations." Dialogue among White family members, between self and media, and learning within public schools often emphasized the "all it takes to move up is hard work." Sarah noted, "I was told that people who were poor just didn't care and were unmotivated ... you know, lazy." What these participants came to understand centered on recognizing the need to question why specific populations in schools and within society were still marginalized. Barbara noted, "We realize the nation is changing...White people will be the minority very soon and yet we know this and it's as though the promise of schools in the United States is somewhat of a joke. We mock this promise with all things we read and discussed with each other."

Greater levels of critical consciousness provided participants with greater clarity regarding their identity as school leaders, and commitment to addressing issues of social justice and understanding their work as a larger part of their future lives and careers. Tyrone said, "It's time for all of us to join forces...to form an alliance of sorts because we can't do this work alone. We have to live these ideals we are talking about. We concluded that standing still is no longer an option. We have to rise to the challenge and rid the notion of second class citizens in our schools and communities." By increasing their critical consciousness, participants continued to engage in developing themselves as school leaders, specifically maintaining a critical awareness of inequities within public schools and their individual agency as school leaders.

> When I think about what it means to lead now, I think about real leadership, not what I have seen in schools up until now. It involves putting ourselves in positions that tend to be quite uncomfortable ... it's about understanding that education is power ... and we have the ability to promote ideals ... we have a job to do ... and our communities have a right to know about the world ... to think about the world ... to contribute ... and to aspire to something bigger than themselves, but all of this begins with me, because I am the one working with the students and the teachers. (Patrick)

They perceived their capacity to address issues of social justice and equity within public schools through individual or collective action. Participants drew upon their increased critical consciousness as an internal resource to cope with the challenges associated with oppressive school practices.

DEVELOPING EFFECTIVE DIALOGUE

Participants recognized how often they identified conversation as effective dialogue despite their tendency to remain closed to new ideas. What they realized was the need to learn how to listen to those they serve, to develop empathic responses, and to come to an understanding of what was meant by building meaningful relationships. Karrie noted, "It's not just about talking for the sake of talking or fulfilling a reflection assignment. It makes you realize that what you say, how you think and how you respond are all matters of the heart. If I don't listen with my heart, then I am not sure anyone I serve will perceive me as someone who cares ... and if I am someone who cares, I will hear what people are telling me and I will develop meaningful relationships with them because I know how important that work is to promoting social justice at my school."

Their inquiries suggested that developing an effective dialogue develops in a safe public space in which their perspectives, beliefs and abilities move people's thinking forward. Within this space, participants stressed the need for making meaning from their experiences. The dialogue seemed to afford them with spaces to build ideas, and commit to taking a stand as a collective and evolving new understanding. For these participants, there was a need to broaden understandings by engaging in dialogue beyond race and class to include immigration, sexual identity, religion, native language, ableness, and gender. Maxwell said, "It takes a leader with a strong mind and heart to be able to have these courageous conversations with people. I realize I have the ability to do this kind of work. It begins by being aware of those I serve, whose who and really engaging in real dialogue with families, my peers and especially with students." Participants emphasized that effective dialogue afforded them with opportunities to deepen their understanding of the experiences of people who do not align themselves with the dominant culture.

DEEPENING EMPATHIC RESPONSES

Participants recognized the need for school leaders to pay closer attention to the lived experiences of underserved people. Sharon said, "I understood by looking at the equity audit data that we often overlook people who are disenfranchised in our schools. It's because they don't count unless someone speaks up for them or there aren't enough of 'those' students in our building or district. It's sad to admit it, but it's true. That's what we do on our campus. Listening to what it means to be student in special education on our campus make me realize there is a need for a new era, a new regime…a call for a new reform movement … it's past due."

They realized the need to deepen understanding as they worked together and alongside those they served. Their understanding deepened by listening attentively and reconsidering their responses so that those they served felt supported, valued, and honored. Alice said, "I don't know what it's like to be Black, to be poor or to be a man, but I'm learning I don't need to in order to be understanding. I need to learn how to listen, to empathize and break through barriers that encouraged me to stay in my bubble and demand everyone join me there."

SELF-TRANSFORMATION

Moving beyond their desire to make schools better places for children and wanting to utilize their new ways of understanding the lived experiences of those who are marginalized was critical to affecting change. As Roger noted, "I want to be part of something bigger than myself and make real change." They believed that in order to interrupt oppressive systemic practices, there was a need for self-transformation. However, such change was often perceived as difficult, challenging, and for some participants, "at first, impossible." Nicole noted, "If you would have told me that I would have been a leader for social justice, I would have laughed at you. I cannot believe the transformation I have made. It's incredible." Participants recognized the need reflect on their practices and the impact of their decision-making on those they serve. Jim stated, "I'm not the same person I was when I first walked through those doors. These experiences have changed me for good. I realize I cannot just sit here and watch these injustices occur in my school or any other school for that matter." For some, self-transformation was not only unexpected, they did not expect to believe they could make changes within, because they did not know how to make such change or if such change was necessary to work in schools.

> It's like I see myself in the mirror and realize it's me, but it's not really me … it's a new me. I may look the same on the outside, but if you know what I think about the world now and listen to my thoughts and watch me in action, you will know I have changed for the better. I didn't know how to do this work or even if I could really do it, but I did. It didn't feel comfortable, but what I did mattered. I see myself as a leader for social justice and I didn't even know what those words meant when I started here. (Matthew)

The complexities of biases and prejudices, of institutional practices both written and unwritten rules, and of recognizing how the rules have shaped beliefs and practices were essential to leading for social justice in schools. There was a need for participants to not only work on themselves, but continuing their social justice work in schools at the same time. Marsha stated, "This is not easy work, but I realize that once I know what I know, I can't just stand there and pretend I don't. I have a responsibility to do something about it. What is at the center of this work is tension. It's uncomfortable for me and I know it's uncomfortable for the teachers I work with. But that's what is going to move us forward. I feel it... I changed ... and now they see the new me ... I have to work with that tension now and work with it in my favor. I want people to work together to hold social justice at the center of everything that we do in school." They recognized how often the choices they make have the potential to lead to new beginnings and as Patrick noted, "New ways of seeing the world." Participants realize leading for social justice is not the work of individuals. As Sonia noted, "This work is about making connections among yourself, children, families and the community."

Participants noted the need to create spaces for "real transformation." As Reginald stated, "The change has to start from within. This is critical, because ism-blindness is dangerous to the idea of challenging the status quo." They realized the need to reflect on their identity as aspiring school leaders – what lived experiences shaped their beliefs, values and school practices. Their need to look within was critical to understanding their need for self-transformation. Cathy said, "I have the power to look within and move myself in new ways ... I also have the ability to touch other people's lives and move them too. We have to move away from surface stuff and get to the real issues and the real work to dismantle these barriers that stop certain groups from being marginalized. Now that's powerful!" Participants noted discussing injustices in schools was not enough. As George noted, "I need to do something about it, because standing still is no longer an option, especially when we can't say we don't know what's happening in our schools." They recognize the need to continue exploring categories of race, class, gender, sexual identity, religion, immigration status, and ableness. And within the exploration, participants stressed taking action is critical to leading for social justice. As Roseanne noted, "We don't have the infrastructure to empower those from disenfranchised populations. We don't give children and families the tools they need to be successful. It's time we invest in our children." Such actions, which included equity and curriculum audits in addition to conducting home visits and facilitating discussions on race in schools, seemed to afford them with a sense of empowerment in the face of the sometimes overwhelming social issues their children and families face in US schools. Their ability to understand their role to intervening in this type of work in schools provided participants with clarity.

DISCUSSION

The purpose of the study was to explore how participants understood what was meant by leading for social justice in US public schools. They concluded social justice work centered on not only immersing themselves in holistic humanistic approaches such as critical reflection and effective dialogue, but deepening their empathic responses as a means of transforming their sense of self to impact their school practices. The main concern of participants was recognizing their role in perpetuating oppressive practices within schools. They realized developing the ability and capacity to understand the lived experiences of those who live on the margins was the first step to understanding social justice. Participants recognized they engaged in meaning making with their peers, they also deepened their empathic responses, which influenced how they understood themselves as school leaders as well as their role in addressing these issues in schools. That is: participants were more successful with an increased critical consciousness that encouraged a dialogue around issues of social justice work in schools in order to utilize their new understanding as a platform to promote this work (see Fig. 1). Understanding how leading for social justice in US public schools does or does not happen has implications for school leadership preparation programs as well as schools engaged in professional development.

Their capacity to engage in social justice work was essential to considering new possibilities for meaningful change. However, the transformative change started from within the individual. Such change seemed to enhance participants' understanding and actions toward promoting equity, social justice, and civic responsibility to empower underserved populations. They recognized social justice work required an increased consciousness, passion, courage, and risk-taking (Dantley & Tillman, 2006; Marshall & Oliva, 2010; Tooms & Boske, 2010). They took seriously the need to listen to the voices of silenced, and reconsider their role in empowering children and families from disenfranchised populations. Their self-transformed leadership shifted from passive observer to activist-oriented (Bogotch, 2002). Such change encouraged participants to engage in being morally transformative, and

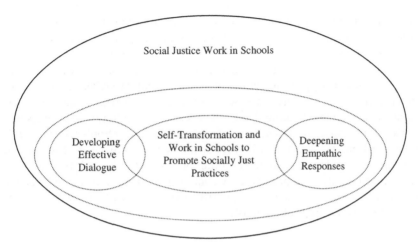

Fig. 1. Social Justice Work in Schools.

pursue social justice work with the intent of eliminating unjust practices (Dantley & Tillman, 2006). In many ways, these participants promoted transformative leadership by challenging the status quo in quiet, strategic ways.

Participants expressed the need for critical thought and reflection with regard to personal beliefs, lived experiences, and cultural identity. Their attempts included building the capacity and will to transform their sense of self to deliver policies and practices that addressed the lived realities of disenfranchised populations (Theoharis, 2007; Tooms & Boske, 2010). Sometimes these discussions center on disparities facing Children of Color (Ladson-Billings, 1994), discriminatory school practices and policies that failed children from disenfranchised populations (Marshall, 1993; Marshall & Gerstl-Pepin, 2005), or long-standing achievement gaps between mainstream and marginalized children in US public schools (Apple, 1993; Darling-Hammond, 1997; Marshall & Oliva, 2010).

School leadership positions were noted as powerful intervening variables in determining whether children from diverse backgrounds were afforded opportunities in school to be successful and to be empowered (Scheurich & Skrla, 2003). They examined programmatic decisions that seemed to influence curricular activities, content, and pedagogy in an effort to foster transformational experiences centered on social justice work (Tooms & Boske, 2010; Young & Brooks, 2008). They believed their ability and willingness to raise the academic achievement of all the students in schools, to prepare students to live as critical citizens, and to provide those interested in social justice work required school leaders to work in inclusive, hetero-geneous spaces that enrich their experiences and meaning making. Critical to this work were opportunities afforded to candidates to reflect in safe spaces and reconsider how their increased critical consciousness influenced their capacity to make meaning from their effective dialogue and deepened empathic responses to promote social justice work in schools (Boske, 2012; Terrell & Lindsey, 2009). Leading for social justice involved the fostering of critical consciousness – understanding of self, others, and the world – deepening empathic responses, and committing themselves to an effective dialogue that engaged them in committing themselves to addressing issues of societal relevance in public schools.

CONCLUSION

School leaders who led for social justice translated into their ability and capacity to transcend their identity, ways of understanding and situation through action. These actions seemed to represent concrete forms of solidifying this transcendence of self. Future research should strive to elucidate relationships more clearly among critical consciousness, effective dialogue, empathy and transformation of self to continue to illuminate constructs that assist school leaders in engaging in social justice work in schools.

REFERENCES

Alston, J. A. (2004). The many faces of American schooling: Effective schools research and border crossing in the 21st century. *American Secondary Education, 32*(9), 79–93.

Apple, M. (1993). The politics of official knowledge: Does a national curriculum make sense? *Teachers College Record, 95*(2), 222–241.

Bogdan, R. C., & Biklen, S. K. (1998). *Qualitative research for education: An introduction to theory and methods.* Needham Heights, MA: Allyn & Bacon.

Bogotch, I. (2002). Educational leadership and social justice: Practice into theory. *Journal of School Leadership, 12*(2), 138–156.

Boske, C. (2011). Using the senses in reflective practice: Preparing school leaders for non-text-based understandings. *Journal of Curriculum Theorizing, 27*(2), 82–100.

Boske, C. (2012). Educating leaders for social justice. In C. Shields (Ed.), *Transformative leadership reader.* New York, NY: Peter Lang.

Boske, C., & McEnery, L. (2010). Taking it to the streets: A new line of inquiry for school communities. *Journal of School Leadership, 20*(3), 369–398.

Bourdieu, P., & Passeron, J. C. (1977). *Reproduction in education, society and culture.* London: Sage.

Brown, K. (2004). Weaving theory into practice: Preparing transformative leaders for social justice. *Scholar-Practitioner Quarterly, 2*(2), 13–37.

Brown, K. (2006). Leadership for social justice and equity: Evaluating a transformative framework and andragogy. *Educational Administration Quarterly, 41*(5), 700–745.

Charmaz, K. (2003). Grounded theory: Objectivist and constructivist methods. In N. K. Denzin & Y. S. Lincoln (Eds.), *Strategies for qualitative inquiry* (2nd ed., pp. 249–291). Thousand Oaks, CA: Sage.

Charmaz, K. (2006). *Constructing grounded theory: A practical guide through qualitative analysis.* London: Sage.

Cooper, C. W. (2009). Performing cultural work in demographically changing schools: Implications for expanding transformative leadership frameworks. *Educational Administration Quarterly, 45*(5), 694–724.

Dantley, M., & Tillman, L. C. (2006). Social justice and moral transformative leadership. In C. Marshall & M. Oliva (Eds.), *Leadership for social justice: Making revolutions in education.* Boston, MA: Pearson.

Darling-Hammond, L. (1997). *The right to learn: A blueprint for creating schools that work.* San Francisco, CA: Jossey-Bass.

Delpit, L. (1995). *Other people's children: Cultural conflict in the classroom.* New York, NY: New Press.

Fielding, N. G., & Fielding, J. L. (1986). *Linking data: Qualitative research methods.* Beverly Hills, CA: Sage.

Furman, G. C., & Shields, C. M. (2005). How can educational leaders promote and support social justice and democratic community in schools? In W. A. Firestone & C. Riehl (Eds.), *A new agenda for research in educational leadership* (pp. 119–137). New York, NY: Teachers College Press.

Gay, G. (2010). *Culturally responsive teaching: Theory, research, and practice* (2nd ed.). New York, NY: Teachers College Press.

Glaser, B. G., & Strauss, A. L. (1967). *The discovery of grounded theory: Strategies for qualitative research.* New York, NY: Aldine de Gruyter.

Harry, B., Sturges, K. M., & Klinger, J. K. (2005). Mapping the process: An exemplar of process and challenge in grounded theory analysis. *Educational Researcher, 34*(2), 3–13.

Hooks, B. (1994). *Teaching to transgress: Education as the practice of freedom.* New York, NY: Routledge.

Kozol, J. (2006). *Shame of the nation: The restoration of apartheid schooling in America.* New York, NY: Crown Publishers.

Ladson-Billings, G. (1994). *The dreamkeepers.* San Francisco, CA: Jossey-Bass.

Lincoln, Y., & Guba, E. (1985). *Naturalistic inquiry.* New York, NY: Sage.

Marshall, C. (Ed.). (1993). *The new politics of race and gender.* London: Falmer Press.

Marshall, C., & Gerstl-Pepin, C. (2005). *Re-framing educational politics for social justice.* Boston, MA: Allyn & Bacon.

Marshall, C., & Oliva, M. (Eds.). (2010). *Leadership for social justice* (2nd ed.). Boston, MA: Allyn & Bacon.

Maxwell, J. A. (1992). Understanding and validity in qualitative research. *Harvard Educational Review, 62,* 279–300.

Maxwell, J. A. (2005). *Qualitative research design: An interactive approach* (2nd ed.). Thousand Oaks, CA: Sage.

Scheurich, J., & Skrla, L. (2003). *Leadership for equity and excellence: Creating high-achievement classrooms, schools, and districts.* Thousand Oaks, CA: Corwin Press.

Shields, C. (2003). *Good intentions are not enough: Transformative leadership for communities of difference.* Lanham, MD: Scarecrow Education.

Sleeter, C. E. (1996). *Multicultural education as social activism.* Albany, NY: State University of New York Press.

Strauss, A. L., & Corbin, J. (1998). *Basics of qualitative research grounded theory procedures and techniques.* Newbury Park, CA: Sage.

Terrell, R. D., & Lindsey, R. B. (2009). *Culturally proficient leadership: The personal journey begins within.* Thousand Oaks, CA: Corwin Press.

Theoharis, G. (2007). Social justice educational leaders and resistance: Toward a theory of social justice leadership. *Educational Administration Quarterly, 43*(2), 221–258.

Tooms, A. K., & Boske, C. (2010). *Bridge leadership: Connecting educational leadership and social justice to improve schools.* Charlotte, NC: Information Age Publishing.

Valenzuela, A. (1999). *Subtractive schooling: U.S. Mexican youth and the politics of caring.* Albany, NY: SUNY.

Young, M. D., & Brooks, J. S. (2008). Administration preparation programs: Faculty perspectives on supporting Graduate Students of Color in educational best practices, possibilities, and problems. *Educational Administration Quarterly, 44*(3), 391–443.

CHAPTER 10

A TALE OF TWO SCHOLAR-PRACTITIONERS: TRANSFORMING PRACTICES AT THEIR SITES AND BEYOND

Peg Winkelman and Michelle Collay

ABSTRACT

This chapter presents case studies of two doctoral students in a program designed to develop leadership for social justice. Amidst criticisms that doctorate programs promote neither research nor professional expertise, the question of program relevance is addressed by asking a different question. How are urban school leaders uniquely positioned to conduct research that can transform schools? The tale of two scholar-practitioners illustrates the changes in site and district practices that result from collaborative, site-based studies. Inquiries were grounded in critical theory: by collaborating with those most affected by policy, school leaders and participants transformed inequitable practices at and beyond their schools.

In problem-posing education, people develop their power to perceive critically the way they exist in the world with which and in which they find themselves; they come to see the world not as a static reality, but as a reality in process, in transformation. (Freire, 2000, p. 83)

Global Leadership for Social Justice: Taking it from the Field to Practice
Advances in Educational Administration, Volume 14, 173–189
Copyright © 2012 by Emerald Group Publishing Limited
All rights of reproduction in any form reserved
ISSN: 1479-3660/doi:10.1108/S1479-3660(2012)0000014014

Recent studies and policy papers address the limitations of education doctoral degrees, criticizing them as neither research nor professional programs (Anderson & Jones, 2000; Auerbach, 2011; Levine, 2005; Young, 2006). We recognize elements of this tension within our own preparation and scholarship, coming from schools and districts ourselves and seeking balance within our own professional practice. We believe education doctorates have an essential role holding the third space between theory and practice, and that our colleagues are bridging (Wenger, 1998) two worlds. We addressed the question about program relevance by asking a different question: How are school leaders who are scholar-practitioners uniquely positioned to conduct research that can transform schooling?

PROGRAM DESIGN

This program is designed to support experienced school and district leaders striving to transform the world of schooling to create more equitable outcomes for students. Transformative learning is defined by Brown (2006) as "a process of experiential learning, critical self-reflection, and rationale discourse that can be stimulated by people, events, or changes in contexts that challenge the learner's basic assumptions of the world" (p. 706). Program participants work in settings where institutional racism, language discrimination, and generational poverty frame their leadership practice and fuel their desire to effect change at their sites and beyond. Shields (2011) has synthesized research on transformative leadership, suggesting that:

> Early in the 21st century, the theory of transformative leadership has been consistently articulated as a form of leadership grounded in an activist agenda, one that combines a rights-based theory that every individual is entitled to be treated with dignity, respect, and absolute regard with a social justice theory of ethics that takes these rights to a societal level. (p. 571)

Leaders in urban schools work within deeply flawed systems, replete with equity concerns at their sites and beyond. Through the process of conducting applied research, these leaders attempt to disrupt patterns of inequity and change systems that allow those patterns to persist. How does their research influence more equitable schooling practices?

This chapter describes the research of two scholar-practitioners leading for equity. Through their site-based inquiries, these leaders addressed inequities by collaborating with and empowering those positioned to make a difference for students. Their collaborative inquiries influenced changes in policy implementation at their districts as their efforts uncovered systemic obstructions to social justice. In the next section, we describe the tenets of a doctoral program designed to develop scholar-practitioners who enact their values of social justice in schools.

Theoretical Frame for the Development of Socially Just Scholar-Practitioners

Urban school leaders are powerfully positioned to conduct research at their sites, and professional preparation should support them in this endeavor. Rather than accepting the portrait of school administrators as ill-prepared to engage in legitimate knowledge construction about the world of schooling, we believe school site and district leaders offer unique and valuable perspectives on school- and system-level reform (Anderson & Herr, 1999; Sagor, 2005; Schmuck, 2006). Course readings, applied research activities, and formative assessments in this program propel doctoral students toward inquiry about access, equity, and efficacy as they work to transform educational processes at their sites. The curriculum is problem-based, reflects tenets of adult learning, and applies critical social theory (Baxter Magolda, 1998; Brown, 2004, 2006; Cranton, 2002; Friere, 1970, 2000, Mezirow, 1998) to all coursework.

The curriculum framework integrates several levels of inquiry as doctoral students pose questions about practice within their work settings (Savery & Duffy, 2001; Wenger, 1998). Through engagement in short, applied research tasks including an analysis of knowledge construction within the school setting, program evaluation, policy analysis, and a participatory action research pilot study, scholar-practitioners refine their research question. The specific equity concern they identify leads them back into literature with a particular emphasis on critical social theory. Doctoral students are guided to move beyond measurement and description of what exists to examine deeper, social constructions that create inequitable practices, policies, and institutions (Shields, 2011). Finally, doctoral students as school leaders develop an applied research question for their dissertation that addresses a problem of equity and social justice in schooling (Lincoln & Guba, 2000; Yin, 2003).

METHODOLOGY: CASE STUDIES OF SCHOLAR-PRACTITIONERS' RESEARCH

Two dissertation studies were selected from the seven completed in this cohort. The two cases were drawn from an earlier study of the same cohort in which dissertation topics were analyzed for their adherence to a social justice stance. The class set of studies was analyzed to evaluate how program assessments guided research topics (Collay & Winkelman, under review). The case selection was "purposeful" (Lincoln & Guba, 2000; Merriam, 1991; Rueschemeyer, 2003) to examine how scholar-practitioners in a doctoral program for social justice took action for more equitable outcomes in schools. These two studies were similar in specific ways: they were conducted at single school sites, engaged teachers and parents as collaborators, focused on transforming exclusionary practices, and changed the lived experiences of teachers and parents at their schools. While both studies focused on educational inequities, one included teachers as coresearchers while the other engaged parents in the inquiry process. These two cases exemplify collaborative site-based research.

The studies were analyzed in relation to the participants studied, the framing of the problem (site specific, district level, societal), the boundaries of the cases, and the findings and recommendations. Cross-case analysis (Stake, 2006; Merriam, 1991) provided a more detailed assessment of the ways in which these scholar-practitioners positioned their equity concerns. School leaders developed their studies in response to direct observation and experiences at their sites, through a series of research activities, and by connecting their inquiry to greater forces beyond the site.

Scholar-Practitioner Research – Two Cases

Scholar-Practitioner	Research Questions	Findings	Significance for Participants
Middle school vice principal	"How do teachers define culturally responsive pedagogy?" "What role can a leader play in facilitating the implementation of culturally responsive teaching practices?"	Leader facilitated teacher-centered examination of culturally responsive pedagogy that increased student engagement and achievement.	District adopted top-down "equity walkthrough" protocols that yielded no demonstrated change in CRP practices across sites. A teacher-centered model increasing student engagement and academic improvement has been presented to other scholar-practitioners and to district leadership.

| Elementary school principal | How do Latino parents of ELL students become empowered and build leadership capacity through their involvement in the implementation of a parent center. | Leader facilitated development of a parent-created center, Mesa Directiva, that addressed community needs. | Though tensions about the role of parent leadership were evident, district leadership has revisited site-based governance, refined parent leadership policies, and now uses the Mesa Directiva as a model. |

In these two case studies, scholar-practitioners observed patterns of exclusion from educational opportunities within the context of district-level reform efforts. In the first case, the leader worked side-by-side with teachers to define, plan, and examine culturally responsive teaching, while in the second case, the focus was on strengthening family involvement. In both cases, site leaders responded to district-level policy by engaging those most affected by the mandate, teachers in the first instance and parents in the second instance, in a collaborative inquiry process. In both cases, district-level directives were "re-directed," leading to productive outcomes for students and families.

Culturally Responsive Pedagogy: A Study of Implementation

The first scholar-practitioner, an African-American woman serving as vice principal of a middle school, studied the implementation of "equity walkthroughs" mandated by her district leadership. While she pragmatically implemented the district policy, she worked directly with teachers at her site to reframe their experience of the district policy as a transformative collaboration to improve instruction for students of color. She contrasted the district approach with her own in the following excerpt from her dissertation:

> The district traditionally disseminates a plethora of information from the "top down." This is what occurred in the implementation of the district equity walkthroughs. This study revealed a different, possibly a more effective model for implementation of culturally responsive pedagogy. (Greenwood, 2011, pp. 143–144)

In this case, the site leader's district superintendent launched a well-intended, systemic initiative to implement culturally responsive teaching practices (CRP). He invited leadership teams from each school to a day of professional development. The event provided teams with the super-intendent's rationale for CRP (including his personal experiences with schooling), his vision for CRP implementation, and selected examples of CRP. Leadership teams were to share the district directive and have teachers vote on their site equity walkthrough objective. Equity walkthrough teams composed of district administrators and site leaders were to observe teachers in classrooms and evaluate the degree of implementation, adherence to, the agreed upon objective. The results of these walkthrough observations would be tallied and then presented to the sites as a measure of accountability and progress two to three times a year.

At this leader's site (and others in the district) teachers chose the objective to "clearly post rules and curricular objectives." While this leader recognized the selection of such a simple objective as a sign of passive resistance, she did not confront teachers about their choice. She followed the prescribed district plan, but pursued a parallel process to collaborate with teachers on implementing culturally responsive teaching practices. She drew from research on critical social theory to shape her practice. Borrowing from the Freirean notion that students must not be viewed as empty vessels, this scholar-practitioner believes teachers must make their own meanings and produce their own knowledge. This leader understood that a directive treating teachers as "empty vessels" could not advance a socially just movement even if the intent of the directive was meant to address the inequitable experiences of students. She began her work by discussing CRP with teachers and asking how she, as a leader, could support their teaching practices. The following teacher response encompasses the sentiments of a majority of teachers at her site.

> A leader can do the following: Assess what teachers already know about culturally responsive pedagogy. Build upon teacher prior knowledge of culturally responsive pedagogy (to reduce teacher resistance of what might be construed as a new "teacher mandate" that will come and go). Outline what will be teachers and administrators' "next steps" after each group discussion of culturally responsive pedagogy. Give teachers opportunities to jointly create lesson plans that actively incorporate culturally responsive pedagogy. Conduct peer observation of culturally responsive pedagogy, and provide observed teachers with peer "critical friend" feedback. (Greenwood, 2011, p. 110)

This teacher's response portrayed a more complex and teacher-centered approach to culturally responsive pedagogy implementation than was prescribed in the district equity walkthrough model. This teacher clearly articulated a plan for implementation that included drawing upon teachers' prior knowledge and experience of culturally responsive pedagogy. The joint planning and peer observation cycles were not included in the district plan. This teacher's "plan" correlated with the scholar-practitioner's study. In her study, the leader examined culturally responsive teaching with her teachers by discussing their plans, videotaping their lessons, and listening to their analyses. At the school site she met with teachers to share strategies and co-taught lessons in classrooms. The leader described her stance in the conclusion of her dissertation.

> As our schools become increasingly diverse, we as educators must embrace diversity in our classrooms. We must reflect on own practices and be open to methods that may feel uncomfortable at first but will improve student outcomes. If I want teachers to value students I, as a leader, must value teachers. If I want teachers to take risks I, as a leader, must take risks with them. (Greenwood, 2011, p. 145)

This leader facilitated a model to implement culturally responsive pedagogy that valued teacher knowledge, teacher practices, teacher questions, teacher reflections, and co-construction of knowledge. Her understanding of critical theory including the liberatory roots of equity pedagogy, culturally relevant, and culturally responsive pedagogy led her to coresearch culturally responsive practices with teachers in their classrooms. The scholar-practitioner incorporated support for culturally responsive teaching as defined in her dissertation (Gay, 2000). Culturally responsive teachers validate, facilitate, liberate, and empower ethnically diverse students by simultaneously cultivating their cultural integrity, individual abilities, and academic success. This scholar-practitioner knew that the implementation of CRP would not "transform" classroom teaching and the learning experience of students if it were reduced to a directive for teachers to use district-prescribed strategies in their classrooms. She applied a critical lens to her leadership role within a larger system and, in facilitating the development of culturally responsive teaching practices leading to more equitable student outcomes at her site, she disrupted the status quo in the larger system. After one of the equity walkthroughs a district leader pointedly asked, "How did you get your teachers to do this?" This statement clearly represents a bureaucratic practice of directing teacher actions to comply with stated district goals, rather than engaging teachers in a transformative process of professional development.

Latino Parent Leadership in the Initial Implementation of Parent Centers

A foundation of critical social theory was also evident in the second scholar-practitioner's conceptual framework, drawing on the research of De

Gaetano (2007), Delgado-Gaitan (1991, 2005), Dyrness (2008), and Elenes (1997), among others. The leader's choice to engage Mexican immigrant mothers of school-age children as key stakeholders reflected her deliberate advocacy for a marginalized population. This leader drew upon the tenants of critical race theory and LatCrit theory acknowledging that the experiential knowledge of people of color is critical to understanding racial subordination in the field of education (Solorzano & Delgado-Bernal, 2001). She described her approach to the work in the following excerpt from her dissertation:

> In the exploration of parent empowerment, placing the parents' experiential knowledge at the forefront as they interact with the school system will allow their experiences to be better understood. The experiential knowledge is looked at as a strength and draws on the lived experiences of people of color by allowing the methodology of storytelling, family histories, scenarios, and narratives to be used as a way to collect oral history (Solorzano & Delgado-Bernal, 2001). The incorporation of the lived experiences of Latino parents with participation in schools can allow for a deeper examination of how parents survive their struggle in the road to empowerment. (Zanipatin, 2011, p. 20)

This scholar-practitioner applied a critical definition of empowerment to her work with parents. She understood that empowerment can be viewed from lived experiences and that those who are oppressed must take action on their own behalf (Freire, 2000).

> To surmount the situation of oppression, people must first critically recognize its causes, so that through transforming action they can create a new situation, one which makes possible the pursuit of a fuller humanity. But the struggle to be more fully human has already begun in the authentic struggle to transform the situation. (Zanipatin, 2011, p. 47)

This leader's work with parents was influenced by other scholars (Shatkin & Gershberg, 2007) who demonstrated that when empowered parents engage in meaningful production of knowledge, their situations can be improved. The scholar-practitioner described implementation of the parent center as an opportunity for Latino parent leaders to participate in their children's education.

> This can be applicable when we consider that the parents of Latino language minority students can begin to take advantage of a policy that will support a network with other parents as they work to build new relationships with the schools and take action to guide the pattern of change. (Zanipatin, 2011, p. 20)

Building on the empowerment work of Delgado-Gaitan (1991), this scholar-practitioner supported an ongoing intentional process centered in the school community to promote caring actions, critical reflection, and an awareness of social actions and strengths. The leader elaborated on how this collaborative work among parents gathered momentum and was designated as the Mesa Directiva.

> ... they discovered that together they had different strengths that would help them take action to gain the resources they needed to make the implementation of the parent center successful. One of their strengths was that some of their members had previous experience with being on a leadership team. These members had expressed that their confidence in being part of the Mesa Directiva came from the fact they had been on other leadership committees. Other members gained confidence in being part of a leadership team because they observed other parents benefiting from the actions that resulted from their involvement. (Zanipatin, 2011, p. 99)

The implementation of district policy to develop a parent center included typical parent involvement activities such as school information sessions and the organizing of a Book Fair. However, through surveys and meeting discussions, specific community needs emerged. The Mesa Directiva offered workshops addressing parental stress, diabetes in children and adults, asthma, domestic violence, nutrition, and immigrant rights. The scholar-practitioner captured their work in her field notes.

> Throughout the year the Mesa Directiva revisited the topic of establishing a support system for parents in the parent center. Although this was not an area of need that was identified in some of the initial meetings, parents on many occasions had informal conversations with other parents about offering their support for families and providing them contact information for outside community agencies. On occasion, after spending time together in the parent center building it was not uncommon to hear parents discuss personal experiences about their children's behaviors or habits to get advice from one another. (Zanipatin, 2011, pp. 71–72)

The Mesa Directiva took action as they interacted with district policies. Their reaction to some of the challenges posed by policies affected the relationship that they had with both site and district leadership. In some cases the interactions served to create a positive collaboration with leadership, while other interactions raised doubt about the intentions of district policy.

In her field notes, this scholar-practitioner described how the Mesa Directiva organized a special meeting to address the new district policy on volunteer fingerprinting. Members of the Mesa Directiva were concerned because the district would no longer allow parents to volunteer in the schools or on field trips without first being fingerprinted and producing a record of tuberculosis immunization. Prior to the policy, parents were afforded the opportunity to go on a field trip under the supervision of the teacher without meeting these requirements. Members recognized that given these new requirements, only parents who could navigate the bureaucracy of completing paper work, paying the 65-dollar fingerprinting fee, and providing immunization documentation would be able to volunteer. This would exclude many participants at the meeting as well as a high percentage of parents at the school. The leader summarized the parent meeting in the following statement: "As a result they rallied in the parent center because they knew that because of their different fiscal or immigration circumstances this policy would exclude them" (Zanipatin, 2011, p. 85).

The leader supported the Mesa Directiva in strategizing with teachers and community members to address this exclusion. They held a subsequent meeting to assist parents in completing paperwork, lobbied the School Site Council members to reallocate funding to cover the cost of the fingerprinting, and brought in a consultant to advise individual parents whether or not to proceed with the process, due to concerns over immigration status. The Mesa Directiva organized a group of parents, who secured all of their documentation, to be surrogate field trip chaperones for any classroom. This allowed parents to feel confident that their children would not be excluded from field trips due to the lack of documented parents in a given classroom. The leader reported on their collaborative action, indicating that: "The Mesa Directiva and the site administrator took a proactive stance together in troubleshooting the barriers that were created by this policy" (Zanipatin, 2011, p. 86).

At times the "proactive stance" of Mesa Directiva included not only collaborative effort to overcome barriers, but also demands for district support. A reoccurring head lice outbreak affecting half the classrooms prompted the Mesa Directiva to petition the district to move beyond the normal protocol. Parents asked the district to send a team of nurses to conduct school wide checks and provide a workshop to explain the health concerns and treatment to parents. They also negotiated to cover the cost incurred by some families for the treatment of their student. The Mesa Directiva volunteered to be trained by the nurses in order to help them with the checks but, due to the student confidentiality policy, this was not allowed.

A Latina principal, serving a majority Latino-enrolled school, worked to establish collaborative leadership at the site by building relationships with Spanish-speaking parents. Her efforts were initially prompted by district and state policy requiring parent representation, yet she learned that there was no infrastructure and little support for actualizing such parent leadership. During the first year of the doctoral program, she had become more familiar with central office bureaucracy through a policy internship and was able to draw on that experience. Even with background knowledge, however, she described the uncertain terrain she encountered in the following passage from her study.

> ... there was no evidence of any mandated parent committees that supported compliance such as the English Learner Advisory Committee (E.L.A.C). Similarly there was no evidence of the establishment of any parent participation in decision-making committees that are required by board policy such as the School Site Council or Site Based Decision Making (S.B.D.M). (Zanipatin, 2011, p. 38)

The lack of systemic support for family involvement was problematic. This leader reported that district leaders raised concerns about the level of parent activism at her school, implying it was the leader's role to "deal with" parent concerns, not to refer them to district-level offices for resolution. In this case, a site-based leader striving to enact a district-level policy came face to face with resistance from the very agency charging principals to create parent centers. Mandates or policies emanating from the district and beyond only lead to socially just transformation if leaders at every level engage in true partnerships. The leader described her participatory role as follows:

> As the researcher and administrator it was imperative that I embrace a fundamental concept of allowing myself to be a true participant in supporting the work that was being generated by the Mesa Directiva in implementing the parent center. I practiced this by assuring them that my role as a researcher/administrator participant held dialogue as indispensable to the act of cognition. This is a concept that Freire (2001) refers to as "problem-posing education." (Zanipatin, 2011, p. 110)

As a scholar-practitioner, this leader purposefully structured collaborative change processes that reflected both professional experience and recommendations from the literature. Her observations at the school site as principal and at the district office informed her knowledge of the journey required to align district policy about establishing parent centers and the engaging parent leaders at her site.

> As co-participants with the researcher, the Mesa Directiva occupied itself in what Freire (2000) refers to as "thematic investigation," meaning that they were striving towards awareness of reality and towards self-awareness. In doing so they were successful at using this to build the leadership capacity that helped surface the need for schools to invest in, such as valuing parents' personal experiences, building support systems that will make their efforts sustainable, establishing collaborative relationships, and making space to accept parents as true partners in empowering parents and thus transforming our schools. (Zanipatin, 2011, p. 111)

This leader walked a careful path between responding to federal, state, and district mandates and responding to her parent leaders, brokering policies in ways that reflected parent leaders' values and goals. Finally, her methodology was not only collaborative, but was designed to facilitate parent advocacy throughout the implementation process.

District Policy is Transformed

Both leaders and participants responded to district directives meant to address inequities. In the first case there was persistent low achievement of students of color. In the second case there was a lack of parent involvement in school activities and governance among the families of Latino students. Further investigation indicated that these inequities were pervasive, often undergirded by systemic practice. The site-based inquiries co-constructed by site leaders and stakeholders initially transformed educational processes at the school site. Through the change process at individual schools, however, scholar-practitioners created forums for dialogues with community members, other site leaders, and district-based administrators. In the first case the leader, a vice principal who was appointed to a principal position, has begun to share teachers' collaborative work on culturally responsive practices with other district leaders and has begun collaborative work on CRP with teachers at her new site. In the second case, the parent cooperative has continued to advocate on behalf of Latino students and their families for more equitable practices, and parents working to develop parent centers at other sites have visited the Mesa Directiva.

CONCLUSIONS

The research conducted by two scholar-practitioners illustrates the power of engaging teachers and parents, often excluded from decision-making, to transform schooling. Scholar-practitioners and their collaborators conducted research that disrupted inequitable practices in their schools and districts. As we examine these cases in relation to our theoretical frame for the development of socially just scholar-practitioners, three critical components emerge: (1) consistent use of critical social theory to examine problems; (2) authentic collaboration with participants to define and implement the research; (3) persistent engagement in recursive inquiry.

Use of Critical Theory

Two scholar-practitioners acting from a social justice standpoint intertwined their beliefs, experiences, and grounding in critical social theory to effect change at their sites and beyond. Their inquiries were grounded in critical theory: by collaborating with those most affected by policy, school leaders and participants transformed inequitable practices at their schools. "One cannot expect positive results from an educational or political action program which fails to respect the particular view of the world held by the people. Such a program constitutes cultural invasion, good intentions notwithstanding" (Friere, 2000, p. 95). These scholar-practitioners respected the worldview of teachers and parents. The CRP and parent center policies were well-intended, but such mandates focus on "directing" or "remediating" participants (parents, teachers, and students) rather than addressing fundamental changes in classrooms, school communities, districts, and systemic notions of schooling.

Collaboration with Participants

Leaders who are scholar-practitioners worked directly with their constituents to identify equity concerns, conduct cycles of inquiry to examine concerns, and transform practices at their sites. School leaders conducted research in their schools by framing their inquiries as leaders addressing educational inequity. The actions of school-based leaders influenced district-level practices initially through their efforts to implement district-level reform. Their initial questions led to further study at the site and beyond, engaging their questions with members of the school community and district leadership.

Recursive Nature of Inquiry

As they collaboratively examined and worked to address inequities at their sites, these scholar-practitioners were cognizant of the deeper, social constructions that create inequitable practices, policies, and institutions. Their initial questions led them to further questions, inquiry, and action. As they implemented participatory research at their own schools, they drew upon both local knowledge and empirical data, then carried implications of their findings to district level and regional leaders, making specific recommendations to the larger educational community. Their research provided a forum for imagining change and powerfully informed the district and the greater society educational leaders serve. Their leadership as scholar-practitioners supported participants to take action at the school site, while their formal research can now influence educators, teachers, and community members beyond their sites.

IMPLICATIONS: SCHOLAR-PRACTITIONERS' UNIQUE POSITION

This chapter provided a description of two scholar-practitioners engaged in community (societal) transformation through their actions at school sites. While we need to further examine the other five dissertation studies completed in their cohort, these cases demonstrate how scholar-practitioners are uniquely positioned to conduct research to transform schooling. As we consider implications for preparation programs, we offer the following insights. First, critical social theory must not be simply designated in course readings and literature reviews, it must be consistently employed as the lens for examining all aspects of educational leadership including finance, curriculum development, program evaluation, policy analysis, and research methodology. Second, in order to enact critical theory, emerging scholar-practitioners and their faculty must consistently engage in authentic collaboration with participants most affected by educational policies and practices. Finally, a program designed to address social justice must support emerging scholar-practitioners in understanding the recursive nature of inquiry. Educational leadership students typically enter such a program with a set of questions and an area of inequity already identified. Each course and assignment should engage emerging scholar-practitioners in deeper and broader investigations of the inequities they observe in schools.

The research of these two scholar-practitioners exemplified critical components for university program design and inspired further action in the educational community. Findings from their dissertation studies led to recommendations and significant changes in site and district practices and policies. These leaders' actions should influence the lived experiences of principals, teachers, parents, and students at other schools. As they publish their work, scholar-practitioners not only offer models of transformation on practical levels, they challenge and expand current conceptual and theoretical frames of social justice. Their research must not be marginalized because of its local, case-based approach (Lincoln & Guba, 2000; Rueschemeyer, 2003). Rather, scholar-practitioners are uniquely positioned to reach across obsolete boundaries and integrate theory and practice through collaborative inquiry.

The work of scholar-practitioners acting with conviction illuminates the potential of a participatory, liberatory approach to educational transformation. We close with Freire's words about leading for social justice and transformation:

> The revolutionary leaders must realize that their own conviction of the necessity for struggle (an indispensable dimension of revolutionary wisdom) was not given to them by anyone else – if it is authentic. This conviction cannot be packaged and sold; it is reached, rather, by means of a totality of reflection and action. Only the leaders' own involvement in reality, within an historical situation, led them to criticize this situation and to wish to change it. (Freire, 1970, p. 54)

REFERENCES

Anderson, G., & Herr, K. (1999). The new paradigm wars: Is there room for rigorous practitioner knowledge in schools and universities? *Educational Researcher, 28*(5), 12–28.

Anderson, G., & Jones, F. (2000). Knowledge generation in educational administration from the inside-out: The promise and perils of site-based, administrator research. *Educational Administration Quarterly, 36*(3), 428–464.

Auerbach, S. (2011). "It's not just going to collect dust on a shelf": Faculty perceptions of the applied dissertation in the new California State University (CSU) Ed.D. programs: Leadership education from within a feminist ethos. *Journal of Research on Leadership Education, 6*(3).

Baxter Magolda, J. (1998). Developing self-authorship in graduate school. *New Directions for Higher Education* (11), 41–54.

Brown, K. (2004). Leadership for social justice and equity: Weaving a transformative framework and pedagogy. *Educational Administration Quarterly, 40*(1), 79–110.

Brown, K. (2006, December). Leadership for social justice and equity: Evaluating a transformative framework and andragogy. *Educational Administration Quarterly, 42*(5), 700–745.

Collay, M., & Winkelman, P. (under review). Focusing scholar-practitioner research on social justice and equity. *Scholar-practitioner Quarterly*.

Cranton, P. (2002). Teaching for transformation. *New Directions for Adult & Continuing Education. 93*, 63–71.

De Gaetano, Y. (2007). The role of culture in engaging Latino parents' involvement in school. *Urban Education, 42*(2), 145–162.

Delgado-Gaitan, C. (1991). Involving parents in the schools: A process of empowerment. *American Journal of Education, 100*(1), 20–46.

Delgado-Gaitan, C. (2005). Family narratives in multiple literacies. *Anthropology and Education Quarterly, 36*(3), 265–272.

Dyrness, A. (2008). Research for change versus research as change: Lessons from a mujerista participatory research team. *Anthropology and Education Quarterly, 39*(1), 23–44.

Elenes, C. A. (1997). Reclaiming the borderlands: Chicana/o identity, difference, and critical pedagogy. *Educational Theory, 47*(3), 359–375.

Freire, P. (2000, 1970). Pedagogy of the oppressed (New Rev. 20th-Anniversary ed.). New York, NY: Continuum.

Gay, G. (2000). *Culturally responsive teaching: Theory research, and practice.* New York, NY: Teachers College Press.

Greenwood, S. (2011). *Culturally responsive pedagogy: A study of implementation.* Unpublished dissertation. California State University, East Bay, Hayward, CA.

Levine, R. (2005). *Educating school leaders.* New York, NY: Columbia University.

Lincoln, Y., & Guba, E. (2000). The only generalization is: There is no generalization. In R. Gomm (Ed.), *Case study method* (pp. 27–44). London: Sage.

Merriam, S. B. (1991). *Case study research in education: A qualitative approach.* San Francisco, CA: Jossey-Bass.

Mezirow, J. (1998). On critical reflection. *Adult Education Quarterly, 48*(3), 185–198.

Rueschemeyer, D. (2003). Can one or a few cases yield theoretical gains? In J. Mahoney & D. Rueshemeyer (Eds.), *Comparative historical analysis in the social sciences* (pp. 301–336) England: Cambridge University Press.

Sagor, R. (2005). *The action research guidebook: A four-step process for educators and school teams.* Thousand Oaks, CA: Corwin Press.

Savery, J., & Duffy, T. (2001). *Problem based learning: An instructional model and its constructivist framework.* CRLT Technical Report 16-01, Center for Research on Learning & Technology, Indiana University. Retrieved from: http://www.dirkdavis.net/cbu/edu524/resources/problem%20based%20learning%20An%20instructional%20model%20and%20its%20constructivist%20framework. Accessed on May 7, 2011.

Schmuck, R. (2006). *Practical action research for change.* Thousand Oaks, CA: Corwin Press.

Shatkin, G., & Gershberg, A. (2007). Empowering parents and building communities: The role of school-based councils in educational governance and accountability. *Urban Education, 42*(6), 582–615.

Shields, C. (2011). Transformative leadership: Working for equity in diverse contexts. *Educational Administration Quarterly, 46*, 558–589.

Solorzano, D., & Delgado-Bernal, D. (2001). Examining transformational resistance through a critical race and LatCrit theory framework: Chicana and Chicano students in an urban context. *Urban Education, 36*(3), 308–342.

Stake, R. (2006). *Multiple case study analysis.* New York, NY: Guilford Press.

Wenger, E. (1998). *Communities of practice: learning, meaning, and identity.* England: Cambridge University Press.

Yin, R. (2003). *Case study research: Design and methods* (3rd ed.). Thousand Oaks, CA: Sage.

Young, M. (2006). The M.Ed., Ed.D., and Ph.D. in educational leadership. *UCEA Review*, 45(2), 6–9.

Zanipatin, Z. (2011). *Latino parent leadership in the initial implementation of parent centers*. Unpublished dissertation. California State University, East Bay, Hayward, CA.

PART 4
THE FUTURE OF EDUCATIONAL
LEADERSHIP PROGRAMS

CHAPTER 11

TOWARD A FRAMEWORK FOR AN INCLUSIVE MODEL OF SOCIAL JUSTICE LEADERSHIP PREPARATION: EQUITY-ORIENTED LEADERSHIP FOR STUDENTS WITH DISABILITIES

Barbara L. Pazey, Heather A. Cole
and Shernaz B. Garcia

ABSTRACT

This chapter offers an integrated framework for the design of educational leadership preparation programs that situate disability in the vision of social justice leadership (SJL) and equity for all students. We examine the extent to which current standards for building-level administrators inform their ability to implement programs for students with disabilities. Utilizing Theoharis' (2007) definition of social justice leadership (SJL), we propose a broader framework for SJL that accounts for students with disabilities and present four key components upon which the broader framework of SJL rests. We align the updated standards for building-level leaders with the professional standards for special education

Global Leadership for Social Justice: Taking it from the Field to Practice
Advances in Educational Administration, Volume 14, 193–216
Copyright © 2012 by Emerald Group Publishing Limited
All rights of reproduction in any form reserved
ISSN: 1479-3660/doi:10.1108/S1479-3660(2012)0000014015

administrators and describe how the skill sets for special education leaders complement and inform the design of leadership preparation programs to support candidates' ability to create, sustain, and implement programs that meet the needs of all children. Finally, we argue for an integrated framework of professional standards that provides a more comprehensive set of skills necessary for meeting the needs of each and every student in the school, and we provide recommendations for leadership preparation programs to achieve this integration.

Within the past two decades, a commitment to social justice has taken center stage in the reconfiguration of many educational leadership preparation programs. Specialized professional associations for school leaders in educational administration (National Policy Board for Educational Administration [NPBEA], 2011) and accreditation agencies (National Council for the Accreditation of Teacher Education [NCATE], 2008) have articulated the need for more equity-minded approaches to education. If educational leaders are to embrace and perform social justice and equity-oriented work, they must be adequately prepared to ensure that schools provide equitable educational opportunities for each and every student including children and youth with diverse abilities, English language learners, and students from diverse sociocultural communities. Until recently, however, the concept of social justice has been linked with issues of race, socioeconomic status, and gender (Polat, 2011; Shepherd & Hasazi, 2008; Theoharis, 2009), with relatively little attention to disability. As a result, this content has been relatively absent in conversations about the design of social justice-oriented administrator preparation programs (Osterman & Hafner, 2009; Pazey & Cole, 2012). In light of the limited preparation of many educational leadership faculty related to disability (Cusson, 2010), there is a need to develop frameworks for leadership preparation that will produce candidates with the requisite dispositions, knowledge, and skills to serve students with disabilities.

The language of the newly updated Educational Leadership Constituent Council (ELCC) standards (NPBEA, 2011) implicitly calls for leadership preparation programs to incorporate curriculum related to meeting the needs of students from diverse sociocultural and linguistic communities *and* students with disabilities. This requires a view of learners as complex individuals, with multifaceted identities reflective of their race, ethnicity, language, religion, *and* (dis)abilities (e.g., Capper, Theoharis, & Sebastian,

2006; Shepherd & Hasazi, 2008). It also requires leadership preparation programs to be guided by frameworks that simultaneously expand social justice leadership (SJL) theory to explicitly incorporate topics related to special education, even as conceptual frameworks related to disability are expanded and embedded in more complex views of difference (Pugach, 2001). Given the role of leadership standards in shaping professional identities (Boscardin, McCarthy, & Delgado, 2009), a commitment to equity for each and every student (McKenzie, Scheurich, & Skrla, 2006) requires us to integrate issues related to students with disabilities into the conversation.

In this chapter, we offer a preliminary, integrated framework for the design of educational leadership preparation programs, to explicitly situate disability in the vision of SJL and equity for all students. To achieve this integration, we examined the extent to which current standards for building-level educational leaders inform their ability to guide the implementation of programs for students with disabilities. Focusing on the updated ELCC standards for building-level administrators (NBPEA, 2011), we aligned these standards with those developed by the Council for Exceptional Children (CEC) for special education administrators (CEC, 2008). Many of the dispositions, knowledge, and skills identified by the latter are also relevant for building-level leaders. We conclude our chapter with implications for the design of leadership preparation programs to support candidates' ability to create, sustain, and implement programs that meet the needs of all children.

FRAMING SOCIAL JUSTICE IN THE CONTEXT OF EDUCATIONAL LEADERSHIP PREPARATION

An inclusive view of SJL entails making "issues of race, class, gender, disability, sexual orientation, and other historically and currently marginalizing conditions in the United States central to their [school leaders] advocacy, leadership, practice and vision" (Theoharis, 2007, p. 223). A focus on eliminating marginalization necessitates an ongoing adherence to inclusive schooling practices for *each and every* student, despite opposition and resistance from outside and inside forces. In other words, a truly inclusive model of education is a model based on social justice (Sapon-Shevin, 2003).

Theoharis (2007) provides a basic, working definition of social justice that accounts for disability and creates a broad outline that distinguishes the characteristics of a social justice leader: (a) values and respects diversity; (b) eliminates segregated programs that eliminate the possibility for academic and emotional success; (c) enables diverse students to access the core curriculum through instructional leadership practices; (d) supports professional development and collaborative efforts to strengthen under-standing of race, class, gender, and disability; (e) recognizes the imperative of providing an opportunity to learn, socially and academically, for all students; (f) addresses the need for every child to achieve success; (g) collaborates with others to maintain an activist stance; (h) examines data through an equity lens; (i) understands the importance of working colla-boratively to provide differentiated instruction to ensure student success; and (j) engages fully with the life and substance of the school.

Drawing upon Theoharis' definition and leadership characteristics and a broader definition of SJL presented in an earlier paper (see Pazey & Cole, 2012), we propose that SJL can be conceptualized in terms of core principles. These principles are reflected in the following four key components, which serve as pillars on which the broader social justice framework rests.

A Belief, Vision, and Leadership Orientation for the Success of all Children

When leaders operate within their schools with this view of how schools function, they recognize that the cultural and organizational aspects of schools and communities must fundamentally change. As change agents, they must possess a sense of will and purpose and demonstrate a strong advocacy orientation: to have a vision of what a better school and a better world might look like. Further, they must be able to articulate their goals and the underlying foundation of those goals. Guided by an informed consciousness and sheer determination of what is possible, they must be able to translate their belief in creating a better world for every child into action.

A Commitment to Eliminate Marginalization

Socially just leaders are driven by a social and legal history that is based on the premise that marginalization, whether by race, class, gender or disability, is unacceptable and are willing to take action toward eliminating its practice. They possess an "equity consciousness" (McKenzie et al., 2006) derived from an understanding that each and every child can achieve academic success, regardless of race, social class, gender, sexual orientation, learning difference, culture, language, religion, and so forth. Recognizing that traditional school practices do not necessarily yield equitable results and frequently perpetuate inequalities, they assume responsibility for moving adults in their school community toward a common vision so that all students can achieve their greatest success (McKenzie et al., 2006).

A Willingness to Advocate in the Best Interest of Every Learner

Advocating on behalf of children means standing up to ensure that all children can benefit from their public school experience, yet knowing that certain students, i.e., students from poor and racial/ethnic minority communities, face an uphill battle toward its accomplishment (Artiles, 2009; Losen & Orfield, 2010). Students who are inappropriately labeled and placed in special education programs, as well as those whose special education needs are overlooked (e.g., Asian Americans, English language learners), face a greater risk of being inappropriately and inadequately served by the educational system (García & Ortiz, 2008; Ortiz, Wilkinson, Robertson-Courtney, & Kushner, 2006). A social justice leader's ability to advocate effectively requires a deeper understanding of the complexity of these issues (McCall & Skrtic, 2009), and the recognition that "it is not that U.S. teachers and students cannot succeed when they are well supported, it is that the system fails to support so many of them" (Darling-Hammond, 1997, p. 27).

Accountability for Diversity, the Opportunity to Learn, and the Promotion of Inclusive Practices

As an advocate for including students with disabilities, a socially just leader possesses a full grasp of the challenges of inclusion including the paradox that can arise from individualizing instruction within the context of school-wide accountability (Voltz & Collins, 2010). It is imperative that leaders are aware of the unique needs of all students, particularly those with disabilities and those disproportionally represented in their ranks. To attain equity in education, leaders must be committed to the implementation and practice of social justice in its broadest form, and ensure a full array of learning opportunities that allow diverse students to be included in the public education system.

SOCIAL JUSTICE AND PROFESSIONAL STANDARDS FOR LEADERSHIP PREPARATION

Thus far, research that addresses leadership behaviors in connection with student achievement in the context of addressing *all student* populations has been generally silent in reference to students with disabilities (Boscardin, 2011; Brown, 2004; Capper et al., 2006; Cusson, 2010; Marshall, 2004; Powell, 2010). As a case in point, the expectation that building-level administrators fulfill the instructional leadership function that "promotes the success of every student" (NBPEA, 2011, p. 9) is threaded throughout the ELCC standards; however, "every student" is not well defined. No mention is made in terms of students with diverse learning needs or abilities. Issues related to children with disabilities tend to be relegated to the purview of specialized teachers and administrators who are designated as the "experts" (Capper et al., 2006; Riester, Pursch, & Skrla, 2002). Little, if any, alignment with the specialized professional standards for special education administrators (Council for Exceptional Children, 2008) exists, even though the ELCC (2011) and CEC (2008) standards for building-level administrators and administrators of special education are both grounded in knowledge and skills-based practices and actions to support student learning.

TOWARD AN INTEGRATED FRAMEWORK OF INCLUSIVE SOCIAL JUSTICE LEADERSHIP

Despite assertions that the professional standards for educational leadership have provided a weak interpretation of social justice in terms of leadership, Marshall, Young, and Moll (2010) remind us that the standards provide a "baseline" for use to generate curriculum and programmatic decisions. A commitment to social justice as a value-orientation for leadership preparation courses in educational administration as suggested (NCATE, 2008; NPBEA, 2011) involves integration of these values throughout the curriculum and a willingness to integrate programs and services for students with disabilities into the discussion. The framework we present in this section reflects the overlapping knowledge, skills, and dispositions contained within and across professional standards for educational administration and special education administration. Of particular relevance to our focus is the integration of special education leadership skills in the preparation of building-level educational administrators.

To ascertain the correspondence between the skills identified as essential for educational leaders and those delineated for special education administrators, we conducted a side-by-side comparison of the skills listed in both documents (CEC, 2008; ELCC, 2011) (see Table 1). Because the two documents do not follow the same organization and conceptualization of knowledge and skills, and given our primary focus on the preparation of building-level administrators (i.e., principals, assistant principals), we retained the organizational structure and sequence of the ELCC document (Table 1, column 1). Next, we considered the applicability of each CEC skill item to each ELCC skills standard (Table 1, column 2). CEC items were repeated if they related to more than one ELCC standard. We discuss our findings below.

ELCC Standard One

As presented in Table 1, the first ELCC standard addresses the ability of building-level education leaders to collaboratively facilitate the "development, articulation, implementation, and stewardship of a shared school vision of learning" (NPBEA, 2011, p. 7) through various actions. School leaders must be prepared to use a data-based approach to decision-making, promote and sustain continuous school improvement, and align evaluation efforts with the vision of school stakeholders. We identified six CEC skills standards for special education administrators that align with and support the implementation of the ELCC standard with respect to students with disabilities. Although both support the development and articulation of a shared school vision and mission, the CEC standards further stipulate the need for an inclusive mindset and framework for meeting the exceptional learning needs of students and their families. For example, the ELCC requirement for data-based decision-making efforts focuses broadly on developing plans to reach school goals, the effectiveness of the organization, and continuous improvement efforts whereas the CEC standards call attention specifically to skills pertinent to students with disabilities. School improvement efforts cannot be realized or sustained unless administrators are willing to advocate for students with disabilities to be fully prepared and able to participate in local, state, and national accountability systems. Student performance data obtained from such systems can be used to inform school personnel to improve student outcomes; assist administrators when evaluating student progress and education personnel within general and special education classrooms; and guide decisions reached by the school

Table 1.　Alignment of Essential Special Education Administration Skills with Standards for Building-Level Educational Leaders.

ELCC (2011) Standard Elements	Special Education Administrator Skills (CEC, 2008)
ELCC 1.1: Collaboratively develop, articulate, implement, and steward a shared vision and mission for a school.	SA1S5: Communicates a personal inclusive vision and mission for meeting the needs of individuals with exceptional learning needs and their families.
ELCC 1.2: Collect and use data to identify school goals, assess organizational effectiveness, and create and implement plans to achieve school goals.	SA3S1: Engages in data-based decision-making for the administration of educational programs and services that supports exceptional students and their families.
ELCC 1.3: Promote continuous and sustainable school improvement.	SA4S1: Advocates for and implements procedures for the participation of individuals with exceptional learning needs in accountability systems.
	SA4S3: Provides ongoing supervision of personnel working with individuals with exceptional learning needs and their families.
	SA5S2: Develops and implements professional development activities and programs that improve instructional practices and lead to improved outcomes for students with exceptional learning needs and their families.
ELCC 1.4: Evaluate school progress and revise school plans supported by school stakeholders.	SA4S2: Develops and implements ongoing evaluations of education programs and personnel.
ELCC 2.1. Sustain a school culture and instructional program conducive to student learning through collaboration, trust, and a personalized learning environment with high expectations for students.	SA6S1: Utilizes collaborative approaches for involving all stakeholders in educational planning, implementation, and evaluation.
	SA6S2: Strengthens the role of parent and advocacy organizations as they support individuals with exceptional learning needs and their families.
ELCC 2.2: Create and evaluate a comprehensive, rigorous, and coherent curricular and instructional school program.	SA2S1: Develops and implements a flexible continuum of services based on effective practices for individuals with exceptional learning needs and their families.
ELCC 2.3: Develop and supervise the instructional and leadership capacity of school staff.	SA4S4: Designs and implements evaluation procedures that improve instructional content and practices.

Table 1. (*Continued*)

ELCC (2011) Standard Elements	Special Education Administrator Skills (CEC, 2008)
ELCC 2.4: Promote the most effective and appropriate technologies to support teaching and learning in a school-level environment.	SA1S1: Interprets and applies current laws, regulations, and policies as they apply to the administration of services to individuals with exceptional learning needs and their families.
ELCC 3.1: Monitor and evaluate school management and operational systems.	SA3S1: Engages in data-based decision-making for the administration of educational programs and services that supports exceptional students and their families.
ELCC 3.2: Efficiently use human, fiscal, and technological resources to manage school operations.	SA1S3: Develops a budget in accordance with local, state, and national laws in education, social, and health agencies for the provision of services for individuals with exceptional learning needs and their families.
	SA1S4: Engages in recruitment, hiring, and retention practices that comply with local, state, and national laws as they apply to personnel serving individuals with exceptional learning needs and their families.
ELCC 3.3: Promote school-based policies and procedures that protect the welfare and safety of students and staff within the school.	SA1S1: Interprets and applies current laws, regulations, and policies as they apply to the administration of services to individuals with exceptional learning needs and their families.
ELCC 3.4: Develop school capacity for distributed leadership.	SA6S5: Implements collaborative administrative procedures and strategies to facilitate communication among all stakeholders.
	SA6S6: Engages in leadership practices that support shared decision-making.
ELCC 3.5: Ensure teacher and organizational time focuses on supporting quality school instruction and student learning.	SA4S4: Designs and implements evaluation procedures that improve instructional content and practices.
ELCC 4.1: Collaborate with faculty and community members by collecting and analyzing information pertinent to the improvement of the school's educational environment.	SA6S1: Utilizes collaborative approaches for involving all stakeholders in educational planning, implementation, and evaluation.
ELCC 4.2: Mobilize community resources by promoting an understanding, appreciation, and use of the diverse cultural, social, and	SA6S3: Develops and implements intra- and interagency agreements that create programs with shared responsibility for

Table 1. (*Continued*)

ELCC (2011) Standard Elements	Special Education Administrator Skills (CEC, 2008)
intellectual resources within the school community.	individuals with exceptional learning needs and their families.
ELCC 4.3: Respond to community interests and needs by building and sustaining positive school relationships with families and caregivers.	SA6S4: Facilitates transition plans for individuals with exceptional learning needs across the educational continuum and other programs from birth through adulthood.
ELCC 4.4: Respond to community interests by building and sustaining productive school relationships with community partners.	SA6S4: Facilitates transition plans for individuals with exceptional learning needs across the educational continuum and other programs from birth through adulthood.
ELCC 5.1: Act with integrity and fairness to ensure a school system of accountability for every student's academic and social success.	SA2S2: Develops and implements programs and services that contribute to the prevention of unnecessary referrals. SA3S1: Engages in data-based decision-making for the administration of educational programs and services that supports exceptional students and their families.
ELCC 5.2: Model principles of self-awareness, reflective practice, transparency, and ethical behavior as related to their roles in the school.	SA5S1: Communicates and demonstrates a high standard of ethical administrative practices when working with staff serving individuals with exceptional learning needs and their families.
ELCC 5.3: Safeguard the values of democracy, equity, and diversity within the school.	SA3S2: Develops data-based educational expectations and evidence-based programs that account for the impact of diversity on individuals with exceptional learning needs and their families.
ELCC 5.4: Evaluate the potential moral and legal consequences of decision-making in a school.	SA1S1: Interprets and applies current laws, regulations, and policies as they apply to the administration of services to individuals with exceptional learning needs and their families. SA2S2: Develops and implements programs and services that contribute to the prevention of unnecessary referrals.
ELCC 5.5: Promote social justice within the school to ensure that individual student needs inform all aspects of schooling.	SA1S1: Interprets and applies current laws, regulations, and policies as they apply to the administration of services to individuals with exceptional learning needs and their families.

Table 1. (*Continued*)

ELCC (2011) Standard Elements	Special Education Administrator Skills (CEC, 2008)
ELCC 6.1: Advocate for school students, families, and caregivers.	SA6S2: Strengthens the role of parent and advocacy organizations as they support individuals with exceptional learning needs and their families. SA6S7: Demonstrates the skills necessary to provide ongoing communication, education, and support for families of individuals with exceptional learning needs.
ELCC 6.2: Act to influence local, district, state, and national decisions affecting student learning in a school environment.	SA5S2: Develops and implements professional development activities and programs that improve instructional practices and lead to improved outcomes for students with exceptional learning needs and their families. SA5S3: Joins and participates in local, state and national professional administrative organizations to guide administrative practices when working with individuals with exceptional learning needs and their families. SA6S8: Consults and collaborates in administrative and instructional decisions at the school and district levels.
ELCC 6.3: Anticipate and assess emerging trends and initiatives in order to adapt school-based leadership strategies.	SA1S1: Interprets and applies current laws, regulations, and policies as they apply to the administration of services to individuals with exceptional learning needs and their families. SA1S2: Applies leadership, organization, and systems change theory to the provision of services for individuals with exceptional learning needs and their families.

leadership team on professional development targeting students with disabilities.

To steward an inclusive school vision, administrators must be able to effectively use data that is aversive to a deficit-based approach to assessment and evaluation: an approach that is inherent in special education and that intersects with issues of race, poverty and class, gender, disability, and language. According to Skrla, Scheurich, Garcia, and Nolly (2010), the foundational basis of marginalization between and across groups exists due to "substantial and persistent patterns" (p. 265) that are both external and internal to schools.

A well-developed skill and value-orientation toward performing equity audits is imperative. Suggested questions to investigate through data-based decision-making efforts are as follows: Are these students being taught by highly qualified and experienced general and special education teachers? Are students being placed at a disproportional rate into special education programs due to accountability or discipline-based concerns? Are students being selectively excluded from consideration for gifted or advanced placement classes and opportunities for future careers or postsecondary options due to issues of race, class, language, or (dis)ability?

ELCC Standard Two

The second standard calls educational leaders to implement the inclusive school vision in a school culture of trust, personalized learning, collaboration, and high expectations. We identified five CEC skills standards for special education administrators that add further detail and support for this standard in regard to students with disabilities (see Table 1).

The CEC standards address the imperative of developing a school culture that fosters a team-focused approach toward the development of a personalized learning program as it applies to person-centered Individualized Education Programs (IEPs). All stakeholders in the education of the student with disabilities are important stakeholders in this process. The building leader serves as a facilitator who extracts information critical to the creation of an IEP that, in addition to focusing on the best interests of the student, recognizes the unique strengths of the student and addresses the specific concerns of the parent. Rather than expecting the parent or caregiver to defer to the authority of the professionals on the team, the parent is treated as a major contributor to the IEP process. Through the empowerment of voice, the parent's expertise is honored, regardless of whether the input agrees or disagrees with other members of the IEP team. If conflicting viewpoints are presented, the building-level leader provides an inclusive environment where every voice has equal weight.

To create a school program that meets the curricular and instructional needs of students with disabilities, administrators need to be able to interpret and apply legal mandates related to educational placement decisions to ensure the student has access to the general education curriculum and instruction provided within the least restrictive environment (LRE). Thus, an "inclusive" vision must consider the full continuum of services. Further, an understanding of the legal requirements contained within the Assistive Technology Act (see CEC, 2005) and that includes accessibility guidelines and requirements stresses the need for leaders to move beyond an understanding of the technologies available.

Administrators need to possess skills in building consensus with teachers, staff, parents, and other external stakeholders. For students with disabilities, they must be willing to facilitate a collaborative approach toward meeting the social, emotional, and academic needs of students from a diverse array of cultures, linguistic backgrounds, and learning needs. Administrators must operate at both levels of analysis to ensure that each student receives appropriate services that go beyond placement. They must monitor the quality of instruction provided and ensure that teachers are including the adaptations and modifications in their instructional practice to meet the educational needs of students with disabilities (Styron, Maulding, & Parker, 2008).

ELCC Standard Three

As presented in Table 1, the third ELCC standard addresses the ability of educational leaders to effectively manage their schools through (a) monitoring and evaluation, (b) distribution of resources, (c) appropriate policies, (d) shared responsibility, and (e) quality instruction. These five components of the standard correspond with seven different CEC skill standards, aligning and complementing the more general leadership requirements with specific focus on the needs of students with disabilities.

The CEC skill standards delve deeper into the core management directives by defining the way in which leaders are to address the needs of a diverse student body. Simply monitoring and evaluating school systems are not enough. Leaders must account for their students with disabilities by using the data to administer educational programs for exceptional children and their families. This is the proactive principle of SJL. Similarly, maintaining a balanced budget and managing resources whether they be financial or human requires an understanding of how those budgets fit within the larger context of local, state, and federal laws regarding individuals with disabilities.

The larger legal framework in which all social justice minded leaders must be aware is heavily implicated in the third ELCC standard and the corresponding CEC skills. Effective management requires not only an appreciation but also a thorough understanding of the obligations of leaders to comply with laws that fund a portion of their budgets for students with disabilities. Policies, much like budgets, must also account for these laws. Failure to comply not only denies access to services to which students with disabilities are entitled but also raises liability concerns for leaders.

The final two components of the third ELCC standard call upon the need for a distributed leadership model and support for quality teaching. The corresponding CEC skills are much the same but expand the notion of distributed leadership to include "all stakeholders." This is a far more inclusive ideal for leadership in which both those inside and outside of the school are given voice to improve the welfare of students. With respect to appropriate instruction, both standards are somewhat vague in how to ensure this happens. But, the CEC skill standard squarely places responsibility for design and evaluation on the shoulders of the administrator. Such an approach expands the notion of distributed leadership to include instructional leadership. Administrators take on personal responsibility to ensure the instruction provided in their schools is serving all children. Administrators must expand the notion of simply monitoring instruction to take on a greater role in actually providing for adaptations and modifications in the instructional practice of their schools (Styron et al., 2008).

ELCC Standard Four

As presented in Table 1, the fourth ELCC standard focuses on collaborating with individuals, both inside and outside the school, utilizing the community and its resources, and responding to the community's interests and needs through understanding and support. In our analysis, we identified three CEC skills standards for special education administrators that support the implementation of the ELCC standard with respect to students with disabilities.

Perhaps more than any other of the standards, this is where ELCC and CEC overlap the most. Both clearly emphasize the importance of getting information from the community and garnering its support toward improving the school's environment. It is interesting that it is the ELCC standard, not CEC, which specifically accounts for the diversity of the school community. While the CEC standards should be representing the voice of marginalized populations, they are silent in this regard. However, the corresponding CEC skill is much more directive in how to achieve community support and mandates agencies to establish shared agreements and responsibilities in regard to programming that addresses the diversity of student needs, particularly students with disabilities.

The more fully articulated course for obtaining community support is further exemplified by ELCC's call to respond to community interests and to build sustainable relationships with parents and with community partners and corresponds with the CEC skill to develop transition plans for exceptional students from birth to adulthood. There is no better way to show good faith in a relationship than to commit to the success of students for not just the duration of their educational enrollment but for their presence before and after they attend an educational institution. CEC's skill creates a blueprint for how to ensure that both parents and the community view school leaders as partners. The responsibility does not begin and end at the doors of the school. Leaders must demonstrate a sincere commitment to all children which aligns with the first pillar we identified as key to social justice: the belief, vision, and leadership for the success of all children. To build trust in a community, leaders must, through deliberate and daily action, go above and beyond what is expected on behalf of the children they serve. Such action will resonate with the community and sustain their support.

ELCC Standard Five

As presented in Table 1, the fifth ELCC standard highlights the moral and ethical underpinnings of school leadership in action, particularly in terms of accountability for the "academic and social success" of every student and advocacy for "the values of democracy, equity, and diversity" (NPBEA, 2011, p. 18) across all aspects of the school. School leaders are expected to examine the motives behind their practice and remain open to others regarding their roles and the "potential moral and legal consequences" (p. 18) of their decisions. They place the individual needs of each student at the forefront of their planning and decision-making efforts as they pertain to all aspects of schooling. The overall intent of the Individuals with Disabilities Education Act (IDEA, 2004) since its original inception (EAHCA, 1975, P.L. 94-142, 20 U.S.C. Sec. 1400(d)) is expressed in this standard. The requirements of each element link the inclusion of students with disabilities to administrator responsibilities and roles as they relate to SJL.

In our analysis, we identified six CEC skills standards for special education administrators that support the implementation of the ELCC standards with respect to students with disabilities. The most closely aligned skill standard invokes leaders to communicate and demonstrate ethical practice in relation to the delivery of services for students with disabilities and their families. To "act with integrity and fairness" (NPBEA, 2011, p. 18) and illustrate a commitment to the academic and social success of every student, the school leader must be willing to draw upon the expertise of others. As the instructional leader, s/he must coordinate an effort to gather and analyze data on school programs and services and investigate whether each student is exposed to "evidence-based programs that account for the impact of diversity" (CEC, 2008, p. 1). Attention to detail and informed decision-making enables the school leader to guard against premature or inappropriate referrals to special education.

To evaluate the potential consequences of specific decisions that are reached on behalf of students with disabilities, the school leader must be able to interpret and apply specific laws and policies to ensure adherence to IDEA in terms of the following mandates: (a) the implementation of response-to-intervention strategies and pre-referral interventions; (b) knowledge of assessment practices and nondiscriminatory evaluation requirements that may contribute to inappropriate labeling of certain students and their marginalization within the school context; (c) the ability to obtain access to the general education curriculum to the greatest extent possible, within the LRE; and (d) the guarantee that each student is provided with instructional and social supports necessary to meet the goals and objectives of his/her IEP.

Building-level administrators who embrace the value of equity, access, and inclusion must provide services within a merged learning environment and increasingly requires a common set of skills. For example, social justice-oriented building administrators who embrace advocacy need to be versed in problem-solving strategies at both the micro level and macro level when arranging for system-level approaches to educate the full range of strengths and learning abilities of a diverse student population (Passman, 2008). Inspiring school staff to embrace a vision of inclusion that recognizes and honors the diversity and difference of each student through an asset, strengths-based perspective is one of the most challenging roles that a school administrator faces (Styron et al., 2008).

Central to the definition of social justice in the leadership preparation literature is the concept of inclusion. In the majority of cases, such services can be supplied within the general education classroom through a co-teaching arrangement. For other situations, a more socially just approach may call for the need to balance advocacy for full inclusion with the intent of the LRE mandate of IDEA that allows the student to benefit from the types of "intense, individualized, and explicit/skill strategy instruction provided by specialists" (Zigmond, Kloo, & Volonino, 2009, p. 201) that are more adequately provided in a more individualized setting or arrangement.

For building-level administrators to lead programs for special population students and to provoke change to address inequities inherent in the current era of accountability and requirements for equity and excellence (Lashley, 2007), they need training programs in educational leadership, multicultural education, and special education administration (DiPaola & Walther-Thomas, 2003; Lashley & Boscardin, 2003; Voltz & Collins, 2010). Perhaps more importantly, negotiated interactions must occur between and among multiple stakeholders who are held accountable to multiple policies and practices ensuring that the instructional and learning needs of students with disabilities are met (Crockett, 2011). Despite a commitment to social justice and educational equity, the fullness of this commitment will go unfulfilled unless administrators filter the (dis)ability needs of individuals as a function of their work (Deshler, 2009, cited in Crockett, 2011).

ELCC Standard Six

The sixth ELCC standard integrates the previous five standards and translates them into a more global set of administrative skills and behaviors. The language contained within this standard and the seven CEC skills standards we identified as supportive of the implementation of this ELCC standard in terms of students with disabilities and their families clarifies the language contained within our four pillars of SJL. The first element calls for leaders to adopt an advocacy stance on behalf of the best interest of students as well as their parents or caregivers. The CEC standards provide substance to this element. In order to advocate for students and their families, school leaders must begin with a belief that all children can achieve success. When parents need additional information or express concern or dissatisfaction with current practices or decisions that may affect their child, they extend themselves to respond to their concerns or rectify any issues that remain rather than engage in avoidance behaviors that ultimately marginalize students or their families. If necessary, they refer students and their parents to other organizations that can assist them in obtaining the supports they need to satisfy their concerns.

The second element continues this stance and calls for school leaders to prepare to take action after careful consideration of how they may be able to influence local, district, state, and national policies or decisions in terms of their impact on student diversity and student learning. At the building and district level, the administrator must work in concert with individuals at the school and central office to determine the specific needs of general and special education personnel and support staff who are responsible for improving student learning. Decisions regarding the design and implementation of professional development and training activities for building-level staff should be based on filling whatever knowledge or skills gaps exist so that they can address the diverse needs of every student.

The administrator must also be able to apply knowledge about the academic, cultural, language, social, emotional, and behavioral characteristics of diverse students as well as the specific types of accommodations, modifications, interventions, differentiated instruction, and learning environments necessary for maximized learning to occur (Passman, 2008). S/he must move beyond the parameters of the school and district boundaries to engage in conversations with individuals at the state and national level through participation in professional associations and specific training activities made available to improve one's knowledge, skills base, and practice in terms of working with and meeting the needs of students with disabilities.

The third element speaks to the need for leaders to be mindful of potential trends or initiatives in order to appropriately adapt the way they react or prepare for change at the school-site level. Building-level administrators must be able to apply knowledge of current laws, regulations, and policies in relation to overseeing the delivery of services to individuals with disabilities and their families. In addition, they must be attentive to potential leadership adjustments to be made due to changes in federal law and policies as it applies to both general and special education and be ready to respond to the needs of students with disabilities.

School leaders can no longer afford to base their leadership strategies and actions on current or past practice and knowledge of special education and special education law. They must continue to build on the knowledge base that intersects leadership, organizations, and change theory and use that information to hone their skills toward fostering an "equity consciousness" (McKenzie et al., 2006). Through an "equity consciousness" approach, school leaders will act on a belief that all children can achieve academic success, regardless of race, social class, gender, sexual orientation, learning difference, culture, and language. Moreover, they will recognize that traditional school practices have failed to yield equitable results and may even perpetuate inequalities. They will acknowledge that they are responsible for moving their school community toward a common vision so that students can achieve their greatest success (McKenzie et al., 2006).

IMPLICATIONS FOR EDUCATIONAL LEADERSHIP PREPARATION PROGRAMS

To promote social justice within their schools, the ELCC standards call for school leaders to keep the needs of the individual student at the forefront of their efforts, which implicitly highlights special education as a core skill for school administrators. Twenty years ago, Valesky and Hirth (1992) alerted states of the need for coursework pertaining to special education in their general education administrative endorsement program. Other scholars (Quigney, 1997; Sirotnik & Kimball, 1994) confirmed their concern, finding that special education had "little or no place at all" (Sirotnik & Kimball, 1994, p. 599) in the curriculum of leadership preparation programs.

An integrated framework for inclusive SJL is needed because neither the ELCC nor the CEC standards provide a comprehensive set of knowledge or skills necessary for meeting the needs of each and every student in the school. Together, however, they set the stage for taking the first steps toward the development of a socially just leadership preparation program, articulated through a specific program of study and sequence of courses with curriculum objectives to address the diverse needs of the students we have been charged to serve. Below, we identify four broad areas for the enhancement of leadership preparation programs to achieve this integration.

A Commitment to an Inclusive Framework of Social Justice on the Part of Educational Leadership Faculty in Higher Education

Thus far, the current social justice approach to leadership preparation has failed to fulfill the call advanced by Marshall et al. (2010) for a "revolutionary" approach in education. Before we can consider the possibility of developing leadership preparation programs that honor diversity in terms of race, gender, (dis)ability, language, and culture, higher education faculty in educational leadership need to move beyond a discussion of its importance and take ownership of their own responsibility by positioning social justice and diversity within the courses they teach. Such a commitment requires a willingness to explore what is possible within the confines of their classroom, their program areas and departments, across the college, and, ultimately, extend the outcome of their conversations into their own research and practice (e.g., eliminating marginalization of special education topics in their own programs and courses; accountability for leadership dispositions, knowledge, and skills that support leadership candidates' ability to foster educational success for students with disabilities; advocating for the best interest of the student through a course dedicated to knowledge of special education and law).

An Increased Focus on Special Education Knowledge and Skills Development

The need for greater knowledge of students with disabilities and special education continues to be identified as a critical component in the preparation of future school administrators (Bays & Crockett, 2007; Crockett, Becker, & Quinn, 2009; DiPaola & Walther-Thomas, 2003; Johnson, 2009; Lashley, 2007; McLaughlin, 2009; Passman, 2008; Powell, 2010). To provide services and supports necessary to achieve a more inclusive learning environment for each and every student, building principals need skill sets similar to those who support the needs of students with disabilities (Passman, 2008). These skill sets can be further informed by specific sets of knowledge, also provided by the CEC (2008) standards for administrators of special education. For example, to create a strong curriculum and instructional school program for every student (see ELCC 2.2 and SA2S1, Table 1), administrators must be knowledgeable about how to design educational programs, instruction, and services that allow students with disabilities to access the general education curriculum. They must be cognizant of universal design for learning (UDL) principles and able to coordinate the use of assistive technology to support student learning.

Integration of Special Education Content into Existing Courses and Curriculum

In most cases, relevant curriculum has been embedded in one or two courses, at best (Powell, 2010). This approach displaces a social justice orientation to meeting the needs of students with (dis)abilities with other priorities (Marshall et al., 2010), thereby marginalizing them from the conversation, and viewing these topics as "add ons" rather than essential.

To fully address the knowledge and skills sets as well as the dispositions inherent in the standards, courses that focus on school business management must be supplemented by an examination of school structures and the ways in which current structures marginalize certain student populations. Content related to multicultural education, special populations, and special education processes and procedures must be integrated into discussions about school law, school finance, ethics and values, organizational behavior and theory, instructional leadership and supervision, and data-based decision-making.

Interdisciplinary Collaboration and Faculty Development

In light of the limited special education preparation of many educational leadership preparation program faculty (Cusson, 2010), the suggested integration and infusion of special education content will require interdisciplinary collaboration within and across departments of educational administration, special education, and multicultural education. Additionally, faculty development opportunities relevant to both sets of standards and their intersection with SJL will be needed to support faculty in these efforts.

CONCLUSION

The call to address social justice in educational leadership preparation programs is not new. The traditional knowledge base and standards guiding the curriculum and instructional focus of administrator preparation programs and state licensure exams have been critiqued for their minimal focus on social justice concerns (Marshall, 2004). Similarly, others have noted that administrator preparation programs have marginalized individuals with differences in abilities, as well as other equity-oriented educational issues (Brown, 2004; Capper et al., 2006; Marshall, 2004; Pazey & Cole, 2012). As leadership preparation programs begin the process of examining their course content with the goal of integrating the knowledge, skills, and dispositions contained within and across leadership preparation program standards, empirical studies of successful leadership preparation programs will help to move us from the traditional model of school leadership into a more socially just framework of leadership, on behalf of all student learners.

REFERENCES

Artiles, A. J. (2009). Re-framing disproportionality research: Outline of a cultural-historical paradigm. *Multiple Voices for Ethnically Diverse Exceptional Learners, 11*(2), 24–37.

Bays, D. A., & Crockett, J. D. (2007). Investigating instructional leadership for special education. *Exceptionality, 15*(3), 143–161.

Boscardin, M. L. (2011). Using professional standards to inform leadership in special education. In J. M. Kauffman & D. P. Hallahan (Eds.), *Handbook of special education* (pp. 378–390). New York, NY: Routledge.

Boscardin, M. L., McCarthy, E., & Delgado, R. (2009). An integrated research-based approach to creating standards for special education leadership. *Journal of Special Education Leadership, 22*(2), 68–84.

Brown, K. (2004). Leadership for social justice and equity: Weaving a transformative framework and pedagogy. *Educational Administration Quarterly, 40*(1), 79–110. doi:10.1177/0013161 x 03259147

Capper, C. A., Theoharis, G., & Sebastian, J. (2006). Toward a framework for preparing leaders for social justice. *Journal of Educational Administration, 44*(3), 209–224. doi:10.1108/09578230610664814

Council for Exceptional Children. (2005). *Public policy update: CEC's summary and update of PL 108-364, the Assistive Technology Reauthorization Act of 2004.* Retrieved from http://www.cec.sped.org/Content/NavigationMenu/PolicyAdvocacy/CECPolicyResources/CEC_AT_Update.pdf

Council for Exceptional Children. (2008). *Advanced knowledge and skill set for administrators of special education.* Retrieved from http://www.cec.sped.org/Content/NavigationMenu/ProfessionalDevelopment/ProfessionalStandards/?from = tlcHome

Crockett, J. B. (2011). Conceptual models for leading and administrating special education. In J. M. Kauffman & D. P. Hallahan (Eds.), *Handbook of special education* (pp. 351–362). New York, NY: Routledge.

Crockett, J. B., Becker, M. K., & Quinn, D. (2009). Reviewing the knowledge base of special education leadership and administration. *Journal of Special Education Leadership, 22*(2), 55–67.

Cusson, M. M. (2010). *Empirically based components related to students with disabilities in tier 1 research institution's educational administration preparation programs.* Unpublished doctoral dissertation. University of Texas at Austin: Austin, TX.

Darling-Hammond, L. (1997). *The right to learn: A blueprint for creating schools that work.* San Francisco, CA: Jossey-Bass.

Deshler, D. (2009, July). *Seeking solutions to wicked problems.* Keynote address, OSEP Project Directors' Conference, Washington, DC.

DiPaola, M., & Walther-Thomas, C. (2003). *Principals and special education: The critical role of school leaders.* Gainesville, FL: University of Florida.

Education for All Handicapped Children Act. (EAHCC). (1975). Pub. L. No. 94-142, U.S.C. § 1400 *et seq.*

García, S. B., & Ortiz, A. A. (2008, copyright 2009). A framework for culturally and linguistically responsive design of response-to-intervention models. *Multiple Voices for Ethnically Diverse Exceptional Learners, 11*(1), 24–41.

Individuals with Disabilities Education Act (IDEA), 20 U.S.C. § 1400 (2004).

Johnson, J. A. (2009). Special education: Whose responsibility is it? *International Journal of Special Education, 24*(2), 11–18.

Lashley, C. (2007). Principal leadership for special education: An ethical framework. *Exceptionality, 15*(3), 177–187.

Lashley, C., & Boscardin, M. (2003). *Special education administration at a crossroads: Availability, licensure, and preparation of special education administrators.* Gainesville, FL: University of Florida.

Losen, D. J., & Orfield, G. (2010). *Racial inequity in special education.* Cambridge, MA: Harvard University Press.

Marshall, C. (2004). Social justice challenges to educational administration: Introduction to a special issue. *Educational Administration Quarterly, 40*(1), 3–13. doi:10.1177/00136161X 03258139

Marshall, C., Young, M. D., & Moll, L. (2010). The wider societal challenge: An afterword. In C. Marshall & M. Oliva (Eds.), *Leadership for social justice: Making revolutions in education* (pp. 315–327). Boston, MA: Allyn & Bacon.

McCall, Z., & Skrtic, T. M. (2009). Intersectional needs politics: A policy frame for the wicked problem of disproportionality. *Multiple Voices for Ethnically Diverse Exceptional Learners, 11*(2), 3–23.

McKenzie, K. B., Scheurich, J. J., & Skrla, L. (2006). Preparing instructional leaders for social justice. *Journal of School Leadership, 16*(2), 158–170.

McLaughlin, M. (2009). *What every principal needs to know about special education* (2nd ed.). Thousand Oaks, CA: Corwin Press.

National Council for Accreditation of Teacher Education. (2008). *Professional standards for the accreditation of teacher preparation institutions.* Washington, DC: National Council for Accreditation of Teacher Education.

National Policy Board for Educational Administration. (2011, November). *Educational leadership program recognition standards: 2011 ELCC building level.* Retrieved from http://www.ncate.org/LinkClick.aspx?fileticket = zRZI73R0nOQ%3d&tabid = 676

Ortiz, A. A., Wilkinson, C. Y., Robertson-Courtney, P., & Kushner, M. I. (2006). Considerations in implementing intervention assistance teams to support English language learners. *Remedial and Special Education, 27*(1), 53–63.

Osterman, K. F., & Hafner, M. M. (2009). Curriculum in leadership preparation: Understanding where we have been in order to know where we might go. In M. D. Young, G. M. Crow, J. Murphy & R. T. Ogawa (Eds.), *Handbook of research on the education of school leaders* (pp. 269–317). New York, NY: Routledge.

Passman, B. (2008). CASE in point: Knowledge, skills, and dispositions. *Journal of Special Education Leadership, 21*(1), 46–47.

Pazey, B., & Cole, H. (2012). *The role of special education training in the development of socially just leaders: Building an equity consciousness in educational leadership programs.* Manuscript submitted for publication.

Polat, F. (2011). Inclusion in education: A step towards social justice. *International Journal of Educational Development, 31*(1), 50–58. doi:10.1016/j.ijedudev.2010.06.009

Powell, P. R. (2010). *An exploratory study of the presentation of special education law in administrative preparation programs for aspiring administrators.* Doctoral dissertation. Retrieved from Dissertation Abstracts International (Order No. AAI3390580). Interlibrary Loan Services, University of Texas, Austin.

Pugach, M. C. (2001). The stories we choose to tell: Fulfilling the promise of qualitative research for special education. *Exceptional Children, 67,* 439–453.

Quigney, T. A. (1997). Special education and school administrator preparation programs: Finding the missing link. *B.C. Journal of special Education, 21*(2), 59–70.

Riester, A. F., Pursch, V., & Skrla, L. (2002). Principals for social justice: Leaders of school success for children from low-income homes. *Journal of School Leadership, 12*(3), 281–304.

Sapon-Shevin, M. (2003). Inclusion: A matter of social justice. *Educational Leadership, 61*(2), 25–28.

Shepherd, K., & Hasazi, S. B. (2008). Leadership for social justice and inclusion. In L. Florian (Ed.), *The sage handbook of special education* (pp. 475–485). Los Angeles, CA: Sage.

Sirotnik, K. A., & Kimball, K. (1994). The unspecial place of special education in programs that prepare school administrators. *Journal of school leadership, 4*(6), 598–630.

Skrla, L., Scheurich, J. J., Garcia, J., & Nolly, G. (2010). Equity audits: A practical leadership tool for developing equitable and excellent schools. In C. Marshall & M. Oliva (Eds.), *Leadership for social justice: Making revolutions in education* (pp. 259–283). Boston, MA: Allyn & Bacon.

Styron, R. A., Maulding, W. S., & Parker, G. A. (2008). Preparing administrators to serve diverse populations of students with learning challenges. *Journal of Diversity Management, 3*(1), 55–66.

Theoharis, G. (2007). Social justice educational leaders and resistance: Toward a theory of social justice leadership. *Educational Administration Quarterly, 43*(2), 221–258.

Theoharis, G. (2009). *The school leaders our children deserve: Keys to equity, social justice, and school reform.* New York, NY: Teachers College Press.

Valesky, T. C., & Hirth, M. A. (1992). Survey of the states: Special education knowledge requirements for school administrators. *Exceptional Children, 58*(5), 399–406.

Voltz, D. L., & Collins, L. (2010). Preparing special education administrators for inclusion in diverse, standards-based contexts: Beyond the council for exceptional children and the interstate school leaders licensure consortium. *Teacher Education and Special Education, 33*(1), 70–82.

Zigmond, N., Kloo, A., & Volonino, V. (2009). What, where and how? Special education in the climate of full inclusion. *Exceptionality, 17*(4), 189–204. doi:10.1080/09362830903231986

CHAPTER 12

THE FUTURE OF EDUCATIONAL LEADERSHIP PREPARATION: CREATING THE CAPACITY FOR CARING, EQUITY, AND LEADING FOR SOCIAL JUSTICE

Christa Boske and Sarah Diem

ABSTRACT

As school leaders across the world wrestle with ways to think about, respond to, and act upon social justice, this chapter provides a way for school leaders to think about what it means to lead for social justice in schools. The chapter offers a template to ground school leaders in socially just practices. The authors contend those interested in leading schools do not need to wait for external agencies to take actions that align with their beliefs and vision to serve school communities in socially just ways. School leaders have the capacity to demonstrate their convictions and commitment to foster meaningful change. The authors suggest such changes promote opportunities to frame a new common discourse in educational leadership: pursuing a new vision for leading for social justice in schools.

Global Leadership for Social Justice: Taking it from the Field to Practice
Advances in Educational Administration, Volume 14, 217–231
Copyright © 2012 by Emerald Group Publishing Limited
All rights of reproduction in any form reserved
ISSN: 1479-3660/doi:10.1108/S1479-3660(2012)0000014016

Recent national discussions, documentaries (e.g., *Waiting for Superman* and *Race to Nowhere*), and newscasts have mainly focused on the quality of teachers and teaching in U.S. public schools. During most of these discussions, those who work in the trenches, such as teachers, have mostly been blamed for the issues facing schools. However, for the purpose of this chapter, we would like to emphasize the need for those who prepare school leaders and those who lead schools to be mindful of the degree of denial and depreciation of serving those who live on the margins. In this vein, it becomes critical for those committed to interrupting oppressive practices to enhance their awareness and deepen their knowledge base in order to better understand how systemic issues shape the education and educational environments for children and families, especially populations most under-served and underrepresented (see Boske, 2010; Marshall & Oliva, 2006; Tooms & Boske, 2010). This chapter creates a space for educators to be more mindful of their rationale, actions, policies, and practices they support that tend to embrace or affirm unjust practices in schools, and the need for school leadership programs to create a space in which leaders have strong dispositions, commitment, and capacity toward leading for social justice.

In this chapter, because there are many layers to addressing educational and social inequities, we recognize institutionalized organizations are often hesitant to undergo significant transformations and tend to be slow to change. Therefore, we contend there is a need for practitioners, school-community members, universities, and national organizations to seek out ways to build upon each others' efforts to overcome resistance as an alliance versus school leaders naively thinking their efforts alone will change both the school and external environment. We begin by discussing the future of programmatic planning for those who prepare school leaders. Next, we explore broader school-community efforts that collectively conceptualize what it means to interrupt oppressive practices by utilizing voice and power-ful segments of society to prevail in schools and communities-at-large. We then address the need to reconsider how those who engage in educatio-nal research have the moral responsibility to revisit and conceptualize an evolving understanding of what it means to engage in social justice-oriented work.

PROGRAMMATIC PLANNING

This section extends the discussion of leading for social justice by exploring what higher educational institutions can provide to candidates to engage in creating and sustaining more equitable schools. Being engaged in implementing practices embedded within actions of idealistic and well-informed school leaders is not enough to make the necessary changes. What is necessary is faculty who are willing and have the capacity to engage in hypersensitive assessment of their preparation practices (Carpenter & Diem, forthcoming), which may be a daunting task at best. However, leadership matters, and those interested in leading schools will need to place social justice at the core of their work, especially faculty who provide initial preparation, experiences, and knowledge to engage in this development.

Faculty who espouse a strong ethic of care (see Noddings, 1984) emphasize the significance of caring and relationships as educational goals and fundamental aspects of education. In utilizing an ethic of care, school leaders can focus more on the needs of the individuals rather than groups, allowing them to humanize the consequences of the decisions they make on behalf of their schools on a daily basis (Larson & Murtadha, 2002). What is at the heart of the planning collaborative preparation programs is preparing school leaders to be thoughtful and critical about imparting specific knowledge, beliefs, and practices to those they serve. Indeed, in order to prepare leaders to care about and support social justice, programs should not only teach their students about the existent social and cultural inequities in society such as racism, sexism, homophobia, poverty, and disability (Marshall & Gerstl-Pepin, 2005), but also teach them how to advocate on behalf of children, families, and communities who experience these inequities everyday (Gerstl-Pepin, Killeen, & Hasazi, 2006). Very few collaborative programs are characterized by advocacy, which emphasizes the need for school leaders to pay close attention to attitudes, beliefs, and mind-sets of those who work with children and families (see Boske & Tooms, 2010; McKenzie et al., 2008).

Leadership preparation programs should seek to promote authentic experiences of learning. We encourage those who prepare school leaders to reconsider to what extent programmatic practices insist on imposing ideas versus creating spaces in which faculty and aspiring school leaders make meaning together. Collectively, they should respond to the growing critique and challenge of preparing school leaders to engage in renewed thought, discussions, and actions centered on improving educational experiences for all children. Therefore, the preparation itself encompasses dialogic pedagogy: the goal is as much about social change as individual change (Freire, 1993). The faculty member as expert and learner as an empty shell must be under question. According to Freire (1993), authentic learning takes place when there are two learners. These learners, both faculty and student, occupy different spaces, but engage in an ongoing dialogue. Within this process, together, both faculty and student illuminate potential within their renewed intellectual community. And within this community, in which both participants bring knowledge to the relationship, they explore what each of them know and what they can learn from each other. This new learning affords participants to accept the responsibility to engage in actions that are systemic, deliberate, and serve as catalysts for change.

Critical Pedagogy

Although the expectations for leaders to be equipped to lead in diverse settings has increased in recent years, preparation programs continue to be unenthusiastic and indifferent to revising their curricula in order to provide the knowledge necessary for future leaders to be able to address issues of social justice and diversity (Brown, 2006; Cambron-McCabe & McCarthy, 2005; Hawley & James, 2010). Further, while the field of educational leadership has been "calling for" institutions of higher education to prepare school leaders with the ability to lead equitable and socially just schools for many years (Blackmore, 2009; Jean-Marie, 2010; Jean-Marie, Normore & Brooks, 2009; Marshall & Oliva, 2006; McKenzie et al., 2008; Rusch & Horsford, 2009; Theoharis, 2007, 2009, 2010), the field has done little to prepare school leaders with the critical pedagogical skills necessary to facilitate social justice-oriented conversations within their schools (Diem & Carpenter, 2012)

If students are to acquire the skills and knowledge necessary to lead socially just schools, the programs that prepare them must incorporate critical pedagogies into their curricula. Pedagogy here refers to how content is delivered within a preparation program (Capper, Theoharis, & Sebastian, 2006). According to Capper et al. (2006), critical pedagogies within preparation programs should include teaching methods associated with raising the consciousness of leaders, deepening leader knowledge, and building leadership skills. Examples of teaching strategies that could help future school leaders gain insight into their feelings toward issues of equity, diversity, and social justice and prepare them to lead equitable schools include but are not limited to conducting equity audits of schools (McKenzie & Scheurich, 2004); engaging in critical self-reflective practices such as writing cultural autobiographies and maintaining journals (Brown, 2004, 2006; Hernandez & Marshall, 2009; Ridenour, 2004); and stimulating rational discourses, which includes examining alternative viewpoints, testing assumptions, and weighing supportive evidence through critical incidents, controversial readings, and group activities (Brown, 2004, 2006).

Jean-Marie et al. (2009) echo these sentiments, highlighting the need for preparation programs to promote opportunities for critical discourse and critical pedagogy as it relates to issues of social justice. Further, Furman and Gruenewald (2004) suggest through their model of a "critical pedagogy of place," educators and students need to situate the social justice discourse within an ecological perspective in order to gain a better understanding of how local economic, environmental, and cultural issues may impact their lives. Faculty within preparation programs can assist their students in developing this socioecological perspective by designing curricula to include readings and activities students can engage in, which help to make connections between education and larger societal issues (Furman, 2012; Jean-Marie et al., 2009; Goddard, 2005). Such programmatic modifications can serve to help prepare leaders to be conscious of the world around them and how their practices must be continuously examined and reflected upon in order to ensure a social justice-oriented pedagogy is woven into the fabric of the schools they will lead.

Strong Sense of Self

In his notion of principled leadership, leadership grounded in Cornel West's notion of prophetic spirituality, Dantley (2008) states:

> there is a very strong sense that justice and fairness ought to prevail in all personal and societal affairs ... Principled leadership is all about being able to look at yourself in the mirror or to lay your head down at night and know that the administrative decisions you have made have been in the best interest of the children and are in fact indicative of the ways you would want your own children to have been treated. (p. 455)

Within principled leadership, Dantley (2008) discusses the concept of individual moralism, where leaders take time out to self-reflect on where they stand in regards to issues such as racism, classism, sexism, and inclusion. Leaders are asked to look inside themselves and question whether the decisions they are making are based on a standard of ethics and social justice. Through critical self-reflection and auto-inquiry individuals can gain a stronger sense of self, and reflect on who they really are as leaders and how their own issues and prejudices may be impacting their ability to lead for equity and social justice (Dantley, 2008).

The process of developing a stronger sense of self is critical in preparing educational leaders to become more aware of injustices occurring within and outside of their schools, and how they can make changes in their everyday practice that can have an impact on the larger structure of society. Therefore, in leadership preparation programs, it is crucial for students to engage in tasks associated with critical self-reflection and inquiry help so that they can become more conscious of both the moral and ethical implications their schooling practices may have on students and the communities which they are called to serve (Brown, 2006).

Love and Respect for All People

School leaders need to show in their behavior what it means to care. We cannot merely tell them to care or read journal articles or scholarly books on caring for those they serve. Faculty must demonstrate their caring in their relations with students and afford them with spaces and support to do caring with those they serve (Boske, 2012a, 2012b; Boske & Tooms, 2010; Noddings, 1992; Starratt, 1994). Centering love within the educational leadership and social justice discourse can help to create a space where individuals commit themselves to improving the lives of others by establishing relationships in which the individuals assume responsibility for and are held accountable to each other (Larson & Murtadha, 2002).

Dantley, Beachum, and McCray (2008) emphasize the importance of establishing caring relationships within educational leadership, specifically, as they relate to addressing issues of social justice. Indeed, students and professors concerned with social justice issues must form relationships and build alliances in order to work against oppressive structures existent within their schools. The type of "visionary social justice" Dantley et al. (2008) envision "should be relationship driven, holistic, and morally grounded." They further elaborate:

> Relationships are at the crux of educational leadership, and they are important to all human interactions and organizations ... The power of relationships cannot be under-estimated because it is in relationships that we are equipped to come to engage others' perspectives and predispositions, which have a monumental impact on our own. (p. 128)

Building caring relationships and establishing mutual respect are key to providing opportunities for dialogue around social justice within school settings. By engaging in such conversations, more people are afforded the space to be a part of the conversation, including marginalized groups who have to overcome many obstacles to share in the schooling experience, which can result in greater school effectiveness.

Insatiable Hunger for Truth and Knowledge

Some argue the phrase "social justice has lost its potency," because at times, it is perceived as a trite rallying call; those who use it are essentialized as non-scholars with an agenda or as the scholars who are the "ists" (as in *Feminists, Queer Theorists, Critical Race Theorists,* and *Post Modernists*). Authors afford us with a wide range of understandings about what social justice is and to what extent, if any, school leadership is predicated on social justice work. Combined, their scholarship reflects a lifetime of social justice work across the arenas of diversity, ethics, and service dedicated to improving the lives of leaders and learners in schools around the world. What we know is for the authors in this book, the passion to improve the lives of others is a core value of both leadership development and social justice.

The issues that galvanized our passion for leadership as it is linked to social justice intensified for both of us over the last several decades because of personal and professional experiences. These significant experiences included Teresa's work to build a school for girls in Kenya to Pollock's (2010) work on engaging faculty members in conversations surrounding race and Rusch and Horsford's (2009) conceptualization of a theory of self-contribution that seeks to understand the skills both faculty and school leaders need in order to move from a color blindness to a color consciousness discourse that promotes constructive conversations about race across all color lines.

Together, their work and challenges encourage and energize us to become more committed to a sense of urgency to consider school's role in communities around the globe. Authors may disagree with each other about what social justice means, how it is interpreted in scholarship, and how it can affect the preparation of school leaders. We realize this is not a unique phenomenon once we read Anthony Normore's foreword. Unfortunately, as a profession, we still argue about what social justice *is*; however, the current discourse brings with it the aforementioned sense of urgency, because technology has served to effectively shrink our profession along with our world.

We were compelled to chronicle the historic social justice moments in our fields because it is directly aligned with the mandatory call for "glocality" (which refers to the ability to think globally and act locally) as an administrative skill set (see Wellman, 2002 for a greater discussion of the term). Glocality for school leaders is an act of consciousness, recognizing the interconnectedness of both self and place. For twenty-first century international school leaders, engaging in minimal external perspectives is no longer enough to lead and respond to the call for social justice. School leaders conscious of self and place realize the influence of the global matrix extends itself through communication and technology. Whether school leaders are comfortable with such interconnectedness or not, they live in glocalities. Such glocalities influence their consciousness, beliefs, and actions. Edward Relph (1976), an academe geographer, notes understanding the influence of place, such as glocality, is essential to understanding human experience, because place provides meaning for people's lives and permeates everyday life.

As we live multiple experiences within these glocalities, Relph (1976) classifies such experiences as insideness and outsideness. Insideness is living within the place or locale and identifying the place as part of their identity. By contrast, outsideness refers to people identifying with superficial qualities of the place, separating themselves emotionally from the places in which they are planning or restructuring. School leaders encounter spaces in which they may also identify as insiders and outsiders, choosing to live and work in spaces without ever fully integrating into the spaces, such as local schools, government, agencies, or community groups. Together, we have the ability to choose to exit places psychologically without physically leaving them in order to find people who are more to our liking. This leaves school leaders with the ability to be both inside and outside the locale at the same time. For example, a school leader who identifies as LGBTQIA and feels isolated within the school community may find support through online global chat rooms or international organizations for educators undergoing similar experiences. So, in essence, the extent to which a school leader is conscious of the interconnectedness of place and identity, such as glocality, the more a school leader is able to experience the qualities of place, bridging the gap between place, needs, and resources. Experiencing the qualities of place encourages school leaders to consider the rich impact of place, human experience, and community resources as of crucial importance in addressing issues of social justice as a school leader.

Doing and Being a Catalyst for Change

Dr. Harvey Sacks, who was an ethnomethodologist at the University of California at Berkeley, focused on understanding how people "do" particular actions, which often make their actions unnoticeable. His 1970 lecture on "Doing Being Ordinary" provided an understanding of the significance of doing everyday work, and in the case of this book, *doing* social justice work in schools. Sacks developed his notion of "ordinary" as daily life and business as usual (Sacks, 1985, p. 215). Being ordinary suggests people who go about their everyday business are invisible to themselves. For people identified as non-ordinary or "not one of us," normative social demands are heightened (Bogdan & Taylor, 1994, p. 14). We intentionally or unintentionally group our efforts into those that translate into professional capital and the other stuff of an ordinary day.

Sacks (1985) noted we tend to organize, understand, and relate our lived experiences to each other in terms of events that are storyable. That is to say they are exciting or epic. The rest of our existence we tend to quantify as *ordinary*. Inevitably we are socialized to describe the contributions we make that carry the greatest cultural capital. However, the rest of our efforts are often deemed as part of the everydayness of people's ordinary lives. For example, people have ordinary days at the office and ordinary lives at home that are interrupted with epic events such as publication, professional recognition, marriage, divorce, or even the death of a cherished colleague. For those who work in schools promoting social justice issues, doing being ordinary has the potential to promote systemic or catalytic responses.

For these school leaders, being committed to serving as a catalyst for educational and social change is part of their everyday work experience. The authors of this book, as well as educators they highlight, work to seek positive changes for marginalized populations because they do not "fit" what is deemed to be the "standard" in educational settings (Allen, 2006; Brooks & Tooms, 2008). What is needed is leadership preparation programs that afford candidates with spaces to empower them to act in just ways.

School leaders are working at the front lines of educational reform and can potentially create a new social order where all students are afforded the same educational opportunities, which eventually can lead to more equitable social opportunities for traditionally disenfranchised individuals (Jean-Marie et al., 2009). Revisiting the programmatic vision and mission as well as strategies to assess student growth with preparation programs is essential to improving learning communities. One element to engaging in revolutionary changes is to continually seek to understand and learn how to improve this learning community (e.g., Glasman, Cibulka, & Ashby, 2002).

BROADER SCHOOL-COMMUNITY EFFORTS

Building on the earlier discussion regarding programmatic planning, it is critical for those involved in preparing school leaders to reconsider what it means to collectively engage in social justice work, given the diverse contexts within schools, and often times, challenging obstacles and resistance to change that does not lead toward empowerment. Addressing these critical issues calls for school leaders to search for practices that affirm students' home cultures, increase family–community involvement, and advocate for societal change. There is little discussion in the field of educational leadership regarding the significance of building bridges and school–community relations (e.g., Boske & Benavente-McEnery, 2012; Boske & McEnery, 2010, 2011; Giles, Jacobson, Johnson, & Ylimaki, 2007; Larson & Murtadha, 2002; Theoharis, 2007). Building home–school relations is critical to diverse communities in which families experience isolation from schools and district leadership. Culturally responsive practices empower families, cause us to rethink curricular practices, and promote systemic school reform (Gonzalez, Moll, & Amanti, 2005; Marshall & Olivia, 2006). Preparing school leaders to address the lived realities of marginalized children and their families links intentions of equity with local school communities (Hallinger & Heck, 1986; Marshall & Oliva, 2006). Such approaches dare school leaders to venture beyond school walls to learn from and advocate for children, families, and community members.

A case example of promoting social justice work through building home–school–community connections is evident when considering the work of Boske and McEnery (2010) and Gonzalez et al. (2005). Scholars present findings from empirical studies centered on home visits as to deepening empathic responses and understanding culturally diverse experiences as knowledge. School leaders and teachers assessed the needs of their school community and aligned their school practices accordingly. They validated the lived cultural experiences of children and their families as essential to perceiving household as dynamic, interactional, and emergent entities. After conducting home visits, teachers and school leaders deepened their understanding, willingness, and ability to engage with children and families who had been shut out by the school and district leadership.

Throughout these studies (see Boske & McEnery, 2010; Gonzalez et al., 2005), educators recognized the existence of oppressive school practices and its influence in undermining the quality of human life played a significant role in driving their work (Derman-Sparks & Phillips, 1997). Teachers and school leaders initially perceived school as an entity that prescribed cultural norms, as opposed to recognizing knowledge as a reflection of the children, parents, and community members (Moll, 1992). Often times, educators initially conducted home visits with a perception that insinuated race, class, and language difference were to blame for academic issues and if families would just "buy in" to the school's mission, their children would be successful (Gonzalez et al., 2005). They perceived family and student knowledge as an attempt to teach parents how to do school and not as one that harnessed the strengths inherent in each family unit.

Families and children understood the resistance they faced by teachers who were not interested in conducting home visits or whose beliefs conflicted with their purpose reflected a complex and ongoing process. Home visits provided participants with an entry point into pursuing socially just school practices to improve the learning experiences of children and their families. Sharing and discussing their lived experiences with home visits provided spaces for vigorous conversation regarding issues of race, class, language, and immigration status.

Case examples as well as experiential learning in which school leaders engage in making meaningful connections with disenfranchised populations is critical to deepening understanding and ways of knowing about what it means to lead for social justice (Boske, 2012a; Young & Laible, 2000). Building bridges between school and home (see Merchant & Shoho, 2010), affording school leaders with spaces to engage more explicitly in social justice educational practices within surrounding school sites (see Boske, 2012a; Jean-Marie & Normore, 2010), and living what it means to be a bridge builder (see Tooms & Boske, 2010) are significant to this work in schools.

EDUCATIONAL RESEARCH

Although the education and welfare of those who live on the margins has increasingly become a primary concern for those who work in U.S. schools, it is clear this concern should not only be strengthened, but re-examined to bear witness to the multiple realities within wider societal contexts. This body of research, taken as a whole, does not often send a clear message about what social justice means within diverse contexts; however, several questions remain: how much success has taken place in preparing school leaders to actively engage in leading for social justice work? How do school leaders construct meanings and act on them to improve the lived experiences of those who are underserved? How do we design research to consider what it means to lead for social justice and to establish theories of justice and democracy in public schools? What does social justice mean within global communities? These questions, as well as many others, suggest those who prepare school leaders and work in schools look deeper into how successful leaders for social justice is understood within and beyond leadership preparation (e.g., Firestone & Riehl, 2005; Lytle, 2004). School leaders might reconsider the intersections of their personal lived experiences and their leadership practices in an effort to deepen their understanding of what it means to live on the margins and how living on the margins shapes students' meaning making and experiences in school.

CONCLUSION

As school leaders across the world wrestle with ways to think about, respond to, and act upon social justice, our chapter provides a way to think about this process. We believe all aspects identified throughout this chapter offer a template to ground their work in social justice. As they engage in the process, school leaders may find themselves somewhere along the continuum to resist change or to help bring about change to empower school communities, especially those from disenfranchised populations. Those interested in leading schools may discover that there is no need to wait for external agencies to take actions that align with their beliefs and vision to serve school communities in socially just ways. School leaders have the capacity to demonstrate their convictions and commitment to foster meaningful change. Such change promotes opportunities to frame a new common discourse in educational leadership: pursuing a new vision for leading for social justice in schools.

REFERENCES

Allen, L. A. (2006). The moral life of schools revisited: Preparing educational leaders to "build a new social order" for social justice and democratic community. *International Journal of Urban Educational Leadership, 1,* 1–13.

Blackmore, J. (2009). Leadership for social justice: A transnational dialogue. *Journal of Research on Leadership Education, 4*(1), 1–10.

Bogdan, R., & Taylor, S. J. (1994). A positive approach to qualitative evaluation and policy research in social work. In E. Sherman & W. Reid (Eds.), *Qualitative research in social work* (pp. 293–302). New York, NY: Columbia University Press.

Boske, C. (2010). A time to grow: Workplace mobbing and the making of a tempered radical. In A. K. Tooms & C. Boske (Eds.), *Building bridges: Connecting educational leadership and social justice to improve schools* (pp. 29–56). Charlotte, NC: Information Age Publishing.

Boske, C. (2012a). *Educational leadership: Building bridges among ideas, schools and nations.* Charlotte, NC: Information Age Publishing.

Boske, C. (2012b). Whose social justice counts? Addressing issues of social justice and equity in schools. In J. Martin (Ed.), *Women as leaders in education: Succeeding despite inequity, discrimination, and other challenges.* Santa Barbara, CA: Praeger.

Boske, C., & Benavente-McEnery, L. (2012). Breaking the mold of education for culturally and linguistically diverse students: Tapping into the strengths of families. In A. Honigsfeld & A. Cohan (Eds.), *Breaking the mold of education for culturally and linguistically diverse students: Innovative and successful practices for 21st century schools* (3rd ed.). Lanham, NY: Rowman and Littlefield.

Boske, C., & McEnery, L. (2010). Taking it to the streets: A new line of inquiry for school communities. *Journal of School Leadership, 20*(3), 369–398.

Boske, C., & McEnery, L. (2011). Catalysts: Assistant principals who lead for social justice. In A. R. Shoho, B. G. Barnett & A. K. Tooms (Eds.), *Examining the assistant principalship: New puzzles and perennial challenges for the 21st century.* Charlotte, NC: Information Age Publishing.

Boske, C., & Tooms, A. K. (2010). Social justice and doing "being ordinary". In A. K. Tooms & C. Boske (Eds.), *Building bridges: Connecting educational leadership and social justice to improve schools* (pp. xvii–xxviii). Charlotte, NC: Information Age Publishing.

Brooks, J. S., & Tooms, A. K. (2008). A dialectic of social justice: Finding synergy between life and work through reflection and dialogue. *Journal of School Leadership, 18*(2), 134–163.

Brown, K. M. (2004). Leadership for social justice and equity: Weaving a transformative framework and pedagogy. *Educational Administrative Quarterly, 40*(1), 79–110.

Brown, K. M. (2006). Leadership for social justice and equity: Evaluating a transformative framework and andragogy. *Educational Administration Quarterly, 42*(5), 700–745.

Cambron-McCabe, N., & McCarthy, M. M. (2005). Educating school leaders for social justice. *Educational Policy, 19*(1), 201–222.

Capper, C. A., Theoharis, G., & Sebastian, J. (2006). Toward a framework for preparing leaders for social justice. *Journal of Educational Administration, 44*(3), 209–224.

Carpenter, B. W., & Diem, S. (forthcoming). Talking race: Facilitating critical conversations in educational leadership preparation programs. *Journal of School Leadership.*

Dantley, M. E. (2008). The 2007 willower family lecture reconstructing leadership: Embracing a spiritual dimension. *Leadership and Policy in Schools, 7*(4), 451–460.

Dantley, M. E., Beachum, F. D., & McCray, C. R. (2008). Exploring the intersectionality of multiple centers within notions of social justice. *Journal of School Leadership, 18*(2), 124–133.

Derman-Sparks, L., & Phillips, C. (1997). *Teaching/learning anti-racism: A developmental approach.* New York, NY: Teachers College Press.

Diem, S., & Carpenter, B. W. (2012). Exploring the blockages of race-related conversations in the classroom: Obstacles or opportunity? In J. S. Brooks & N. W. Arnold (Eds.), *Educational leadership and racism: Preparation, pedagogy and practice.* Charlotte, NC: Information Age Publishing.

Firestone, W. A., & Riehl, C. (2005). *A new agenda for research in educational leadership.* New York, NY: Teachers College Press.

Freire, P. (1993). *Pedagogy of the oppressed*. New York, NY: Continuum Books.

Furman, G. (2012). Social justice leadership as praxis: Developing capacities through preparation programs. *Educational Administration Quarterly, 48*(2), 191–229.

Furman, G. C., & Gruenewald, D. A. (2004). Expanding the landscape of social justice: A critical ecological analysis. *Educational Administration Quarterly, 40*(1), 47–76.

Gerstl-Pepin, C., Killeen, K., & Hasazi, S. (2006). Utilizing an "ethic of care" in leadership preparation: Uncovering the complexity of colorblind social justice. *Journal of Educational Administration, 44*(3), 250–263.

Giles, C., Jacobson, S. L., Johnson, L., & Ylimaki, R. (2007). Against the odds: Successful principals in challenging U.S. schools. In C. Day & K. Leithwood (Eds.), *Successful principal leadership in times of change: An international perspective* (pp. 155–168). Dordrecht: Springer.

Glasman, N., Cibulka, J., & Ashby, D. (2002). Program self-evaluation for continuous improvement. *Educational Administration Quarterly, 38*(2), 257–288.

Goddard, J. T. (2005). Toward glocality: Facilitating leadership in an age of diversity. *Journal of School Leadership, 15*, 159–177.

Gonzalez, N., Moll, L. C., & Amanti, C. (2005). *Funds of knowledge: Theorizing practices in households, communities, and classrooms*. Mahwah, NJ: Erlbaum.

Hallinger, P., & Heck, R. H. (1986). Exploring the principal's contribution to school effectiveness: 1980–1995. *School Effectiveness and School Improvement, 9*(2), 157–191.

Hawley, W., & James, R. (2010). Diversity-responsive school leadership. *UCEA Review, 52*(3), 1–5.

Hernandez, F., & Marshall, J. M. (2009). "Where I came from, where I am now, and where I'd like to be": Aspiring administrators reflect on issues related to equity, diversity, and social justice. *Journal of School Leadership, 19*(3), 299–333.

Jean-Marie, G. (2010). "Fire in the belly": Igniting a social justice discourse in learning environments of leadership preparation. In A. K. Tooms & C. Boske (Eds.), *Bridge leadership: Connecting educational leadership and social justice to improve schools* (pp. 97–124). Charlotte, NC: Information Age Publishing.

Jean-Marie, G., & Normore, A. H. (Eds.). (2010). *Educational leadership preparation*. New York, NY: Palgrave MacMillan.

Jean-Marie, G., Normore, A., & Brooks, J. S. (2009). Leadership for social justice: Preparing 21st century school leaders for a new social order. *Journal of Research on Leadership in Education, 4*(1), 1–31.

Larson, C., & Murtadha, K. (2002). Leadership for social justice. In J. Murphy (Ed.), *The educational leadership challenge: Redefining leadership for the 21st century* (pp. 134–161). Chicago, IL: University of Chicago Press.

Lytle, J. H. (2004). A superintendent's reaction. *Journal of School Leadership, 14*(5), 573–577.

Marshall, C., & Gerstl-Pepin, C. I. (2005). *Re-framing educational politics for social justice*. Boston, MA: Allyn & Bacon.

Marshall, C., & Oliva, M. (Eds.). (2006). *Leadership for social justice: Making revolutions in education*. Boston, MA: Pearson.

McKenzie, K. B., Christman, D. E., Hernandez, F., Fierro, E., Capper, C. A., Dantley, M., … Scheurich, J. (2008). Educating leaders for social justice: A design for a comprehensive, social justice leadership preparation program. *Educational Administration Quarterly, 4*(1), 111–138.

McKenzie, K. B., & Scheurich, J. J. (2004). Equity traps: useful construct for preparing principals to lead schools that are successful with racially diverse students. *Educational Administration Quarterly, 40*(5), 606–632.

Merchant, E., & Shoho, A. (2010). Bridge people: Civic and educational leaders for social justice. In C. Marshall & M. Oliva (Eds.), *Leadership for social justice: Making revolutions in education* (pp. 120–138). Boston, MA: Allyn & Bacon.

Moll, L. (1992). Funds of knowledge for teaching: Using a qualitative approach to connect homes and classrooms. *Theory Into Practice, 31*(1), 132–141.

Noddings, N. (1984). *Caring, a feminine approach to ethics and moral education.* Berkeley, CA: University of California Press.

Noddings, N. (1992). *The challenge to care in schools: An alternative approach to education.* New York, NY: Teachers College Press.

Pollock, M. (2010). Engaging race issues with colleagues: Strengthening our professional communities through everyday inquiry. *MASCD Perspectives* (Online), Winter 2010. Publication of the Massachusetts Association of Supervision and Curriculum Development.

Relph, E. (1976). *Place and placelessness.* London: Academic Press.

Ridenour, C. S. (2004). Finding the horizon: Education administration students paint a landscape of cultural diversity in schools. *Journal of School Leadership, 14*(1), 4–31.

Rusch, E., & Horsford, S. D. (2009). Changing hearts and minds: The quest for open talk about race in educational leadership. *International Journal of Educational Management, 23*(4), 302–313.

Sacks, H. (1985). On doing being ordinary. In J. Maxwell Atkinson & J. Heritage (Eds.), *Structures of social action: Studies in conversation analysis.* New York, NY: Cambridge University Press.

Starratt, R. J. (1994). *Building an ethical school: A practical response to the moral crisis in schools.* London: Falmer Press.

Theoharis, G. (2007). Social justice educational leaders and resistance: Toward a theory of social justice leadership. *Educational Administration Quarterly, 43*(2), 221–258.

Theoharis, G. (2009). *The school leaders our children deserve: Seven keys to equity, social justice, and school reform.* New York, NY: Teachers College Press.

Theoharis, G. (2010). Sustaining social justice: Strategies urban principals develop to advance justice and equity while facing resistance. *International Journal of Urban Educational Leadership, 4*(1), 92–110.

Tooms, A. K., & Boske, C. (2010). *Building bridges: Connecting educational leadership and social justice to improve schools.* Charlotte, NC: Information Age Publishing.

Wellman, B. (2002). Little Boxes, glocalization, and networked individualism. In M. Tanabe, P. van den Besselaar & T. Ishida (Eds.), *Digital cities.* Berlin: Spinger-Verlag.

Young, M. D., & Laible, J. (2000). White racism, anti-racism, and school leadership preparation. *Journal of School Leadership, 10*(5), 374–415.

EPILOGUE

In an era of changing social environment within the United States and globally, the examination of leadership for social justice has implication on how preparation programs robustly address issues of diversity, access, and equity to equip school leaders to effectively lead schools. The intersection of leadership, social justice, and equity concerns is a growing focus of scholars in the field of educational leadership (i.e., Cambron-McCabe, 2010; Jean-Marie, 2009; Jean-Marie, Normore, & Brooks, 2009; Normore, 2008) challenging traditional paradigms of leadership that are inadequate in preparing 21st century school leaders. Given the complexities of educational policies, increasing diversity of communities (i.e., racially, culturally, ethnically, and linguistically), and pervasive educational disparities in schools as discussed in these chapters, attending to what aspiring and practicing leaders are learning to provide equitable education for all is paramount.

In this book, each chapter makes a contribution to our understanding on the enactment of social justice within the P-20 system. Specifically, the depth of ideas and analysis offers both conceptual and empirical knowledge on the landscape of quality leadership and teacher preparation including research and engaged scholarship around issues on social justice through the perspective of students, teachers and school leaders, program designs and change efforts, and the "what" and "how" of educational leadership practice to advance social justice. As a result, the contributors offer a discussion on the future of educational leadership in the context of social justice, and the current research and policy engagement efforts and practices that are preparing leaders for the demands of an evolving and multi-dimensional context. As such, there are three key areas which merit considerations in an effort to more deeply infuse the practice of social justice in P-20 system so leaders will have the indomitable will to lead equitable schools and engage others (i.e., teachers and staff, students, parents, and community, etc.) in dismantling structural barriers that have been difficult to eradicate.

BEYOND AWARENESS: ROBUST LEARNING EXPERIENCES ON SOCIAL JUSTICE

The facilitation of learning of leadership for social justice involves experiences which go beyond awareness (Cambron-McCabe & McCarthy, 2005; Jean-Marie et al., 2009). Brooks and Miles (2008) contend "awareness of social injustices is not sufficient, school leaders must act when they identify inequity. School leaders are not only uniquely positioned to influence equitable educational practices, their proactive involvement is imperative" (p. 107). However, if school leaders have not been exposed in their preparation programs on the "need to, why, and how to act," they will struggle to challenge inherent practices when they are in school leadership positions. To build capacity for school leaders to take socially just actions, learning experiences about social justice should include critical literature and research that interrogate the principles of equity, access, and equality that vehemently shed light on school practices.

While there have been different efforts employed in leadership preparations, one national effort that is focused on increasing the knowledge and skills of school leaders about social justice issues is the United States Department of Education, FIPSE grant hosted by the University Council of Educational Administration (UCEA). Specifically, the initiative called, *Preparing Leaders to Support Diverse Learners: Curriculum Modules for Leadership Preparation* involves faculty teams from several institutions to develop curriculum modules focused on preparing leaders to support diverse learners. The modules include: developing advocacy leadership, organizing learning and the learning environment, instructional leadership for ELL student populations, family and community involvement, building a community of trust through racial awareness of self, and marshalling and using resources based on data and student needs. These modules are designed to enhance the core curriculum used in University Council of Educational Administration (UCEA) school leadership programs. Further, each of the modules contains powerful learning experiences (PLEs), a learning framework developed by UCEA faculty based on adult learning principles. PLEs include the following characteristics:

1. Authentic, meaningful, relevant problem-finding linking theory, and principal practice
2. Involves sense-making around critical problems of practice
3. Explores, critiques, deconstructs from equity perspective (race, culture, language)

4. Requires collaboration and interdependence
5. Develops confidence in leadership
6. Places both the professor and student in a learning situation
7. Learners are empowered and responsible for own learning
8. Shifts perspective from classroom to school, district, or state level
9. Has a reflective component (Young & Gooden, n.d.)

The value of such national initiative in preparation programs, which should include teacher education, provides a platform for aspiring leaders and educators to experiment with engaging in social justice work. In preparation programs, students are supported through a community of learners (i.e., instructor and colleagues) to go beyond their comfort level and challenge themselves to grapple with difficult questions and ideas, including their own beliefs and values.

Students in preparation programs are often intrigued by diversity, but Shields (2010) observes, "the challenging task is to help students to be both critical of, and open to, new ideas and indeed, to have the agency to shape identities that will be both different from those of their parents and yet connected to the traditions of their communities and countries" (p. 138). While the diverse academic culture in higher education adds to the learning of everyone, it also minimizes the more specific training that could also be useful (Kelly, 2010, p. 8). Learning from other group members within a community of learners provides diversity enrichment and opportunity for productive and innovative learning that is not found in many preparation programs.

ENHANCING STUDENT LEARNING THROUGH FIELD-BASED INTERNSHIPS

Additionally, a field-embedded internship experience with a strong social justice focus provides application of practical knowledge integrated with technical knowledge to promote school leaders' role in transforming schools and communities (Angelle & Anfara, 2009; Jean-Marie et al., 2009). The quality of the internship plays a central role in the development of socially just school leaders. Carefully designed internship help students to identify hands-on, on-site experience under the guidance of practitioner provides the integration of knowledge and skills aspiring and practicing leaders will need to address the challenges of the principalship. Further, duration and intensity, getting experiences in multiple settings, meaningful activities and experiences, and contextual relevance are key in providing quality internships that help students to delve deeper into the experiences of teachers and students (Brown-Ferrigno, 2003: Jean-Marie et al., 2009).

LEARNING TO LEAD FOR DIVERSITY ACROSS CONTEXTS: UNIVERSITY-DISTRICT PARTNERSHIPS

Finally, a concerted effort to develop strong university-school district partnerships to support the development of school leaders for social justice is critical. Partnership with school districts serves a critical role in providing: a quality program to students, developing a different type of educational leadership program, and preparing the next generation of educational leaders (Darling-Hammond, LaPointe, Meyerson, & Orr, 2007). Sustainable partnerships with stakeholders are key through collaboration, cooperation, and commitment to participate in the planning, implementing, and assessment process (Calabrese, 2006). As Young (2009) asserts "we must be clear about what we want, the kinds of leaders our schools and children need, and we must recognize and embrace our responsibilities" (p. 4). Through partnerships, students' learning experiences (i.e., aspiring and practicing) can be enhanced through experiential learning within their school districts. Strong-university partnerships provide opportunities to expose students to various settings including local communities, agencies and other school districts so they can understand the complexities of issues that students and families face. Also through partnerships, multiple perspectives converge and a number of professional strengths have the potential to enhance the depth and quality of preparation programs (Jean-Marie & Normore, 2010; Orr, 2006; Stein, 2006) to more effectively develop school leaders for social justice.

In sum, leadership is pivotal in promoting improvement and contributing to the well-being of children and communities. Rising national and global expectations about schools have been accompanied by increased focused on leadership development in schools and in preparation programs (Jean-Marie & Normore, 2010). The focus of scrutiny on school leadership in recent years raises questions about effective leadership and its impact on the functions of schools. There is an urgency to forge a new direction for school leadership and preparations programs to develop school leaders for social justice and this book provide insights and important lessons on current efforts.

Gaëtane Jean-Marie

REFERENCES

Angelle, P., & Anfara, V. (2009, November 18–22). Leadership for lifelong learning: The Center for Educational Leadership. Paper presented at the annual meeting of the University Council for Educational Administration, Anaheim, CA.

Brooks, J. S., & Miles, M. T. (2008). From scientific management to social justice…and back again? Pedagogical shifts in educational leadership. In A. H. Normore (Ed.), *Leadership for social justice: Promoting equity and excellence through inquiry and reflective practice* (pp. 99–114). Charlotte, NC: Information Age.

Browne-Ferrigno, T. (2003). Becoming a principal: Role conception, initial socialization, role-identity transformation, purposeful engagement. *Educational Administration Quarterly*, *39*(4), 468–503.

Calabrese, R. L. (2006). Building social capital through the use of an appreciative inquiry theoretical perspective in a school and university partnership. *International Journal of Educational Management*, *20*(3), 173–182.

Cambron-McCabe, N. (2010). Preparation and development of school leaders: Implications for social justice policies. In C. Marshall & M. Oliva (Eds.), *Leadership for social justice: Making revolutions in education* (pp. 35–52). New York, NY: Pearson.

Cambron-McCabe, N., & McCarthy, M. M. (2005). Educating school leaders for social justice. *Educational Policy*, *19*(1), 201–222.

Darling-Hammond, L., LaPointe, M., Meyerson, D., & Orr, M. (2007). *Preparing school leaders for a changing world: Executive Summary*. Stanford, CA: Stanford University.

Jean-Marie, G. (2009). "Fire in the belly": Igniting a social justice discourse in learning environments of leadership preparation. In A. Tooms, & C. Boske (Eds.), *Building bridges, connecting educational leadership and social justice to improve schools* (pp. 97–119). Educational Leadership for Social Justice. Charlotte, NC: Information Age.

Jean-Marie, G., & Normore, A. H. (Eds.). (2010). *Educational leadership preparation: Innovation and Interdisciplinary approaches to the Ed.D. and graduate education*. New York, NY: Palgrave MacMillan.

Jean-Marie, G., Normore, A. H., & Brooks, J. (2009). Leadership for social justice: Preparing 21st century school leaders for a new social order. *Journal of Research on Leadership and Education*, *4*(1), 1–31.

Kelly, R. (2010). Developing leaders in the complex adaptive setting of higher education. *Academic Leader*, *26*, 7–8.

Normore, A. H. (Ed.). (2008). *Leadership for social justice: Promoting equity and excellence through inquiry and reflective practice* (pp. 99–114). Charlotte, NC: Information Age.

Orr, M. T. (2006). Research on leadership as a reform strategy. *Journal of Research on Leadership Education*, *1*(1).

Shields, C. M. (2010). Transformative leadership. In E. Baker, P. Peterson & B. McGaw (Eds.), *International encyclopedia of education* (3rd ed.). Oxford, UK: Elsevier.

Stein, S. J. (2006). Transforming leadership programs: Design, pedagogy, and incentives. *Phi Delta Kappan*, *87*(7), 522–524.

Young, M. (2009). The politics and ethics of professional responsibility in the educational leadership professoriate. *UCEA Review*, *50*(2), 1–5.

Young, M., & Gooden, M. (n.d.). Preparing leaders to support diverse learners. Powerpoint presentation slides.

AUTHOR BIOGRAPHIES

Carl Kalani Beyer is the dean of the College and the Founding Dean of the School of Education at Pacific Oaks College in Pasadena, California. Prior to his arrival in May 2011, he was the dean of the School of Education at National University with the rank of professor and full time faculty and chair of the Teacher Education Department at Concordia University (Chicago). He came to higher education after a 34-year career in public education. Multicultural education, Native American education, manual labor and manual training curriculum, education for Hawaiians, and higher education issues are his research interests. Since he became a professor in 2002, his scholarship consists of publishing 18 articles, a chapter in a book, a forward to a book, and 4 book reviews, and presenting over 50 papers at peer-reviewed conferences. He is currently awaiting publication of two additional articles, a chapter in a book, and the manuscript of his reworked dissertation. Dr. Beyer is a high school graduate of Kamehameha School for Boys. He received a BA in mathematics from Beloit College and earned a MA in US history from Northern Illinois University, MA in education and MS in management and organizational behavior from Benedictine University, and Ph.D. from the University of Illinois at Chicago in curriculum design.

Jill Bickett brings 25 years of professional experience in the field of education to her research and writing on educational leadership. She is currently the assistant director for the Ed.D. Program in Educational Leadership for Social Justice at Loyola Marymount University, where she earned her doctorate in 2008. Although her recent research has addressed the efficacy of leadership programs for social justice, previous scholarship has focused on issues of gender, service, and leadership including work on family friendly policies in Catholic higher education, the underrepresentation of girls in special education, and single-sex service programs in Catholic high schools.

Christa Boske is an associate professor in the educational leadership at Kent State University. She works to encourage school leaders to promote humanity in schools. Christa's recent work is published in the *Journal of School Leadership*, *Journal of Research on Leadership Education*,

Multicultural Education and Technology Journal, and the *Journal of Curriculum Theorizing*. Her scholarship is informed by work in residential treatment and inner-city schools as a school leader and social worker. She recently coedited the book titled *Bridge Leadership: Connecting Educational Leadership and Social Justice to Improve Schools* with Autumn K. Tooms in 2010 with Information Age Publishing. Christa has another edited book scheduled for publication in the fall of 2012 titled *Educational Leadership: Building Bridges between Ideas, Schools and Nations* through Information Age Publishing.

Bradley W. Carpenter is an assistant professor in the Department of Leadership, Foundations and Human Resource Education at the University of Louisville. His research focuses on the politics of school improvement and implementation issues related to the Title I School Improvement Grant program; the ways in which school leaders craft and implement policies that shape how parents and communities are able to meaningfully partici-pate in schools; how educational administration professors facilitate conversations surrounding race; and the possibilities that exist for educa-tion leaders asked to realize their role as an advocate at the state and federal levels of policymaking. Dr. Carpenter's primary responsibilities at the University of Louisville include leadership education/development and the fostering of supportive research and mentoring relationships with leaders located within JCPS and OVEC schools. Bradley is a former graduate fellow from The University of Texas at Austin where he received his Ph.D. in educational policy and planning.

Heather A. Cole is a doctoral candidate in the Department of Special Education at The University of Texas at Austin. She is a former attorney, practicing for more than a decade in education and disability rights law. She also holds master's degrees in public administration and education (learning disabilities and behavioral disorders). Heather's research interests include educational policy and reform, law and ethics, special education, and juvenile justice.

Michelle Collay is a professor of education at the University of New England in Maine, where she is director of the online doctoral program in educational leadership. Formerly a faculty member in educational leader-ship at CSU East Bay, Hayward, California, she and her colleagues across the California State University established an education doctorate for school- and agency-based practitioners focusing on educational reform. A former public school music teacher, she is a scholar practitioner who seeks to align teaching and scholarship in higher education and K-12 schools. Her research focus is teacher professional socialization with attention to how race, class, and gender shape teachers' professional identities. Her recent publication, "Everyday Teacher Leadership: Taking Action Where You Are," recognizes and celebrates the power of teacher leadership in schools. Other recent publications include: Collay, Winkelman, Garcia, & Guilkey-Amado (2009). Transformational leadership pedagogy: Implementing equity plans in urban schools. In *Educational leadership and administration*; Collay & Cooper (2008). The role of self-authorship in developing women leaders. *Journal of Research on Leadership Education.* Collay coaches school leaders engaged in professional learning communities, constructive teaching and leading, transformative leadership, and other school reform efforts. She has been active as a parent volunteer in her children's schools and is a bassoonist in community orchestras and chamber ensembles.

Sarah Diem is an assistant professor in the Department of Educational Leadership and Policy Analysis at the University of Missouri. Her research focuses on the social and cultural contexts of education, paying particular attention to how the politics and implementation of educational policies affect outcomes related to equity and diversity within public schools. She is also interested in the ways in which future school leaders are being prepared to address race-related issues that may affect the diverse students and communities they are called to serve. Dr. Diem received her Ph.D. in educational policy and planning from The University of Texas at Austin. Dr. Diem was awarded the 2011 Outstanding Dissertation Award by the Districts in Research and Reform Special Interest Group of the American Educational Research Association (AERA) for her dissertation, "Design Matters: The Relationship between Policy Design, Context, and Implementation in Integration Plans Based on Voluntary Choice and Socioeconomic Status."

Thad Dugan is a doctoral student in the educational leadership department at the University of Arizona. He has worked in various educational positions including special education teacher, instructional coach, assistant principal, and district long-term hearing officer. He is currently a graduate research associate at the University of Arizona as part of a grant that trains principals of corrective action schools in assessment literacy, as well as an assistant principal three days a week at a large urban middle school. His research interests include leadership for social justice, culturally responsive leadership, and effective leadership practices in high achieving schools.

Shernaz B. Garcia is an associate professor of multicultural special education in the Department of Special Education at The University of Texas at Austin, and a fellow in the Lawrence and Stel Marie Lowman College of Education Endowed Excellence Fund. She holds a doctorate in special education administration from The University of Texas at Austin, and earned her master's degree in special education from George Peabody College for Teachers, Nashville, Tennessee. Her research and teaching interests are focused on cultural influences on teaching and learning, factors contributing to educational risk for students from nondominant socio-cultural and linguistic communities; prevention of, and early intervention for academic underachievement; family–professional partnerships; and personnel preparation. Dr. Garcia has more than 25 years of experience as a teacher educator, researcher, and administrator of multicultural/ bilingual special education programs at the university level, and is a nationally recognized expert in the field of bilingual/multicultural special education.

Walter S. Gershon (Ph.D.) is an assistant professor in the School of Teaching, Learning, and Curriculum Studies at Kent State University. His scholarly interests focus on how people make sense of educational contexts and how those understandings are made through the senses. As such, Walter's work examines educational actors' ways of being and knowing, the sociocultural ecologies that contextualize such understandings, and the qualitative research methodologies utilized to study their sense-making. Such questions also speak to understandings of teacher education and possibilities for social justice in schooling. He is the editor of *The Collaborative Turn: Working Together in Qualitative Research* and recent publications include editing and contributing to a special issue of the *Journal of Curriculum Theorizing* on sensual curriculum and a forthcoming article in *Taboo: The Journal of Culture and Education* in which he uses sound files to critically map an urban middle grade student's identity as well as the racial tensions in his home and school communities. In addition to these more traditional modes of scholarship, Walter also represents research findings as public scholarship in an effort to engage communities outside the academy. His most recent example of public scholarship is a sound installation at the intersection of ethnography, art, STEM education, and social justice currently exhibited at the Akron Art Museum through June 2012. Prior to his time in higher education, Dr. Gershon taught in urban schools in the United States and in rural and urban contexts in Japan.

Mark Halx is an independent educational research consultant currently living in San Antonio, Texas. Dr. Halx has worked in educational research for over 10 years. His research interests include critical education, secondary and higher education student development, and qualitative research methods. Dr. Halx is the author of several journal articles. He has presented his research at several national and international conferences. His current research project is a series of four coordinated qualitative studies that explore the viability and benefits of critical consciousness development in marginalized student populations. Through the perspectives of students, teachers, principals, and senior district administrators, with this project he seeks to advance the empowering student development philosophy of a more critical pedagogy. Dr. Halx received his Ph.D. from The University of Texas at Austin.

Frank Hernandez, during his 15 years in public education, has served as a classroom teacher, an assistant principal, a principal, and a district coordinator of multicultural programming throughout several Midwestern urban school districts. Currently, Frank Hernandez serves as an assistant professor in the Hamline University School of Education. He also serves as chair of the Department of Continuing Studies, Partnerships, and Strategic Initiatives. His research interests include the intersection of identity and school leadership and teaching, equity and social justice, the principalship, and Latinos and school leadership. His work has been published in *Educational Administration Quarterly*, *Journal of School Leadership*, *Journal of Research in Leadership Education*, and *Education and the Urban Society*. Dr. Hernandez is currently completing a book on Latinos and school leadership with his co-author Dr. Elizabeth Murakami. Dr. Hernandez holds Ph.D. in educational leadership and policy analysis from the University of Wisconsin-Madison.

Karie Huchting is an assistant professor in the Department of Educational Leadership at Loyola Marymount University and a core faculty member in the Doctoral (Ed.D.) Program in Leadership for Social Justice. Her research focuses on student perceptions of the curricular and cocurricular educational experience. Her recent work, funded by the Conrad S. Hilton Foundation, supports LMU's Center for Catholic Education and examines aspects of social justice tied to Catholic schools. She has also authored numerous manuscripts related to student health. Her expertise is in quantitative methodology and survey construction. She has a Ph.D. in applied social psychology and an MA in education.

Gaëtane Jean-Marie is an associate professor and program coordinator of educational leadership at the University of Oklahoma-Tulsa campus. Her research focuses on leadership development and preparation, effective leadership for educational equity in K-12 schools, women and leadership, and urban school reform. She coedited, *Women of Color in Higher Education: Turbulent Past, Promising Future and Women of Color in Higher Education: Contemporary Perspectives and New Directions* (with Brenda Lloyd-Jones). She is also coeditor of *Educational Leadership Preparation: Innovation and Interdisciplinary Approaches to the Ed.D. and Graduate Education* and has published in numerous journals including *Journal of Educational Administration, Journal of School Leadership*, and *Journal of Research on Leadership and Education*. She is an associate editor of the *Journal of School Leadership*, book reviews editor of the *Journal of Educational Administration*, and president of *Leadership for Social Justice* (AERA/SIG).

Katherine Cumings Mansfield is an assistant professor of educational leadership and policy at Virginia Commonwealth University. Mansfield's interdisciplinary scholarship focuses on the social, historical, and political contexts of education and the relationship of gender, race, religion, and class on educational and vocational access and achievement. Mansfield has presented at American Educational Research Association, *National Summit on Interdistrict Desegregation* at Harvard Law School, *Legal and Policy Options for Racially Integrated Education in the South and the Nation* at University of North Carolina-Chapel Hill School of Law, and University Council for Educational Administration. Mansfield has published in *Journal of Educational Administration, Journal of Research on Leadership Education*, and *Journal of School Leadership*. Mansfield currently serves as program chair for the American Educational Research Association's Leadership for Social Justice Special Interest Group. Dr. Mansfield received her Ph.D. from The University of Texas at Austin.

Miriam Bageni Mwita is an associate professor of Kiswahili and vice chancellor at University of Eastern Africa, Baraton-Kenya. Her areas of research include culture and the education of women and the teaching of Kiswahili in Kenya.

Anthony H. Normore holds a Ph.D from OISE/University of Toronto. He is currently professor and department chair of educational leadership in the Graduate School of Education at California Lutheran University,

Thousand Oaks, Southern California. Dr. Normore's research focuses on leadership development, preparation and socialization of urban school leaders in the context of ethics and social justice. His most recent books include *Discretionary Behavior and Performance in Educational Organizations: The Missing Link in Educational Leadership and Management* (2012, Emerald Publishing Group, and coedited with Ibrahim Duyar); *Education-Based Incarceration and Recidivism: The Ultimate Social Justice Crime Fighting Tool* (2012, Information Age Publishers, coedited with Brian D. Fitch); *Leadership in Education, Corrections, and Law Enforcement: A Commitment to Ethics, Equity, and Excellence* (2011, Emerald Group, coedited with Brian D. Fitch); *Educational Leadership Preparation: Innovation and Interdisciplinary Approaches to the Ed.D and Graduate Education* (2010, Palgrave MacMillan, and coedited with Gäetane Jean-Marie). Dr. Normore is series editor of *Advances in Educational Administration* with Emerald Publishing Group. His research has appeared in *Journal of School Leadership, Journal of Educational Administration, Values and Ethics in Educational Administration, Leadership and Organizational Development Journal, Canadian Journal of Education Administration and Policy, International Journal of Urban Educational Leadership, Educational Policy*, and *Journal of Research on Leadership Education*.

Barbara L. Pazey is an assistant professor in the Departments of Special Education and Educational Administration at The University of Texas at Austin. She holds a doctorate in educational administration/special education administration from The University of Texas at Austin. She earned a master of arts degree in music from The Ohio State University and obtained her special education teaching credential from Francis Marion University and The University of South Carolina. Her research and teaching interests are focused on the development of socially just leadership preparation programs in the context of meeting the academic, social, and emotional needs of special population students; ethical leadership, decision-making, and change made effectual through self-reflection and the empowerment of student voice; and the development of secondary education programs that foster creativity, innovation, and 21st century skills for special population student.

Teresa Wasonga is an associate professor of educational leadership at Northern Illinois University. Her areas of research focus of educational leadership, resilience, and issues of justice in education in Kenya.

Anjalé Welton is an assistant professor in the Department of Educational Policy, Organization, and Leadership at the University of Illinois, Urbana-Champaign. Welton's scholarship broadly explores the social, cultural, and political dynamics of schools; and more specifically examines the opportunity structures (issues of stratification, college, and career readiness) of students of color, from low socioeconomic backgrounds in secondary school settings. Anjalé is published in the *Journal of Educational Administration*, the *Journal of Advanced Academics*, and *Democracy and Education*. Her professional experiences include coordinator of a leadership and empowerment program for urban youth, a facilitator of an urban education teacher preparation program, and a teacher in both Washington DC and Austin, Texas public schools. Dr. Welton received her Ph.D. from The University of Texas at Austin.

Peg Winkelman is an associate professor in educational leadership at California State University East Bay, Hayward, California. Prior to her appointment as a faculty member at CSUEB, Dr. Winkelman served in California public schools as a teacher, principal, and director of curriculum and professional development. As a scholar-practitioner, she has initiated and participated in many district-university partnerships, both as a district administrator and faculty member. She has taught in several teacher education programs and continues to collaborate with her teacher education colleagues on efforts to better serve marginalized students, including linked learning. At CSUEB, Winkelman coordinates the first year of a credential and masters program in educational leadership. She teaches courses and chairs dissertations in the educational leadership for social justice doctoral program. Winkelman uses case study in her educational leadership courses as a teaching strategy, with particular emphasis on how case construction supports emerging leaders to bridge theory and practice. Her publications include works in the areas of after-school programs, arts education, case study as pedagogy, and culturally responsive teaching. Her most recent article is *Collaborative Inquiry for Equity: Discipline and Discomfort* (in press). She spends her spare time learning from her three children.

INDEX